China in the Caribbean

Roger Hosein · Bhoendradatt Tewarie · Rebecca Gookool-Bosland

China in the Caribbean

Trade, Investment, and Geopolitical Influence

palgrave
macmillan

Roger Hosein
Department of Economics
The University of the West Indies
St Augustine, Trinidad and Tobago

Bhoendradatt Tewarie
The University of the West Indies
St Augustine, Trinidad and Tobago

Rebecca Gookool-Bosland
Department of Economics
The University of the West Indies
St Augustine, Trinidad and Tobago

ISBN 978-3-031-71984-4 ISBN 978-3-031-71985-1 (eBook)
https://doi.org/10.1007/978-3-031-71985-1

This Palgrave Macmillan imprint is published by the registered company Springer Nature Switzerland AG
The registered company address is: Gewerbestrasse 11, 6330 Cham, Switzerland

Contents

List of Figures

List of Tables

CHAPTER 1

China in the Caribbean Context

1.1 Introduction

China should consider its growth trajectory in the context of its existing production attributes: 1.4 billion people in a world of about 8 billion people, the world's biggest exporter and importer, a major investment destination, and a significant investor in other countries. Further, China has lifted 87% of its population above the poverty line of $5.50 daily.[1] What would be the next steps? How would China secure its gains? How would China expand its global opportunities? How would China continue to rise? How would China advance national development, expand trade, increase desirable investment inflows, and invest strategically to advance its economic interests while avoiding unnecessary and undesirable conflicts? How does China navigate the world to improve its standing, build alliances, seize opportunities, and stave off threats?[2] Indeed, these are some of the critical questions that Chinese policymakers are grappling with and that other countries are observing in order to orient their policies in a world with China as an economic and geopolitical powerhouse.

R. Hosein et al., *China in the Caribbean*,
https://doi.org/10.1007/978-3-031-71985-1_1

1.2 The Contemporary Chinese Leader: Xi Jinping

This is where China has been for some time. Moreover, the critical thinking involved in devising contemporary strategy has been facilitated by the Chinese Communist Party and the President of China since 2013, Xi Jinping. The Chinese president, one year earlier, had also begun to serve as General Secretary of the Chinese Communist Party[3] as well as Chair of the Central Military Commission. He spent 11 years conceptualizing the Party and Military and ten more years developing a pragmatic approach to government, power and governance in relation to Party philosophy and objectives and Military power in a world of changing geopolitical relations.[4]

This chapter will consider Xi Jinping's thinking as articulated in public documents and will focus on China's policy priorities, alignment of action, and where emerging economies, and particularly the economies of the Caribbean Community (CARICOM) feature and fit into this framework.[5] It is difficult to consider CARICOM's interests without considering China's interests, and China's interest in CARICOM makes little sense if one does not consider China's broader, bigger interests as a global power. Why would CARICOM matter, and how does it matter in the bigger scheme of things? In addition, how would China's consideration of the larger scheme of things affect how much CARICOM would matter to China and how that would affect policy and strategic approaches to the region? On the other hand, how complementary will the mutual need be between CARICOM and China in the context of intensifying renewal of interest by the USA and Canada in the region and the hemisphere. And further what will this look like in the context of fluid and sometimes contradictory alignments of other countries in the Western Hemisphere?[6] The journey from post-WWII financial, economic, institutional, and geopolitical architecture to the present has been turbulent and messy. Change has been constant; combustion has been everywhere. Individual acumen, as well as the world system, has been tested. Navigation through these waters has required both precision and deliberateness, and navigation going forward requires even greater adeptness.

It is against this background that one can appreciate the person of Xi Jinping since his emergence as General Secretary and President and as he consolidated military command. In his first speech, on 15 November 2012, he expressed thanks to the international press for spreading the Chinese voice to other countries noting that "The expectations from all comrades of the Party and the hopes from all ethnic groups of the country are a source of immense encouragement for us to do our jobs well, and it is also a heavy responsibility on our shoulders," which he further elaborates, is a responsibility "towards our nation." Xi Jinping continues further: "Our nation is a great nation. In over 5000 years of civilization, the Chinese people have made indispensable contributions to human development. In recent history, our nation has suffered. The Chinese confronted its gravest moments. Since then, numerous Chinese patriots have waged a hard struggle for the sake of a great revival of the Chinese nation, but time and again they have failed." He spoke of "turning the poor and backward China into a new China ever closer to the goal of national prosperity and strength," and continues: "Our responsibility is to rally and lead the whole Party and the Chinese people from all ethnic groups, take up the historic baton and continue working hard for the great revival of the Chinese nation so that we will stand rock firm amongst nations of the world, and make fresh and greater contribution to mankind." Xi Jinping spoke of his understanding of the people's aspirations for tangible gains such as "better education, more stable jobs, more satisfactory income, more reliable social security, medical services with higher standards, more comfortable living conditions and a more beautiful environment." He aligned himself with the aspirations of ordinary people for a better life. "The people wish that their children will grow better and live better. The people's desire for a better life is simply the target of our endeavour."

"All happiness in this world," Xi Jinping continues, "can only be created with hard work. Our responsibility is to rally and lead the whole Party and the Chinese people of all ethnic groups, in continuing to liberate our way of thinking, carry on reform and openness, further unleash and develop social productive forces, work hard to resolve the difficulties people face in both work and life. And stand firm on the road for prosperity for all." He continued by talking about making the Communist Party less bureaucratic and more responsive to people and by emphasizing "Socialism with Chinese characteristics."[7]

He ended with an emphasis on unity and this reflection: "An individual has limited time in Office, but there is never a limit to serving the people heart and soul." He again reached out to the press, saying that China needs to know more about the world and the world needs to know more about China.[8]

In this speech, he highlighted historical struggles admonishing that China needed to embrace progress and prosperity and forge national unity in a context of ethnic cleavages; reform and modernize the Communist Party in its embrace of the media to tell the world about China and bring news of the world to China and its dedicated commitment to the rejuvenation of China and the achievement of shared prosperity across the Chinese nation; and in the articulated recognition of the need for dedication of leadership commitment to improve the lives of ordinary people over generations.

It is as if he had been preparing for this leadership role all his life; everything seemed to flow and fit naturally. With his Chairmanship of Military strategy and his ascendency to the Presidency, his roles were overlapping, complementary, and complete. All that remained was the consolidation of power in that system. He began to stabilize his own path about eleven years ago and, in the last ten years, has consolidated power to entrench himself for five more years. In the last ten years, China has become a formidable global economic power with a technologically sophisticated presence in the world up to the emergence of COVID-19. With COVID-19, amidst the health crisis and the human loss, there began a general rethinking of everything, by the major world powers; economy, politics, society, trade, investment, development, competitiveness, technology, alliances, geopolitics, business, labour market, inflation, logistics, business strategy, margins, profits, globalization, self-sufficiency, energy, energy transformation to cleaner power for the sake of planet earth, and then the current technological innovations such as algorithms, big data, artificial intelligence, robotics, G5, and the fifth industrial revolution. Amidst these great complexities, all of which are critical in the geo-economics, geopolitical and technological positioning, and repositioning of a country, it is important to take note of strategic thinking and action that led to the significant rise of China as a global power-up to 2020. Indeed, COVID-19 represented a watershed in terms of China's ambitions and economic progress as well as in terms of China's relations with the USA and the West.

Reflecting on Xi Jinping's speeches from 2012, one gets a sense of both perspective and strategic objectives, priorities, and the level of resolve. Despite its significant and major technological leaps, Xi Jinping regards China as the world's largest developing country. He sees China's challenge as making space for itself in a world organized and controlled by Western powers who do not wish to concede space in trade, investment, technology, or political influence to China, whom they view as an adversary with hegemonic ambitions and military might to back it up. At the same time, he sees China's future as being in alliance with the developing world and the ex-colonial world; and views global diversification of trade, investment, access to resources, and collaboration in development, as being good not only for China's economic interests and development strategy but, essential as well, to its global repositioning. In the first instance, the impact of Xi Jinping's public utterances over his years of Chinese leadership, is considered.[9]

1.2.1 Xi Jinping's Thinking 2012–2017

Reflecting on Xi Jinping's speeches from 2012 to 2017, one sees systematic thought at work, focused, first, on China's development, not just as the second-largest economy in the world but also as the largest developing country in the world. Always at the top of mind, is the global economy which demands innovation to compete; the geopolitical positioning of China based on economic, financial, and political stability inside; a changing world outside in which adjusting the balance of power in China's favour is desirable; a transforming world order in which fairer governance arrangements are at stake,[10] and the need for China to effectively manage the opening up of China to the world. There is the desire too, in opening the economy, to play a reasonable and responsible role in global governance, and to productively engage developing countries, beginning with smaller countries of its Asian neighbourhood (The Economist 2024,[11] IMF 2024[12]). In opening up to the outside world, China is starkly sanguine of the need for autonomy, sovereignty, and capacity building in knowledge, applications, and technical competence. Beyond these, China sees world peace as an important goal linked to general economic progress and to China's own prosperity, expansion of trade, investment, and influence. In one of Xi Jinping's speeches, this is spelled out starkly in terms of the behaviour required of China.

Xi Jinping noted on 18 December 2015, in "The New Normal: How to Respond and Adapt": "I have emphasized repeatedly that we must escape the Thucydides trap and the middle-income trap. The former relates to the political sphere—we should carefully tackle the relationships with other major countries such as the United States. The latter is about the economy—we must improve the quality and effectiveness of economic growth… to change the economic growth model and restructure the economy more quickly."[13]

What exactly are these traps for any country but, especially for a big country like China, which is at once an economic powerhouse, a strong power in the world system with a highly centralized political structure, and a country of formidable and considerable military might?

1.3 Middle-Income Country Trap and Thucydides Trap

The term "middle-income trap" was introduced by the World Bank in 2006.[14] Countries that grow to a certain level of GDP and per capita income and find it challenging to move beyond that level remain stuck. The "trap" is that they find it difficult to accelerate growth and development beyond the level already achieved. Since 2006, a lot has been written about the middle-income trap and how to escape it. At the heart of the problem are competitiveness, labour capacity, and productivity at the level of sophistication required to sustain competitive capability, which means knowledge, skills, competence, adaptability, driven by innovation, and continuous capacity building. Although, from the outside, it may seem unlikely that China would be caught in such a trap given China's size, diversity, market, and international reach in trade and investment, not to mention its exponential growth rate over the last several decades, its competitive capacity, its technological evolution and level of sophistication, and its drive to innovation, which Xi Jinping has constantly stressed, it is identified as a significant concern of the Chinese leader. Indeed, the stress-inducing fact of being stuck in middle income has been a source of worry because, for Xi Jinping, it would limit the growth and expansion of the middle class in China. Countries all over the Caribbean and Latin America have been so trapped.[15] This has been a particular concern of the Asian Development Bank, as it seeks[16] to examine and assess the relationship between finance and development in Asia, where significant growth and development progress has been made since the 1990s and as the process of globalization has intensified.

The other trap mentioned, the Thucydides trap, describes the temptation of an emerging power to lean towards militarism and war as its sense of power increases and the earlier power of a hegemonic presence begins to wane. This can also occur if power is perceived as waning for a once powerful country, threatened with displacement. Reaction to changes in the power dynamics of the time as the new, emerging power senses its opportunity of a lifetime[17] and as the existing power ceases to hold on to position can result in increasing tension. We note the rise in tensions, for instance, over Taiwan between China and the USA and mutual outreach by both China and Russia since the beginning of the Russia-Ukraine war to each other.

Graham Allison coined the term "Thucydides trap" and has identified sixteen instances in history in which it emerged and resulted in war or conflict.[18] It should not be missed that when US Secretary of State, Antony Blinken, visited China following a range of tensions that escalated as a war of words built up over former Speaker of the House Nancy Pelosi's visit to Taiwan, Xi Jinping, not only met with Blinken, but also, that the Chinese press reported the Chinese President as saying that "China would not challenge or replace the US." In the same breath, he called on the USA "to respect China and not harm China's rights or interests."[19]

It would be reasonable to claim that all economic and geopolitical strategies, as Xi Jinping is defining them, derive from these fundamentals.[20] The inevitable questions that emerge from China's point of view are: (1) how to become the largest, most competitive economy in the world and manage the navigation and deal with the inevitable, consequential fallout and (2) how to build up military capacity, be autonomous and independent in an interdependent world, secure your strategic interests, expand your global economic and geopolitical interests, manage inevitable conflicts, and avoid war with the US?

1.4 Geopolitical Thrusts

The earth's geopolitical and geoeconomic space includes 193 countries and 2 with associate status in the UN, namely the Vatican and Palestine. Consider that China's important geopolitical concerns and global economic interests from Xi Jinping's point of view, bearing in mind that there is a remarkable consistency of strategy and policy even as leaders change, with shifts in emphasis and re-evaluation of methods.[21]

The Communist Party of China (CPC) drives everything in China. The military derives its mandate from the CPC. The CPC determines the focus and direction of policy by the government. Xi Jinping is a leader and head of all three, Party Military and Government. All are urged to stay close to the people and to enhance their value to the people.[22] At home, the objective is to achieve economic development and stability and to spread prosperity and improvement of lives, enhancing national unity in the process; abroad it is to increase market and boost trade, to gain access to resources, to invest, to spread influence, to strengthen geopolitical power, walking that fine line between increasing power and influence, avoiding conflicts, and maintaining peace. The two are related. All are related. Disharmony among the Party, Military, and Government can cause strife and vulnerability. Hence, Xi Jinping's pleas for discipline, leadership by example, end of corruption by the Party hierarchy, his insistence that the military is accountable to the CPC and must take guidance from it and must ground itself with the needs of the people, and the government commitment to unity among ethnic groups as well as general economic improvements and prosperity—all are related. Internal strengths make China less vulnerable as a nation. Geopolitical reach and power make China more formidable in the world, and it is a source of pride at home, which is good for unification and gives China a basis for internal stability, which is vital to support China's geopolitical ambitions.

China's priorities outside of China begin with its "One China, Two Systems" policy and the fact that the Chinese nation, while inflexible on autonomy and national sovereignty China, will not likely concede Independence nor too much autonomy to either Taiwan, Hong Kong, Macao, or Tibet. From time to time, this is tested. Moreover, there is a range of islands in the Taiwan Straits and in the South China Sea, some in dispute, which China insists upon as its own territory. Thus, while the One China, Two Systems policy is conceded, the issue of autonomy, if not Independence, is in dispute. Moreover, China's territorial claims on multifarious islands continue to be contentious. In much of Asia, China is seen as a big power with hegemonic ambitions, even though Asian nations may be sympathetic to China's drive and ambitions in the world as an Asian nation.[23]

Another important concern for China is good relations through economic partnerships involving trade, investment, and development with its Asian neighbours. Fourteen countries have a land border with China. These are North Korea, Russia, Mongolia, Kazakhstan, Kyrgyzstan, Tajikistan, Afghanistan, Pakistan, India, Nepal, Bhutan, Myanmar, Laos, and Vietnam. There are yet others with substantial Chinese populations with which trade relations have been expanding with China—countries like Thailand, Cambodia, Malaysia, Indonesia, and Singapore.

Two other neighbouring countries are Japan and South Korea. Of these countries, China has either gone to war or had military conflicts with Japan, South Korea, India,, and Vietnam. At the same time, some of those countries have benefitted from China's growth and prosperity, and many of them have a balance of trade in their favour; there is, therefore, some dependence on China by these countries. China's relationship with countries in Asia is a rather complicated one with a clash of sovereignties, tensions over the level of autonomy, territorial disputes, a known history of aggression, overseas Chinese populations who are citizens and nationals of sovereign countries, trade, investment, and commercial relations, competing ambitions (Japan, India, South Korea) as well as big country/small country fears and caution about bullying and hegemonic aspirations. China wants to build an Asia–Pacific Partnership on mutual trust, but this is easier said than done because of the many tensions inherent in this multiplicity of relationships.[24]

China is very strong in building China-Africa relations. Africa is a big continent with 55 countries, extensively exploited and colonized, and rich in natural endowments. "In conducting China's relations with Africa, we apply the principles of sincerity, affinity, and good faith, and uphold the values of the greater good and shared interest," said the Chinese president in a 4 December 2015, speech entitled "A New Era of China—Africa Cooperation and Common Development." In this presentation, Xi Jinping pledges "political equality and mutual trust...mutually beneficial economic cooperation... mutual assistance in security...solidarity and coordination in international affairs...ten cooperative programmes with Africa." The Chinese president closed his speech with the following sentence: "Let us join hands, pool the wisdom and strength of the 2.4 billion Chinese and Africans, and open a new era of China—Africa mutually beneficial cooperation and common development." The aspirations of China for leadership of the developing world is clear.[25]

So much has been written of the China-Africa relationship, a good deal of which is negative on debt, acquisitions, plunder of resources, and related matters. An Institute for Security Studies report, for instance, reports this: "The number of African countries indebted to China and subsequently handing over their assets or resources is in no short supply. Zambia, Angola and the Democratic Republic of Congo (DRC), Mozambique, Ethiopia, Sudan, Kenya, and Djibouti are just some." The article goes on to describe some of the transactions and consequences in detail.

The ISS Africa is the largest independent research institute in Africa dealing with matters of human security.[26]

China appreciates the importance of the EU and bilateral relations with key countries of the EU. It wants to expand relations with the Arab world; it wants good mutually supportive relations with Russia, and Xi Jinping is committed to the idea of BRICS; but its major initiative for inclusion of, first of all, Asian countries with China's future economic development, and then a wider circle of countries in China's orbit, is China's Belt and Road Initiative, the brainchild of Xi Jinping for international cooperation and a China pivot with developing countries for trade, investment, diplomacy, and development, but also for, expanding reach and increasing influence.[27]

1.5 Xi Jinping and the Caribbean

In all of Xi Jinping's thinking and writing, the Caribbean does not feature at all. There is, however, a policy paper published in 2008, before Xi Jinping's time, which outlines China's interest in Latin America and the Caribbean.[28] The Belt and Road Initiative presented an opportunity for Caribbean countries to join this China initiative. Trinidad and Tobago was the first CARICOM country to join, but currently, there are ten countries of the Caribbean involved, eight from CARICOM, plus Cuba and the Dominican Republic. Over 100 countries globally are part of this initiative. Some Caribbean countries are aligned with Taiwan and have benefitted from that relationship, so CARICOM as a regional entity could not join the initiative as a group, nor could those countries individually align with Taiwan since this would signal a lack of recognition of China's "One country, Two Systems" policy. However, when Xi Jinping on an official state visit to Trinidad and Tobago in 2013, he made time to meet individually with each of the leaders of CARICOM who had diplomatic relations with China or did not officially have relations with Taiwan. The Chinese Foreign Ministry posted the important bilateral considerations emerging from each meeting. These reveal some matters of economic interest.[29]

St Lucia, St Vincent and the Grenadines, St Kitts and Nevis, Haiti, and Belize all recognize Taiwan. This, notwithstanding, CARICOM's trade with China was US$8 bn in 2019. China's exports were just over US$6 bn, and imports from CARICOM were just under US$2 mn.When Xi Jinping made his State visit to Trinidad and Tobago in 2013, trade was just US$450 mn. At that time, China and Trinidad and Tobago signed an agreement “to actively advance cooperation in key areas of energy, minerals and infrastructure development and also to advance our cooperation in new energy, telecommunications and agriculture.” Trinidad and Tobago also got a soft loan of $250 mn to build a children’s hospital. In 2017, the TT government and the government of China agreed on the Phoenix Park economic zone project. By 2013, the Belt and Road Initiative had already been publicly announced but no CARICOM country was yet on board. When the Chinese president flew out of Trinidad and Tobago, he also visited Costa Rica, Mexico, and the USA. So, in a vital way, he made it an important visit to the hemisphere. While in Port of Spain, he met with the Prime Minister of Trinidad and Tobago, Mrs. Kamla Persad-Bissessar, as well as other heads of CARICOM nations.

Currently, Cuba, Dominican Republic, Jamaica, Antigua Barbuda, Dominica, Barbados, Grenada, Guyana, Suriname, and Trinidad and Tobago are all signed up to the Belt and Road Initiative. China’s investment in CARICOM countries is over $10 bn, the main recipients being Jamaica (3.16 bn), Guyana (3.01 bn), Trinidad and Tobago (2.28 bn), Antigua and Barbuda (1 bn), and The Bahamas (350 mn). These figures of 2019 have significantly increased in the contemporary period, and available data is included in the various proceeding chapters.[30]

In the Chinese Foreign Ministry’s information on his meetings with heads of individual CARICOM countries, the public documents do not detail much in the way of project areas, projects, or specifics. Priorities are identified in generalities and couched in the framework of building friendly relations, but it is a big country—small country relationship. CARICOM individual countries seem to be seeking development resources; that was the point of view of most CARICOM countries. In addition, the Caribbean produces little that it can offer China and has little to offer that China cannot get elsewhere in terms of produced goods and services outside of natural resources. These countries do not offer investment to China. Chinese investments in infrastructure in receiving countries come with access to resources and finance, it is true, but almost inevitably, with Chinese labour, Chinese loans, and other conditions.[31] The Caribbean being a region in which tourism is the main source of revenue for most nations, is not addressed in any detail in Chinese reports of Xi Jinping‘s Caribbean engagements.[32] The generalization though, is continued bilateral relations between China and the region.

Regarding Guyana, the emphasis is on infrastructure, construction, bauxite exploitation, agriculture, forestry, and fisheries. Airport construction and e-government collaboration are also mentioned and specifically, a hydropower generation plant, which Guyana has been pursuing for some time. All of this was before Guyana found oil, in the period of Donald Ramoutar's Presidency. It is inevitable that priorities would have changed, and an oil-consuming country like China would have an interest in oil as well as fossil fuel spin-offs, not to mention the development potential of a shared border with Brazil, a country with which China has been expanding relations. Since then, and currently, Guyana has partnered with Huawei to establish a face recognition system as part of a Safe City initiative (Stabroek News 2024[33]). Privacy issues have been raised but have not interfered with the execution of the project. Guyana had also been considering engaging Taiwan in commercial matters but with the strengthening of relations with China, this initiative has been sidelined. China National Corporation for Exploration and Development of Oil and Gas (CNODC) owns 30% of a consortium developing the Stabroek block, which is said to be a 6.6 million acreage with the potential for 10 billion barrels of oil equivalent. The Chinese have invested close to US$1 bn in major road and bridges construction in Guyana opening and connecting important points for development in the country.

With Antigua and Barbuda, discussions centred around raising people's livelihoods through tourism, but no specific action issues were mentioned. Environmental protection and the ecological impact of construction were discussed. In addition, the strengthening of relations in economy, trade, culture, and multilateral affairs were also areas of focus (Observer 2024[34]). One may speculate that part of the multilateral focus may well involve global financial rules and the global financial system about which Antigua and Barbuda has often complained. Since then, China has invested US$1 bn, established a Confucius Institute, and actively supported this country as Chair of the Alliance of Small States in 2021 and 2022. Another area of cooperation is oceanography and the green economy (The Daily Herald 2024[35]). Although tourism contributes more than 50% to Antigua Barbuda's GDP, there are currently no specific and direct projects in tourism with China.

Several issues were covered between the Chinese Premier and Prime Minister of Dominica on an official visit by Dominican officials to China in March 2024: agriculture and health care, economic and technical cooperation, clean energy, climate change, personnel training, people-to-people exchange, transportation, and infrastructure. Deepening any relationship between these two countries remains a work in progress.

With the Bahamas, the discussion focused on trade, tourism, economy, culture, and people-to-people relations and investment and financing opportunities with China (Ministry of Foreign Affairs PRC[36]). In 2010, the Export–Import Bank of China provided over US 54 m dollars in preferential loans to build a four-lane highway in the Bahamas. Another US$3 bn loan was also given and the China Corporation (CSEC) purchased the British Hilton Colonial and invested in further construction expansion. Bilateral trade between the two countries reached almost $500 mn, a jump of 40% from 2021 to 2022 and in 2021, both countries signed an agreement to facilitate US$12 m in infrastructure upgrades in the Bahamas. A Chinese company, Hutchinson Port Holdings operates the Freeport container port in the Bahamas, and on Grand Bahama Island, 50 miles from the US coast, China is constructing a US$3 bn deep-water containment port.

In Jamaica, the emphasis was mutual learning on sports, environmental protection, and infrastructure. The two countries have mounted a trade volume of US$816 mn and China has invested over US$3 bn in Jamaica. Jiuquan Iron and Steel (JISco), a Chinese state enterprise, purchased Jamaica's alumina refinery in 2017. China Merchant Port Holdings owns the Port of Kingston, and more than US$1 bn in Chinese government financing has gone into road construction, involving a main highway as well as connector roads. In exchange, the Chinese have been given lands along the highway for development purposes. A framework agreement to build an industrial park is now being executed and China has established a Confucius Institute in Jamaica.

In Grenada, the discussion focused on infrastructure, construction, agriculture, human resources, education, culture, and tourism. The relationship has been slowly building. Trade is now over US$10 bn with most of it being Chinese imports to Grenada. Additionally, China has helped to expand Stadia, build low-cost housing, expand the airport, and support agriculture through technical cooperation, according to the China-Grenada Economic Relations report put out by the Chinese Embassy of Grenada. The irony of this is in the balance of trade, where Grenada's exports to China are just over US$10,000.

In Barbados, the Chinese have focused on infrastructure projects, such as a gymnasium, market, and cultural centre. Some concern has been expressed about Barbados's debt to China, but Barbados is a heavily indebted country, and debt to China constitutes only a small percentage of the total debt.

In Suriname, China's investments have been in the primary products sector like timber, and it has exported a modest amount of manufactured goods to that country. What has happened, though, is that there has been a fair amount of migration from China to Suriname, and retail sector ownership of distribution trade by the Chinese has grown. This has been the source of minor tension but not enough to constitute a problem yet.

In Trinidad and Tobago, China once owned 10% of Atlantic LNG, one of the largest LNG plants in the world, but China has recently divested as the shareholding and business relationships have been restructured. China is involved in the construction of an Economic Zone-styled business park at Phoenix Park and Moruga Agro Park and has been involved in a range of construction projects in TT, including hospitals, sports, and stadium facilities. Steps are being taken to build a partnership between a TT company and a Chinese counterpart to export chocolate and other fine cocoa products to China, and China has helped with the establishment of a Forensic Science centre, police motorcycles, training of TT nationals in short courses and has also with the University of the West Indies, established a Confucius Institute.[37]

At the end of the communique, Xi Jinping stressed that the Caribbean is an important force in the international community and emphasized "comprehensive partnerships" with countries in the region.[38]

If China's active relationship with the Caribbean excludes meaningful engagement with those countries aligned with Taiwan (St Vincent, St Lucia, St Kitts Nevis, Belize, and Haiti), China also has strong relationships with Caribbean countries that are not members of CARICOM. These countries have relationships with CARICOM countries in other fora such as CARIFORUM and the ACS.

1.6 Cuba and the Dominican Republic

China's relationship with Cuba is significant. Cuba manages and controls internet access through a single State company, but all three providers are Chinese—Huawei, TP-Link, and ZTE. China is also heavily involved in construction in the Tourism sector, developing major resorts, Golf courses, and luxury hotels. Both governments have signed a memorandum of understanding to solidify tourism cooperation. Cuba's

Tourism sector is led and controlled by the military. China is also one of Cuba's major trading partners, and in investment, beyond telecommunications and tourism, China is involved in Cuba in mining as well as energy. Cuba is heavily indebted to China, and an outstanding debt of more than US$4 bn has been restructured twice in the last two decades. In 2019, China in partnership with Cuba, began drilling for oil. Cuba has also been the beneficiary of a Confucius Institute but is involved with the deepening and strengthening of military ties with China as well.[39]

The Dominican Republic (DR) has also been strengthening its engagement with China. In exchange for Diplomatic recognition of China, the DR received a package of combined investments and loans of over US$3 bn, and in addition, took a US$600 mn loan to expand and modernize that country's electricity grid.[40]

All 10 countries discussed above have signed on to China's Belt and Road Initiative. According to China's ambassador to Trinidad and Tobago, the initiative now has 152 countries signed on and 32 multilateral organizations and is actively making development happen in countries across the world.[41]

1.7 Caribbean and Latin America in Geopolitics

China has been active in the Caribbean for many decades and, indeed, was active before Xi Jinping‘s visit, and the economic relationship and the diplomatic gains for China have been significant over time. At the same time, benefits in loans and investments have come to Caribbean countries, and the expansion of trade has been in China's favour. Details of these will be illustrated below, but it is important to note that China has been positioning itself to play a bigger and more influential and strategic role, not only in the region but in the hemisphere with the Caribbean and Latin America. The Foreign Affairs Committee of the IDB gives us this snapshot:

China is both a member of the Inter-American Development Bank (IDB) and the Caribbean Development Bank (CDB) with significant "shareholderships" and influence in both banks.[42] Noting also that "The People's Republic of China‘s (PRC) ‘engagement in the Caribbean has focused on infrastructure and developing trade relations." The focus of that article is on trade and economic investment, interest in energy, infrastructure, and on China's soft power in the Caribbean, and, of course, the muting of Taiwan‘s reach and influence, but also on security assistance.[43]

China has always been a big country with a large population and is largely land-based, but today China is a maritime power, building ports all over the world and carving out shipping lanes that are vital for commercial trade but which can be of strategic value for military purposes. China can feel secure in defending its landmass despite its many borders, but China is building two navies for different strategic purposes: a *Blue* water navy to patrol the oceans around it, but, potentially worldwide, and a *Green* water navy to patrol the maritime borders whose waters wash its coasts. China has 34 major ports and more than 2000 minor ports, and Chinese companies own or operate terminals in 96 ports in 53 countries around the world. A recent article in Barron's raises concerns about Chinese-controlled ports because some are being converted for military uses.[44]

Beyond the Caribbean, China is keen on Latin America and views the Western Hemisphere strategically in terms of positioning itself relative to the USA, in terms of expansion of trade and investment opportunities, in terms of building alliances and neutralizing antagonism and resentment and building friendly relations. In this regard, CARICOM is important because of the number of countries involved. China must show those countries in diplomatic relations based on its "One China, Two Systems" policy that its relationship with China has value. It would be better for those countries aligned with Taiwan to shift allegiance with incentives and with a gentle diplomatic nudge rather than the use of muscle, as the votes of all of these small countries are important in international fora and institutions. Other economic issues, such as trade expansion, are important for China, as are the job opportunities that loans and investments in infrastructure create. For some time now, construction projects in China have been waning, and in 2022, it ground to a halt. China has gone from double-digit to single-digit growth. The pandemic has been like a whiplash on the China economy, and China needs to be busy and create jobs for Chinese workers outside of China. China's global strategy has always been not only trade, investment, and loan financing but also the acquisition of natural resources that China needs or can sell and the construction of infrastructure that can be of value not just to the host country but to China's strategic interests. It is not by accident that China has an interest not only in minerals but also in port and airport construction.[45]

In 2013, the Prime Minister of Barbados, Freundel Stuart, raised the issue of imports from the Caribbean to address the imbalance of trade and payments, but this can only be addressed if the region has something to sell that China wants, or if Chinese tourists decide to make the Caribbean one of their preferred destinations. Ronald Sanders, a regional diplomat and newspaper commentator, raised around the time of Xi Jinping's 2013 visit, the issue of local labour in place of Chinese labour in Chinese-led projects and creating the conditions for partnerships with local companies so that procurement rules and enlightened worker-friendly practices can be honoured. He also raised the question of local and regional business, for example, contractors, doing business in China. "China is not the answer to the region's economic difficulties," he concluded, "but it can contribute to overcoming them if the projects that individual countries propose are viable and sustainable."[46] It is in this sense that the former diplomat, at the time, was cautioning countries in the region not to count their chickens before eggs hatch. As we can see, though, some of the chickens have come home to roost in a good way. Trade has grown but the balance is still in favour of China's exports. Loans have grown, which presents its own set of problems of repayment or alternatively, as we have seen in other places, the surrender of assets and/or control (Foreign Affairs Committee 2022,[47] Lewkowicz 2024[48]).

1.8 Where and How Does the Caribbean Fit?

Considering the above, the following are some issues, worthy of note. China has surpassed the World Bank, and the Inter-American Development Bank combined, as Latin America's top lender for Energy and infrastructure projects.[49]

China is the largest export market for Brazil, Chile, Cuba, Peru, and Uruguay currently. Imports from Latin America by the USA have fallen by 40% in the last fifteen years.[50]

The strengthening of military relations between China and Venezuela and Cuba and the deep nexus between Venezuela and Cuba and their connection with Russia and Iran can spell difficulties of increasing magnitude and increase geopolitical tensions in the Western Hemisphere. Moreover, from Peru to Mexico, China has various levels of interest in 40 ports in Latin America. It also has 11 satellite ground stations in Argentina, Brazil, Bolivia, and Venezuela.

In 2008, China released a major policy document on China, Latin America, and the Caribbean. The goal was to establish a "comprehensive and cooperative partnership featuring equality, mutual benefit, and common development."[51] "China's expansion throughout Latin

America is in keeping with that mandate." Its interest in the countries of CARICOM and the Caribbean has to do with the basics of trade, investment, and diplomacy, but also with China's aspirations to lead the developing world and to build numbers in terms of its objectives to rebalance power and influence in the world in key decision-making bodies.

China exhibits a willingness to trade with and invest in any country. It takes a developing country's perspective and articulates a sympathetic and empathetic position towards other developing countries. However, China is a big country. Counterparts with which it is involved in a geopolitical context are the USA, Russia, and Europe. With these, it wants to cooperate and collaborate but also, to compete and to win. What does it need to win? Firstly, a thriving economy and political stability through unification and shared prosperity within China. China needs to import massive amounts of energy and raw materials that it needs to support a thriving economy; it needs to export to create jobs and grow the economy; it needs to keep up with technology and be ahead in some technologies. China also needs to be competitive and innovative. Moreover, beyond that, it must be militarily strong on land, sea, and air, and it must have a commanding capability in technology and in Space. China is competing in all these spheres to win. It is a comprehensive contest. Yet, it wants to change the world order and the balance of power in the world. To do that it must champion the cause of the developing world, whose support China needs, and it must play a role in the further development of the developing world, which it must also finance. All these converge into a highly complex undertaking.

It must also prepare for war while working for world peace on which prosperity depends. China must play a responsible role in governance while working for change in the world order. It must be aggressive as well as defensive in Space. This is a complex undertaking as China must continue evading the middle-income country trap; while resisting the temptation to go to war with the USA. Not only do all of these constitute a complex undertaking, requiring meticulous navigation, but despite every care, things can go wrong.

In his speech on the Governance of China, Xi Jinping says, "The overall trend to multipolarity, economic globalization and democratic international relations remain unchanged." We should help the international community to create a truly just and equitable world order. No matter how the world changes and develops, we must maintain our strategic confidence, faith, and patience. We should develop a global vision of national security, coordinate development and security, combine principles with tactics, and always keep hold of the strategic initiative for national security. Great efforts should be devoted to political, economic, territorial, social, and cyber security, "It is vital for China to proactively create a favourable international security environment, and we must urge the international community to intensify cooperation for global security."[52]

Such an outline clearly outlines the breadth and depth of China's vision, but this articulation also reveals the strength of China's aspirations and ambitions.

Regarding developing countries, this is Xi Jinping's position, "We are firm in our position that all countries, regardless of their size strength and level of development are equal members of the international community and that the destiny of the world should be decided by people of all countries. We will uphold international justice and in particular speak up for developing countries… we should strengthen unity and cooperation with other developing countries and closely associate our development with the common development of other developing countries…We should…promote reform of the international system and global governance, so that Developing countries, China included, will have bigger representation and greater say."[53] Xi Jinping also talks in that speech about "building a global network of partnerships."[54] From this point of view, the Caribbean is part of China's global network of partnerships spread around the globe.

According to Standard and Poor's rankings, China owns the four largest banks in the world: the Industrial and Commercial Bank of China, the China Construction Bank, the Bank of China, and the Agricultural Bank of China.[55] The Export–Import Bank of China and the China Development Bank finance projects in Latin America and the Caribbean. China knows that it takes money to make things happen, and once countries accept their terms or negotiate mutually acceptable terms, those countries can get the funding that they need through a mix of measures and means.

China is likely to become more aggressively defensive of interests that surround her geographically but is likely to become bolder and more aggressive in building a series of alliances in concentric circles across the world, to aggression in defence of sovereignty, territory, and boldness in the quest for global strategic influence and economic and technological competitiveness are likely to inform China's dominant thrust into the future.[56]

For the Caribbean, therefore, the relationship with China is not a purely economic one. It may involve trade, investment, diplomacy, and loans and these are matters that individual countries must manage. The countries of CARICOM, and even in the wider region, would do well to share information and perspectives with each other to have a stronger sense of how each, separately, as well as together, might navigate with what is essentially a big, powerful country from their perspective.

1.9 Western Hemisphere

There are also hemispheric challenges that are unique to the hemisphere and region. For instance, the Western Hemisphere constitutes the most unequal in the world[57]; Trinidad and Tobago and the region are dealing with a mass migration challenge from Venezuela,[58] while the USA deals with a constant flow of migrants, especially from Central America and Haiti.[59] Most migration in the hemisphere is economic,[60] (except perhaps Venezuela), which means that there is a substantial deficit of production, business growth, and jobs with decent incomes, competitiveness, and inclusion in both prosperity and democracy. Support for development and know-how and do-how from China would be welcome, but the USA has been a friend and partner and has strengthened trade, investment, and security support over time.[61] Canada also has played a constructive role in the Caribbean[62] and ideological and geopolitical tensions exist in the hemisphere as China, Russia, and Iran have all become more assertive.[63] These have to be navigated and managed, and there is no doubt that the Caribbean needs to be more productive, competitive, prosperous, and agile and to develop at a faster pace. However, China must manage both development and international relations as it seeks to change the world and make it better and fairer both for itself and for developing countries generally.

1.9.1 Traps for Caribbean Countries to Avoid

There are some traps that the Caribbean must avoid too. One is the middle-income country trap,[64] reliance on one country trap,,[65] food insecurity trap,[66] synergy in the region trap,[67] technology absorption weakness and deployment avoidance trap,[68] diversification, value chain upgrade required to absorb our tertiary graduates (to prevent brain drain), and globalization of labour force in terms of skills and education.[69]

As the Caribbean region engages with China, one opportunity for consideration is the post-COVID movement away from China to nearshoring. Here is an opportunity for investment partnerships for wider regional, hemispheric, and global markets.[70]

The seven traps mentioned above for the Caribbean, and the opportunity for nearshoring because of changing relationships between China and the USA, in particular, need to be frontally addressed in any trade, investment, and development engagement with China or other foreign investors and governments generally.

What is the value of trade, investment, and development engagements with larger, more powerful, more prosperous countries if Caribbean countries cannot rise in per capita income, grow their GDP, increase shared prosperity within their countries, and escape the middle-income country trap? China will understand this, as will the USA, Canada, Europe, and the UK.

Most countries including China, and the major industrialized countries mentioned above, understand the need for as much self-sufficiency as possible and greater food security.

The weakness of regional cooperation, failure of effective collaboration, and the absence of meaningful synergy across the Caribbean region constitute a source of perpetual vulnerability for the region in security, trade and investment alignment and convergence, logistical coherence, and economic competitiveness. This is known by regional leaders, but their actions demonstrate that if they understand the problem they are not doing enough about it. The big players in the world also appreciate and understand the vulnerabilities and indeed, sometimes help, but from time to time, they also seek to exploit it.

One of the gains of engagement of international cooperation and foreign investment in technology absorption and development is to enhance competitiveness and innovation. This should not be missed in the Caribbean‘s engagement with China and other countries that compete for the Caribbean's attention. The plight of the pool of tertiary graduates and the role that they can play in driving knowledge industry diversification in the region should also not be missed. Additionally, the literal abandonment of half of each year's secondary school graduating class of sixteen-year-olds should not continue without a decisive strategic intervention. Development strategies and prosperity interventions must provide tracks for the self-development of annual waves of 16-year-old cohorts coming out of the secondary school system throughout CARICOM.

1.10 Nearshoring Opportunities

The nearshoring opportunity for Trinidad and Tobago and other CARICOM countries as investments pull out of China is real for the countries of the Caribbean. A fair amount of US investment and some Canadian investment have gone into Mexico, Costa Rica, and Panama, for instance. Moreover, Chinese manufacturers and service providers can invest in these islands to engage markets in Latin America and North America.

Trinidad and Tobago, Jamaica, and Barbados for instance, have a large pool of graduates who are English speaking, as do the rest of CARICOM. Further, it should be noted that Trinidad and Tobago, has a significant migrant population that is Spanish-speaking, and for exports to, and tourist, from Latin America, is a valuable asset. Nearshoring is valuable for investments in the CARICOM region as it can diversify both investment and exports, the range of countries from which investors come, as well as the markets targeted. This reduces the investment dependence on any one country, which presents its own set of challenges and can be a healthy opportunity for CARICOM. In outlining the twin challenge of internal stability in China, which depends on shared prosperity and unification strategies inside China, and peace in the world which depend, at least in part, on China's wisdom in resisting provocation and keeping its own military ambitions in check, Xi Jinping, is very alert to his responsibilities and obligations as leader of China. In addition, though, Xi Jinping wants to change the world, to recalibrate the world order. This we have also mentioned earlier in the chapter. This is in keeping with his view of China as a developing country, his commitment to engage the developing world, to align with them, and to express solidarity with them, and this is his reason for pursuing the strengthening of BRICS even while China is an important member of the G20 formation of leading nations of the global economy.

1.11 Conclusion: How Will Emerging Economic Problems in China Affect Its Approach?

China's ascent as a global economic powerhouse is inextricably linked to its strategic vision under the leadership of Xi Jinping. The nation has made remarkable strides in lifting a significant portion of its population out of poverty while positioning itself as a key player in international trade and investment. As China continues to expand its influence, particularly in emerging markets like the Caribbean, Chinese policymakers must navigate the complexities of global politics and economics precisely. This involves balancing domestic aspirations for growth and stability against the need to engage with other nations, especially considering the geopolitical tensions that characterize current international relations.

The significance of Xi Jinping's leadership is evident in the formulation of policies that prioritize national development and global engagement. His approach has focused on sustaining economic growth and addressing the potential pitfalls that could hinder China's progress, such as the middle-income trap and rising tensions with established powers. The emphasis on reform and modernization within the Communist Party underscores the need for adaptability in changing global dynamics. As China seeks to establish itself as a leader among developing nations, it must also confront the challenges posed by its relationships with the US and other Western powers, which often view China's rise with suspicion.

The recovery of China post-COVID has been slow. China has seen a real estate crash at home.[71] Protest demonstrations in China have been increasing.[72] Ethnic problems have emerged as a challenge to unity.[73] COVID-19 has raised suspicions. The post-COVID recalibration of business strategy has had serious impacts on China.[74] This has included sanctions and serious areas of disagreement between the USA and China, including Taiwan and spying air balloons.[75] The invasion of Ukraine by Russia, followed by the Israel/Gaza war, contributed to the global turmoil.[76] All of this has heightened the geopolitics and tensions inside China.

For Caribbean nations, the relationship with China offers both opportunities and risks. The Belt and Road Initiative provides a platform for investment and infrastructure development that could significantly benefit CARICOM member states. However, these countries must approach their engagement with China strategically to mitigate the risks associated with over-reliance on a single economic partner. This requires careful negotiation to ensure that investments align with regional development goals while fostering economic resilience. By cultivating a diversified approach to international partnerships, Caribbean nations can enhance their bargaining power and protect their sovereignty.

The path forward for both China and the Caribbean lies in fostering cooperative relationships that respect the interests of all parties involved. As China navigates its ambitions on the global stage, it must consider the implications of its actions and strategies for regional partners. In doing so, China can help create a more balanced and equitable international order that benefits not only its own development but also the aspirations of countries in the Caribbean and beyond. By emphasizing mutual benefit and shared prosperity, both China and the Caribbean can work towards a sustainable and prosperous future in an increasingly interconnected world. Whether China continues to deepen its reach outward more aggressively towards the small countries of the region or pull back defensively to take stock of other global and geopolitical challenges remains to be seen.

Notes

1. WB estimates the world population to reach 9.8bn, the United Nations 9.2b. by 2050. See also, "World Population Day: what will the world look like in 2050". Al Jazeera https://aljazeera.com Worldometer on October 16th, 2023, recorded the world's population as just over 8 billion, https://wwwworldometer.info. According to the United Nations Population Fund (UNFRA) State of World Population Report for 2023, China's population is 1.4257 billion, surpassed only by India's of 1.4286 billion. Lifting millions of people out of poverty had been a persistent theme of Chinese leadership from Mao Tse Tung onwards. See World Bank documents with the Ministry of Finance, China, and the Development Research Centre (DRC) for International Knowledge on Development (CKID) completed as a joint study. "Four Decades of Poverty Reduction in China: Drivers Insights for the World and the Way Ahead." Xi Jinping has made it one of his priorities to focus on poverty alleviation and lifting people to reasonable income. "Expanding the middle-income group is key to realizing a moderately prosperous society. It is also indispensable to transforming the growth model, reforming economic structures, and maintaining social harmony, stability, and long-lasting national peace." May 16,

2016, included in Xi Jinping, The Governance of China 11 Foreign Language Press Co. Ltd. China (p. 397).

2. In Prisoners of Geography, by Tim Marshall captures China's dilemma well. "China has locked itself into the global economy. If we don't buy, they don't make. And if they don't make, there will be mass unemployment. If there is mass and long-term unemployment, in an age where the Chinese are a people packed into urban areas the inevitable social unrest could be like everything else in modern China- on a scale hitherto unseen" (p. 63).
3. It is clear from reading Xi Jinping's statements over time that the Communist Party is the central command, source of power, and guide of policy, strategy, and action. Xi Jinping stresses three things: the need to weed out corruption, the need for party officials to be grounded in the people and in touch with their aspirations, and the need for party officials to be exemplary leaders.
4. Xi Jinping's awareness of the interdependence of party, military, and central government authority and their connections to the aspirations of ordinary people are evident throughout his speeches. He is also extremely conscious of the need for exemplary leadership in all national spheres by those at the top. His approach is unity and alignment at home.
5. China's International Relations outreach and geopolitical alertness make its interventions deliberate. China's interest in the Caribbean, therefore, is no different in this regard. There are economic, political, regional, and geopolitical dimensions focused on a recalibrated world order.
6. Beyond CBI and CARIBCAN, the trade investment and development relationship between the Caribbean and the USA and the Caribbean and Canada in each case is strong. Moreover, a significant Caribbean diaspora exists in both the USA and Canada. This has been strengthened in the post-COVID era with significant bilateral institutional relationships following the last controversial Summit of the Americas between the USA and the CARICOM, where President Biden engaged CARICOM directly, and Vice President Harris has been put in charge of US relations with CARICOM leaders at this level. Prime Minister Trudeau of Canada has not only extended CARIBCAN without further discussions for another ten years but has also called a meeting in Canada between

himself and all CARICOM leaders. Meanwhile, across the hemisphere, democracy seems to be deteriorating, inequality is growing, and ideology is shifting. See Daniel Zovato "Order from chaos: Foreign Policy in a Troubled World" www.brookings.edu/articles.

7. USC-US-China Institute, Xi Jinping's first speech as General Secretary, November 12th, 2012.
8. Ibid.
9. In 2023, there were two disturbing wars with the potential for catastrophe—the Russia-Ukraine war on the edge of Europe and the Israel-Hamas war in the Middle East. Tensions over Taiwan have also escalated. In addition, the crash of the real estate market in China and US sanctions on trade and investment have made the economic situation more challenging in China, increasing the number of daily protests. World news sources make these facts abundantly clear.
10. This is what Xi Jinping says in his 27 September 2016 speech focused on "Improve Our Ability to Participate in Global Governance." He says: "The pattern of global governance depends on international balance of power, and the transformation of global governance system originates from changes in the balance of power." In this, he sees a direct connection with the developing world. "We must continue to voice opinions on behalf of developing countries and strengthen solidarity and operations with other developing countries." Xi Jinping The Governance of China 11. pp. 488/489.
11. https://www.economist.com/asia/2024/09/10/the-scary-new-map-of-the-south-china-sea.
12. https://www.imf.org/en/Blogs/Articles/2024/09/12/trade-balances-in-china-and-the-us-are-largely-driven-by-domestic-macro-forces.
13. Xi Jinping, The Governance of China 11. (p. 262).
14. See Breda Griffith elibrary.worldbank.org/doi/10.1. "Middle Income Trap." Rising costs and declining competitiveness made it difficult for a country to move from middle income to high income and they become stuck or trapped. The challenge of getting out of this trap is a difficult one. Few countries have been successful in getting out of it.
15. Lisette Pacia Cervanles, Galvan Carlos Carmona, Campo Sevo Stanojevic, and David Villada Azate. https://www.frontras.org.

Evidence of Middle-Income Trap in Latin American countries: Factor analysis approach using regression and the ARDL models. Many Latin American and even Caribbean countries which moved quickly from low income to middle income, either regressed or ended up being stuck.

16. See https://www.adb.orgpublications "Escaping the middle-income trap: Innovate or Perish / Asian Development Bank.
17. The trap is named after the Greek historian who wrote about the Peloponnesian War between Greek and Sparta. He was a strategist who spoke incisively about power relations.
18. Graham Allison's views are expanded in his 2017 book, Harper Collins 2017.
19. See China, Ministry of Foreign Affairs statement of 23-06-19 @ 1840 hrs. "President Xi Jinping meets with US Secretary of State Antony Blinken, which includes both statements."
20. The fundamentals are the avoidance of the Middle-Income Trap and the Thucydides trap.
21. Continuity and change define China's policy over time. Each leader builds on what his predecessor has achieved before and inserts his own priorities based on his assessment of time, context, and necessities. As mentioned in the chapter, the Communist Party (CPC) is supreme and directs military strategy and economic policy. In Xi Jinping's speeches contained in "The Governance of China," one can note his indebtedness to earlier leaders while he acknowledges that "this is a world in which new opportunities and new challenges keep emerging, a world in which the international system and international order are going through a profound adjustment and a world in which the balance of international forces is shifting steadily in favour of peace and development." ("China's Diplomacy Must Benefit Its Major Country Status" in The Governance of China 11.) pp. 480/481.

    In Xi Jinping's 20 August 2014 speech, "A Bright Future for Socialism with Chinese Characteristics" in The Governance of China 11 (pp. 3–15), Xi Jinping acknowledges a debt to his predecessors, continuity of policy under the direction of the party and the significant legacy of Deng Xiaoping who coined the phrase "Socialism with Chinese Characteristics" which the current President of China, Head of the Military, and General Secretary of the party continues to honour. In the context of the focus of this book, the conceptual paper for China's relationship with the Caribbean was prepared in 2008 during the presidency of Hu Jintao, who succeeded Jiang Zamin, but it is emphasized that Xi Jinping is the one who visited the Caribbean and pushed things forward.

22. "The ultimate purpose of economic development is to ensure and improve people's well-being." Xi Jinping 27 October 2016, in "Secure the People's Basic Needs" in The Governance of China 11 (pp. 404–405), in which he also quotes Mao Zedong, who said in 1934 " …all practical problems in the masses' everyday life should claim one's attention. If we attend to these problems, solve them and satisfy the needs of the masses, we shall really become organizers of the well-being of masses, and they will truly rally round us and give us their warm support." So, Xi Jinping asks his CPC members to remember Mao and keep their nose to the ground even as he navigates the complexity of the world system and reaches for the stars in a way that his predecessor, might never have foreseen.
23. "Diplomatically" writes Tim Marshall in Prisoners of Geography in his chapter on China, "they (meaning China) will attempt to pull the South Asian nations away from the United States using both the carrot and stick." Too much carrot and they may not bend to Beijing's will. At the moment, they still look across the Pacific for protection. p. 61.
24. See Tim Marshall's Prisoners of Geography, chapter on China (pp. 40–65) for an exposition, elaboration, analysis, and assessment of China's geopolitical complications and the complexity of the landscape.
25. See "A New Era of China–Africa Cooperation and Development: (pp. 496–501) in The Governance of China" 11.

    See also, www.chatamhouse.org "China-Africa relations" and https:www.economist.com "The Chinese-African relationship is important to both sides, but also unbalanced".
26. https://issafrica.org. "Africa's future depends on a reset of China-West relations".
27. See the Belt and Road section of The Governance of China (pp. 543–568), to understand the concept of the Belt and Road Initiative from Xi Jinping's point of view.

28. The full text of China's policy paper on Latin America and the Caribbean can be found at https://english.www.gov.cn, which was published by the State Council, The People's Republic of China.
29. See "President Xi Jinping holds talk with Prime Minister Kamla Persad-Bissessar of Trinidad and Tobago." (Jm.china-embass.gov.cn) and President Xi Jinping meets with state leaders of Caribbean countries (https://www.fmprc.gov.ca).
30. See CARICOM China Trade https://CARICOM.org and https://wwwresearchgate.net. "The Dragon in the Caribbean: the future of CARICOM—China trade." https://www.researchgate.net and "Trade Relations between CARICOM and China a recap and outlook."
31. See Rasheed Griffith "Assessing China's Preserve and Power in the Caribbean" Lawfare Institute in Cooperation with Bookings June 17th, 2021.
32. See "China's Expanding and Evolving Engagement with the Caribbean" https://www.cc.gov.
33. https://www.stabroeknews.com/2024/01/14/news/guyana/govt-to-use-facial-recognition-to-track-criminals-jagdeo/.
34. https://antiguaobserver.com/symposium-held-at-chinese-embassy-highlights-strong-china-ab-relationship/.
35. https://www.thedailyherald.sx/regional/pm-took-antigua-s-relationship-to-new-heights-during-china-visit-diplomat-says.
36. https://www.mfa.gov.cn/eng/xw/zwbd/202407/t20240716_11454669.html.
37. See Ministry of Foreign Affairs of the People's Republic of China, "President Xi Jinping meets with State Leaders of Caribbean countries to strengthen bilateral cooperation and push for development of China-Caribbean relations," 6 March 2013.
38. Ibid.
39. Mao Xianglin, Adrian H. H. Hearn, and Liu Weiguang, China and Cuba: 160 years and looking ahead in Latin American perspectives Vol. 42 No, 6 (pp. 140–152) "China and Latin America: Processes and Paradoxes" (November 2015) Sage Publications. www.China-briefing.com. See also "China's Bi-lateral Trade and Investment Outlook with Cuba" 25th November 2022. Reuters 27th November 2022 "Cuba wins China debt relief, new funds."
40. Theglobalamericans.org "Chinese Engagement in the Dominican Republic: an update" Latin American News Agency (Prensa Latina)

May 2nd, 2023, "Dominican Republic of China strengthening relations in five years".

41. Belt + Road TT Chinese and Trinidad Guardian, "TT China relations have deepened with the Belt and Road initiative" 14 August 2023. Trinidad and Tobago Newsday ambassador Fang Qui, "China to boost investment in Trinidad and Tobago"
42. China in IDB and CDB 22 February 2017 https://www.1adb.org China joins IDB in a ceremony at Bank Headquarters. Using the Chinese Renminbi could help safeguard the region's access to global finance Committee on Foreign Affairs "China Regional Snapchat: The Caribbean.
43. See Tim Marshall Prisoners of Geography "Having spent four thousand turbulent years consolidating its landmass, China is now building a blue water navy. A green water navy patrols its maritime borders, a blue water navy patrols its oceans", p. 56. Moreover, China's investment in ports around the globe is a way of establishing friendly bases around the world, effective trade links, and logistical strength.
44. https://www.barrons.com January 25th, 2023 "China's Port Investment are Raising Security Fears. How to Deal with Them".
45. https://dialogo-america.com "China's network of ports grow in Latin America" in which China's foothold in some 40 ports in Latin America are identified.
46. See Ronald Saunders: Chinese Eggs waiting to be Hatched: Kaieteur News, October 24th, 2023.
47. https://foreignaffairs.house.gov/china-snapshot-project-the-caribbean/.
48. https://dialogue.earth/en/business/how-is-chinese-investment-in-latin-america-changing/.
49. Council on Foreign Relations "China's growing influence in Latin America" June 15th, 2023.
50. https://repositorio.cepal.org "Latin America and the Caribbean exports to the United States: Analysis of the Competition with China."
51. https://www.gov.cn "Full text of China's Policy Paper on Latin America and the Caribbean."
52. The Governance of China II p. 412.
53. Ibid p. 482.
54. Ibid p. 483.

55. https://spglobal.com "The World's 100 largest banks 2023 / S&P Global Market Intelligence. https://www.investopedia.com "The Four Biggest Chinese Banks."
56. A careful look at China's approach suggests it focused on internal stability and shared economic prosperity and then moved outwards in concentric circles, involving neighbourhood strategies, outreach strategies to other regions in an ever-increasing circle, and global presence, reach, and influence.
57. https://www.weforum.org 2016–01."Latin America is the world's most unequal region. Here is how to fix it".
58. See Roger Hosein, Anthony Gonzales, Bhoendradatt Tewarie and Rebecca Gookool-Bosland, Economic Development, implications of Venezuelan Migrant Crisis: Trinidad and Tobago and the Caribbean Community Springer 2022.
59. Council on Foreign Relations Diana Roy, December 1st, 2022 "See graphics that explain the US Struggle with Migrant Flows 2022.
60. Www.chatamhouse.org "Migration in Latin America."
61. There have been attempts to invigorate the Trade and Investment Council between CARICOM and the USA since the last summit of the Americas. See https://CARICOM.org "CARICOM and the United States Hold Ninth Meeting Trade and Investment Council", 16th October 2023.
62. The Canadian prime minister hosted a CARICOM Heads' delegation in Ottawa on October 18th. For a joint communique, see https://CARICOM.org.
63. dialoga-americas.com "Confronting China, Iran, Russia against Threats to Democracy" March 2023. Also, Wall Street Journal 12th June 2023 "Russia, China, and Iran in America's Backyard."
64. The Caribbean comprises high-income and middle-income countries, but the quest for sustainable growth, structurally sound economies, and sustainable development is elusive.
65. Traditionally, the UK and the USA have invested in these English-speaking countries. Most countries in the region think diversification of investment is desirable.
66. Especially post-COVID, most countries are pursuing self-sufficiency and developing neighborhood strategies for economic security.

67. Despite genuine gains, the dream of CARICOM economic integration has not been realised, even though CARICOM is one of the longest-standing regional formations in the world.
68. The CARICOM region is not known for rapid technological absorption and advance.
69. The high failure rate at CSEC is cause for alarm; Douglas (2024 https://newsday.co.tt/2024/08/21/cxc-reports-poor-regional-performance-64-fail-maths/) and Guyana Times (2024 https://guyanatimesgy.com/348058-2/).
70. Nearshoring is simply a growing desire by countries to invest in nearby countries rather than far away ones. The COVID crisis and logistics problems accelerated the movement towards nearshoring.
71. Fortune, 17 August 2023 "China Real Estate Crash is Worse than Official Data".
72. In Prisoners of Geography Tim Marshall indicates that there are now "five hundred mostly peaceful protests a day across China over a variety of issues" p. 55. In the current climate the numbers have increased as has the intensity, see "Human Rights Watch China: unprecedented nationwide Protests against Abuses".
73. https://research.nus.edu.sg/eai/wp-content/uploads/sites/2/2017/11/Vol1No3_LaiHongyi.pdf. "China's Ethnic Policies and Challenges". Tim Marshall points out in Prisoners of Geography how the Han ethnic group constitute a ruling caste.
74. Www.pewresearch.org "Unfavourable Views of China Reach Historic Highs in Many Countries."
75. The Taiwan issue will persist, and the issue of Chinese spying is likely to be a continuing problem between the USA and China even though it is well known that the USA spies on China and countries spy on each other.
76. The Israel-Gaza war, which erupted with the attack by Hamas on Israel in early October 2023, is likely to have serious implications for geopolitical relations going forward and for terrorism, security in the Middle East, and Peace in the World.

CHAPTER 2

The Dragon Can Dance!!!

2.1 Introduction

The growth of China since the 1970s has been spectacular. China has become more and more important in the Caribbean, from a non-player about 25 years ago to a middleweight or even a light heavyweight player today! (Poon, 2021[1]). China approaches the Caribbean region with grants, gifts, and soft loans and increasingly purchases raw materials from the region while providing low-cost goods. As some CARICOM countries increasingly turn to China, there have been growing tensions, and the USA has voiced its concerns and indeed has started to take steps to ramp up its support for the region, competing in some cases directly with Beijing (Montoute, 2023[2]). Carr (2023)[3] reflects China's core interest in the Caribbean. China seeks to secure raw materials and energy to help fuel its thriving economy and expanding middle class. China also sees the region as a place to make strides ahead of Taiwan, which continues to be recognized by Belize, Haiti, St Kitts and Nevis, St Lucia, and St Vincent and the Grenadines.[4]

China's investments in the Caribbean have benefited the region considerably. Between 2005 and 2020, China invested over US$10.8 bn in the Caribbean.[5] Grady (2024)[6] discusses that Chinese investments in the region have been diverse and mainly related to infrastructure and productive capacity enhancements such as ports, 5G telecommunications networks, transport infrastructure, and clean energy. In Jamaica and

R. Hosein et al., *China in the Caribbean*,
https://doi.org/10.1007/978-3-031-71985-1_2

China, investments have been used to build up the country's infrastructure base with the construction of highways, bridges, and ports, which support the expansion of mining and energy sectors. Some noteworthy projects include the 66 km North–South highway linking Kingston to Ocho Rios, Portland Bright Energy Centre, and the Falmouth Cruise Port. Estimates from the Ministry of Foreign Affairs and Foreign Trade indicate that China invested approximately US$3 bn over a 20-year period.[7] Morris (2024)[8] reported that Chinese investments have cumulatively contributed to the employment of more than 40,000 persons over the last decade.

The trade volume between China and Jamaica in 2023 was US$1.28 bn, a year-on-year increase of 25.8 per cent. China continues to be Jamaica's second-largest trading partner.

China has been consistently one of the largest economies in the world in the last 2000 years (Table 2.1). One contemporary Portuguese account of sailors that went to Guangzhou noted, "The ramparts were covered in silken banners, while on the towers reared flagstaffs from which also hung silken flags, so huge that they could be used as sails, ….Such is the wealth of that country, such is its vast supply of silk, that they squander gold leaf and silk on these flags where we use cheap colours and coarse linen cloth" (Shuman, 2020).[9] Bearing this in mind, China's rise to the second-largest economy in the world is not entirely surprising. Using the data presented by Yang (2019), it can be noted that in the year 1700, China accounted for 23% of the world's population, with this increasing to 37% in 1820, and standing at 26% of the global population in 1900. In 1820, China accounted for a third of global GDP. In terms of GDP per capita, it is noted that for China, this increased from US$8265 in 2015 to US$17,210 in 2020 (using 2015 US$). By 2023, China had 18% of the world population and was also generating 18% of global GDP. Per capita GDP in 2023 was only marginally below the international average.

This chapter briefly discusses the contribution of several key factors in the development of modern-day China. The rest of this chapter progresses as follows: The next section provides an overview of the various Chinese Dynasties before reflecting on some of the main leaders. The chapter provides some context for the legacy of socialism before concluding.

Table 2.1 Selected historical indicators for China, 1700–2023

	1700	*1820*	*1900*	*1950*	*2001*	*2015*	*2020*	*2022*	*2023*
Population (millions)									
China	138	381	400	5,47	1275	1387	1439	1412	1410
World	603	1042	1564	2521	6149	7154	7794	7951	8024
China in world (%)	23	37	26	22	21	19	18.18	18	17.6
*GDP (billions of 1990 international dollars)**									
China	83	229	218	240	4570	11,463	14,616.41	16,325.21	17,794.78
World	371	696	1973	5326	37,148	57,947	82,117.36	87,063.96	90,546.52
China in world (%)	22	33	11	5	12	20	17.8	18	19.7
*Per capita GDP (1990 international dollars)**									
China	600	600	545	439	3583	8265	10,358.2	11,223.2	11,178.44
World	615	668	1262	2110	6041	7154	10,499.6	11,037.3	11,258.04
China in world (%)	0.98	0.9	0.43	0.21	0.59	1.16	1.01	0.98	0.99

Source: Yang 2019, and WDI
*2020 and 2022 date is given in 2015 US$

2.2 A Brief Economic Overview of Various Chinese Dynasties

The various Chinese Empires are shown in Table 2.2 below. Chinese civilization peaked during the Tang and Song dynasties (AD 666–1266), but it stagnated during the Ming and Qing dynasties (Yang, 2019). The Tang Dynasty was able to help unify a vast territory and spread culture as well as absorb the culture of the surrounding states. The Tang emperors instituted a system of land reform that involved breaking up large holdings to help the peasants. They also made a system of canals for trade and transport, Holcombe (2001) (Table 2.2).[10]

The Song Dynasty consisted of centrally appointed officials, which gave the Song emperors a greater degree of control than the Tang officials. Under the Song Dynasty, paper money was established, and a unified tax code was formed (Pfaff, 2010).[11] The Song Dynasty has been measured alongside the European Renaissance as China made considerable progress in technology and inventions.

Table 2.2 Empires of China, 618–1911

Dynasty	*Date*
Tang	618–907
Five dynasties	907–960
Northern song	960–1127
Southern song	1127–1279
Yuan	1271–1368
Ming	1368–1644
Qing	1644–1911

Source: https:culturachina.net

At the end of the Tang Dynasty, General Zhao Kuangyin, in the year 960, took charge of the divided parts of China and unified them (Glahn, 2016). He became the first Song Emperor. Gao (2017) notes that Bi Sheng invented the clay movable type printer between 1041 and 1048 (Bi Sheng carried identical characters on pieces of fine clay). The movable bloc could be glued onto an iron plate and easily detached from the plate as needed. In addition, it was during the Song Dynasty that the "Green Sprout" system was introduced. This was a loan scheme for the peasants to assist them in purchasing seeds at an interest rate of about 2% for an average of ten years (Glahn, 2016). Agyekum (2019) noted that under the Song Dynasty, inventions related to shipbuilding increased and helped the Song Dynasty to construct vessels of different sizes never witnessed before. Their building of these ships involved the design of watertight compartments that could store food for the sailors (including people like Zheng He, the greatest Ancient Chinese explorer). Agyekum (2019) notes that in this Dynasty, a compass pointing north was also invented and deployed. One thing that worked well for the Song Dynasty was that the great general Zhao Kuangyin retired all his military men and replaced them with capable civilians. This move helped to bring political stability in the era of the Song Dynasty and allowed active trade to take place (Ting et al., 2019).[12]

During the Song Dynasty, a new type of Southeast Asian rice was brought into China. This rice had a longer shelf life and offered a better yield than in China at the time. Farmers in China were innovative, and as Hansen 2000, p. 266 noted, "Over time, farmers were able to develop hybrids with Indigenous strains to make double-cropped rice, and the resulting increase in production freed some of the working population from having to grow their food. It was those workers who were able to produce goods for market" (Hansen, 2000, p. 266). In this era, agriculture moved from subsistence farming to cash crops to even commercial farming, with Ebrey (1996), p. 141 noting: "Some farmers were even finding specialization profitable. Local farmers near Suzhou, for instance, often devoted themselves to raising silkworms and producing silk thread. In Fujian, Sichuan, and Guangdong, many farmers devoted their land to sugar cane."

Historically, China has been a major centre of manufacturing. During the Song Dynasty, it experienced changes close to an industrial revolution almost seven centuries before the European Industrial Revolution (1760–1840).[13] Even before Vasco da Gama made his way to India in 1498, the Chinese had trading links that stretched from South China to South Asia to across the Persian Gulf and the Red Sea.

The Yuan Dynasty lasted from 1271 to 1368, while the Ming Dynasty existed between 1368 and 1644. One of the big achievements of the Yuan Dynasty was the unification of the whole of China. The unification of China helped to strengthen national integration. During the Yuan Dynasty, the "Chao" banknote was introduced (made from the bark of a mulberry tree). The Chao was the first paper currency in history to be used as the predominant medium. During the Ming Dynasty, China, according to some sources, was the largest economy in the world, with a larger area and more literate people than in other countries (Eckhart, 2016).[14]

The Qings of the Qing Dynasty were from Manchuria and reigned over China for 268 years. The Qing Dynasty focused on two main sectors: agriculture and industry. In the agriculture sector, the Qing leaders influenced people to settle new land by providing seeds, livestock, and tax breaks. Farmers throughout the country established productive agricultural colonies (Zhihong, 2017).[15]

The Qing statesmen considered measures to boost China's wealth and power and began undertakings in transport, industry, and commerce. They obtained new machines powered by steam, which reformed transportation. China's first railroads and steamships were constructed. Qing officials and foreign engineering experts constructed over 300 miles of track by the year 1894.[16] Chinese elites bought and operated machines for spinning and weaving cotton, wool threads, and textiles, pumping water, digging irrigation canals and water wells, and ploughing agricultural areas. In the later part of the nineteenth century, the Qing statesmen had concerns about the location and extraction of coal to power these machines. Statesmen worked with foreign scientists and technicians to extract the coal, which became China's most treasured resource (Lavelle, 2017; Wu, 2015).

From 1700 to 1820, the population of China, according to Maddison (2006), increased from 138 to 381 mn. Significantly, this increase occurred without the decline in standard of living. During this period of the Qing Dynasty, another aspect of achievement was the expansion of the area under imperial control. By 1820, China's national territory was 12 million square km, which is about twice that of what it was in 1680. Mongolia was conquered in 1696–97, Taiwan in 1683, and Tibet in 1720. However, the nineteenth century was very different from the Qing Dynasty, and several factors worked together to end this Dynasty and set the path for modern China (Hang, 2016). Specifically, the White Lotus uprising of 1796–1820 occurred during their reign. This Rebellion was a large-scale uprising in the mountainous regions of China that helped to weaken the Qing Dynasty. The Rebellion consisted of uncoordinated guerrillas using hit-and-run tactics (Yincong Dai, 2019,[17] Miller, 2013[18]).

Another factor that led to the demise of the Qing Dynasty was China's miscalculation of the power of the British military and the consequent "Opium Wars." The first "Opium War" in 1839–42 was between the Qing and Great Britain as the Qing Dynasty targeted the British merchants that sold opium to the Chinese merchants. Only one Chinese Port, the Canton Harbour, was opened to trade with foreigners and only between October and May (Brown, 2004, Kalipci, 2018, p. 34). Britain was bringing opium into China from India for a period, but because of the associated addiction, Chinese officials, first in 1726 and then again in 1796, banned the opium trade. The murder of a Chinese peasant in 1839 helped to spark the First Opium War (Brown, 2017).[19] The Opium War of 1839–42 ended in defeat for the Qing. (Note that things had become so bad that by the 1840s, the Chinese had to export silver to meet their deficit, whereas before, they had an inflow of silver.) With the Treaty of Nanjing, China acknowledged it lost the first war, handed over Hong Kong to the British, and allowed five (5) other ports to be opened for trade with Europe (Loh & Chen, 2019).[20] It also ended the Cohong monopoly on foreign trade and tolerated the import of opium (Glahn, 2016).[21]

Although there was an increase in opium imports, the exports of tea from China grew even more than proportionally. British merchants became disgruntled and pushed their government into the Second Opium War (Maurice Solocitz, 2018). With the second war, from 1856 to 1860, the Qing Dynasty was forced to provide favourable tariffs, trade concessions, and land to the Europeans (Hayes, 2021, Loh & Hao, 2019). The Taiping Rebellion 1850–64 also helped to weaken the Qing Dynasty.[22] The Taiping Rebellion started in the deep south in the Kwangsi province. Maddison (2003)[23] notes that the Taiping war is generally held to be responsible for 20 million deaths. As its weaknesses became exposed, China began to lose power over other peripheral parts of the region to Britain, France, Germany, Russia, and Japan. The balance of power had decidedly moved away from the Qing Dynasty to foreign countries (Charles Rivers, 2018; Maddison, 2007).

2.3 Key Leaders in the Development of the Modern Chinese Empire

Several key players helped to move China forward since 1901. This next section briefly mentions the role of several of these political leaders.

2.3.1 *Sun Yat-Sen, The "Father of the Nation"*

Many people refer to Sun Yat-Sen as the "Father of the Nation" and the First Provisional Premier of the Republic of China. He was born on 12 November 1866 and died on 12 March 1925. Sun Yat-Sen played a pivotal role in the overthrow of the Qing Dynasty during the Xinhai Revolution. Sun studied at a missionary school in Hong Kong and attained a medical degree. During his time spent in the West, he was not satisfied with the Chinese government, and he started his political career by trying to organize reform groups of Chinese exiles in Hong Kong. Since the 1880s, Sun Yat-Sen was the main activist promoting the formation of a nationalist republican movement. Sun failed in a coup that he had planned in 1895, and for 16 years after, he was an exile in Europe, the USA, and Japan.[24] Sun joined dissident Chinese groups in Japan and became their leader (Jensen, 1951). Sun was expelled from Japan and was living in America when the Wuchang uprising broke out (Jensen, 1951). Although it occurred quickly, the Wuchang uprising was, in part, the result of over ten years of hard work by Sun Yat-Sen abroad (Tung, 1964).[25]

On 29 December 1911, Sun Yat-Sen was elected provisional President of the Republic of China (Lane, 2008).[26] Sun Yat-Sen's key proposal was socialism and he proposed that "The State will take over all the large enterprises; we shall encourage and protect enterprises which may reasonably be entrusted to the people…" (Shen & Payne, 1946).

2.3.2 Mao Zedong

Mao was born on 26 December 1893 in the village of Shaoshan in Hunan province, as the son of a peasant who became wealthy by dealing in grain. In 1911, Mao Zedong began a provincial school in Changsha (Glahn, 2016). He took part in the 1911 uprisings for six months as a private soldier. As a symbol of Rebellion against the Manchu, Mao and one of his friends cut off their queue pigtails which was considered a sign of subservience to the emperor (Schram, 1966)).

A very significant event in Mao Zedong's era, was the "Wusi" protest on 4 May 1919.[27] Initially, China had contributed thousands of workers to the joint effort during World War I; however, at the Paris Peace Conference, German belongings in the country were transferred to Japanese control. Protests aimed at Chinese leaders occurred throughout the country against the deal. The Chinese refused to sign the Treaty of Versailles (Linyn, 2019).[28] The protests were successful in demonstrating the power of collective action and constructing anti-imperialist sentiment. This movement led to the formation of the Chinese Communist Party. Panda (2015) indicated that Mao Zedong quoted the movement as a "new stage in China's bourgeois-democratic revolution against imperialism and feudalism."

Mao Zedong would become the first President of the People's Republic of China in 1949. Maddison (2007) noted that the degree of central control was greater than under the Qing Dynasty.[29] Mao Zedong also cut ties in most ways with the outside world. His leadership was classified by his successors as having "7 parts good and 3 parts bad" (Leon Poon, 2010, Lieberthal, 2023).[30] Significantly, though, Mao had won the hearts of the peasants of China and, at one point, instructed his officials not to take a "needle or a thread" from the mass of Chinese people, and the common people appreciated this (Leon Poon, 2010).

Mao facilitated men and women receiving higher education equally in China. He famously said, "funu neng ding ban bian tian," meaning that "women could hold up half the sky," and in many regards, this was very effective in motivating the working efforts of women in China. Although not always well received, other important developments would emerge, one of the more significant being The Centre for Women Studies built at Zhengzhou University in Henan province in 1987, followed by many women's studies programs and research centres throughout China (Wang, 1997).

Another one of Mao's famous slogans at this time was "chao ying gan mei," which translated to "surpass the British and catch up with the Americans." This phrase was first uttered by the First Secretary of the Soviet Union, Nikita Khrushchev, in 1957, when he argued that the Soviet Union would surpass Britain and catch up to America.[31]

One major accomplishment of Mao Zedong was the banning of opium and the intensive education of youths against its use, to the extent that by 1953, with the use of force, opium use in China dramatically declined (Kissinger, 2004).[32]

After 1956, Mao became more subjective and eccentric, and he implemented two (2) disastrous political interventions, *The Great Leap Forward* and *The Cultural Revolution*. The Great Leap Forward was supposed to be part of the second Five-Year Plan, but after just three years, it was stopped. The Great Leap Forward was the expression of the intent of Mao Zedong to push China from a mostly agrarian society to a more modern industrialized nation within 5 years. The fallout from the interventions under this plan was catastrophic and it was not helped by adverse weather conditions.[33] Indeed, the period 1958–1960 became known as the Three Bitter Years. Private industrial enterprise was eliminated by Mao in 1958. Mao promoted the development of small-scale industry in rural areas by pushing rural labour into iron smelting, cement, and fertilizer manufacturing. This was done under quasi-military conditions and involved some 30 million peasants being taken away from farmlands. The result of this was widespread harvest failure and moreover, much of the industrial output produced was useless (Maddison, 2007). The official death toll for that period stands at 14 mn but many agree this was an understatement (Szczepanski, 2019; Joseph, 1986)[34] and was subsequently revised to about 45 mn (O'Neil, 2010).[35]

The Cultural Revolution, launched by Mao Zedong in 1966, was intended to preserve Communism in China by removing whatever elements of capitalism remained within China and within the Chinese Communist Party.[36] One and a half million (1.5 mn) people were killed during the Cultural Revolution (Wang, 2017)[37] and millions were imprisoned.[38] During the this era, the economy plummeted and industrial output by 1968 was 12% less than in 1966.[39] Communes that were created during the Great Leap Forward and which involved the abolition of private property and rural markets were closed (Skinner, 1965). The state, in this period, controlled all marketing and credit arrangements. Families were required to eat in communal kitchens or in mess halls. The communes were expected, according to Maddison (2007), to be basically self-sufficient. In this period, statistical reporting took the form of an exercise to feed the fantasies of the political leadership. The famine deaths and the decline in births from the period 1959–61 led to a fall in the population of about 6 mn as compared to an increase in population of about 28 mn for the previous period 1957–59.

Even so, under Zedong, economic performance in the period 1952–78, improved significantly as compared to previous periods. GDP trebled, and per capita real product increased by 82% and labour productivity by 58%.

2.3.3 Deng Xiaoping

Mao Zedong died in 1976 and Deng Xiaoping gradually rose to power. Deng Xiaoping was born in 1904 and was the son of a middle-class landowner and brought a significant change in Chinese economic policies (Vogel, 2013). Deng turned around the policies of China from being centralized to being liberalized. Deng's vision to promote economic growth was considered by many to be one of "great international circulation" which is a strategy of economic growth led by export-oriented production (Grieger, 2020).[40] Maddison (2007) noted, "...after, there was a major political shift to a cautious pragmatic reformism which relaxed political control and modified the economic system profoundly. These changes brought a more stable path of development and a great acceleration of economic growth." The shift in China's economic policies helped pave the way for the Chinese economy to prosper (Vogel, 2013, Whyte, 2013; Maddison, 2007).

Deng spent part of his early life in France where he studied during the period 1920–24 (Wang, 2009),[41] and he became active in the communist movement and the Soviet Union (1925–6), which allowed him to have a broader outlook on running China than Mao. Deng Xiaoping considered the New Economic Policy the economic model best suited to China (Cable, 2017).[42]

One of Deng's first priorities was the Gu Mu delegation of 1978.[43] Shuyuan (2014) highlighted that the Vice Premier of the State Council, Gu Mu, led an economic delegation to visit five Western European countries, including France, Switzerland, Belgium, Denmark, and the then Federal Republic of Germany. One source notes that before this delegation left China, Deng Xiaoping instructed them to "Have broad contacts, make detailed investigations, and carry on deep research into the issues. Look at how they [Western Europe] manage their economic activities. We ought to study the successful experiences of capitalist countries and bring them back to China." The Gu Mu delegation noted, "… Everything we saw and heard startled every one of us. We were enormously stimulated…We thought capitalist countries were backward and decadent. When we left our country and took a look, we realized things were completely different" (Wang Quangduo, head of the State Planning Commission of Guangdong province, explaining tour member's impressions).[44] When the Gu Mu delegation visited a German coal mine, they found that a German worker was about 80 times more productive than a Chinese worker in coal mining. When the delegation returned, they prepared a Report on the visit to five countries in Western Europe and made an 8-hour oral presentation to Xiao Ping. This report was important, and it included a set of policy recommendations to help expand trade, advance science and technology, learn how to utilize foreign technology, and improve manufacturing.

Deng met the prime minister of Japan on 6 December 1979, and, during their discussion, he indicated that he wanted China to become a well-off society (Hoppens, 2020).

Deng Xiaoping launched The Four Modernizations, one of which was to boost agriculture (the other three modernizations were industry, national defence, and science and technology).[45] China relied on grain imports and needed an increase in its domestic food supply to feed its rapidly growing population. Deng introduced agricultural reforms in December 1978.[46] Glahn (2016) indicated that Deng's policy changes resulted in China having 44,000 markets in 1983, which allowed farmers to sell their foods privately.

Deng also disbanded the commune system and relaxed agricultural controls, production targets, and quotas. The government also made significant revisions to prices paid for farm products. Maddison (2007) documents that between 1978 and 1983, for example, farmers received, on average, 50% more for their produce. Quota prices were also increased. The system of egalitarian payments was dropped, and a new system built around household responsibility contracts (with remuneration linked to output) was introduced. Deng also reallocated collective lands to households, commencing with the Anhwei province, and because of its success, the reallocation continued from 14% in 1980 to 99% by 1984. This disbandment helped to liberalize Chinese peasants, and pesticides and other modern techniques were introduced as an essential feature of the Chinese agricultural system. Deng also granted the peasant farmers greater control over their production and profits, which, after its initiation in 1981, helped to increase agricultural production significantly within just a few years (agricultural value added increased from US$41 bn in 1978 to US$75.1 bn in 1983 an increase of 81.5%).

Under Deng, China became an important trade partner of many countries and embarked on a program of aid and investment to help strengthen other economies.

Deng established Exclusive Economic Zones (EEZs) in China, and these were initially situated in four provinces, Shenzhen, Zhuhai, Xiamen, and Shantou, in 1979. The objective of these EEZs was to help develop trading ties with foreign countries. The second objective of these EEZs was the observance of economic reforms in the Chinese system to reduce the highly centralized and closed system. These new economic reforms were designed to bring changes to the existing system (Butt & Sajid, 2018).[47] China used these economic zones to increase industrial technology and management skills and incorporate features of capitalism in their socialist economy. These were designed as containment zones as these zones depended on the import of foreign capital. These four main EEZs were set up along the coast and away from China's main population centres and were isolated from China's economic and political influence (Zheng, 2012). These zones attracted foreign firms which wanted to operate from China and benefit from its low labour costs without being subjected to restrictions on FDI and the bureaucracy as existed elsewhere in the economy. In the mid-1980s, 14 New Open Port Cities were established, all of which offered incentives similar to the first four.

Mao Zedong noted, "The more people there are, the stronger we are." However, Deng Xiaoping disagreed and implemented the One Child Policy to control China's rapidly growing population. This one-child policy was enforced in 1980 by Deng Xiaoping after the population had increased to 969 million in 1980 from approximately 540 million in 1949 (Mullen, 2021).

Universities and colleges were almost completely closed over the period 1966–1968[48] as no students were admitted over this period. From 1969 to 1976, China's higher education system was partly restored when workers, peasants, and soldiers, social classes that were highly regarded by the government, were allowed to register based on a recommendation system. Deng also restored the National College Entrance Examination, as this had been cancelled for ten years during the Cultural Revolution, and stopped the recommendation system. He also heavily improved tertiary education in China, seeing it as a first step towards social reform therein (Kang, 2004).[49]

However, there was a dark stain in the period of rule by Deng Xiaoping as he permitted Chinese troops to open fire on the pro-democracy gathering of about 1 mn students in 1989 at Tiananmen Square, killing many and arresting as many as ten thousand (Vogel, 2011). Many factors played a role in this uprising, including rising inflation, corruption, and growing expectations.

2.3.4 *Xi Jinping*

Xi Jinping was born in 1953 as the son of Xi Zhongxun (one of the heroes of the Chinese communist revolution). Xi studied Chemical engineering at Tsinghua University and later majored in Marxist Theory and Ideological Education. From early on, Xi Jinping was outspoken and at one point on a tour of Mexico, noted, "Some biased foreigners, with full bellies and nothing better to do than engage in finger pointing at us... First, China does not export revolution; second, it does not export famine and poverty; and third, it does not mess around with you. So what else is there to say?" (Perlez, 2012).[50]

Xi Jinping became President on 14 March, 2013. He changed the One Child Policy to two and, in May of 2021, announced a Three Child Policy in an attempt to address China's flagging birth rate as a strategy to stave off risks to the economy from an ageing population.[51] This policy, which was passed into law in 2021, is to be complemented by a host of support measures that will be consistent with the change in policy alongside the imposition of interventions to cope with an ageing population.[52]

The "Chinese Dream" is a term closely associated with Xi Jinping. Xi has encouraged young Chinese to dream and revitalize their nation. Xi's vision of the Chinese Dream is achieving the Two Centenaries, the first of which is being a moderately well-off society by 2021 and a fully developed nation by 2049, (the 100th Anniversary of the People's Republic of China). In many regards, in pursuing the Chinese Dream, Xi Jinping attempted to tap into the historical consciousness of the Chinese people (von Hein, 2018).[53]

For many years, China seemed to follow a strategy of "hide your strength, bide your time" as advocated by Deng. In 1996 though, China adopted a more proactive approach of "peaceful rise." Goldstein (2020) in commenting on Xi, noted that he: a) sought to reassure others about the peaceful rise of China and b) he progressed China from rhetoric to action in promoting the reform of the international order that helped to facilitate China's rise.

Xi, however, has been more resolutely defiant and resists challenges to what the Chinese Communist Party considers to be its core interests. Indeed, Xi Jinping had his ideology included in the Party's Constitution in 2017, and term limits were scrapped in 2018, indicating a more confident and confrontational China. (Not only were term limits scrapped, but of the 2964 delegates that were present to vote, 2958 voted in favour of scrapping the term limits, and there were two dissents, three abstentions, and one of the votes was invalid (The Wall Street Journal, March 11th, 2018).[54]

2.4 The Legacy of Socialism

After the war years in China, there was considerable damage to its economic infrastructure especially in industry and agriculture. Hyperinflation, which had set into the economy in the war years had disturbed the short-run development process. (Specifically note that for the period September 1945–May 1949, China experienced a bout of hyperinflation. Indeed, Teh-Wei Hu in *Dynamics of Hyperinflation* found this to be 78% on average per month for this period).

The years of foreign aggression experienced by the Chinese from 1839 until 1945, that is, from the Opium Wars through to the anti-Japanese war,[55] resulted in Chinese distrust of Western institutions. At the same time, the Nationalist parties, which were the main opponents of the

Communist Party, lost some political ground as the economy experienced a sharp bout of hyperinflation from 1945 to 1949.

In 1949, China was a poor country, although it had a relatively high level of human capital (Naughton, 2007). Additionally, there was a small university system and a cadre of Chinese citizens with foreign training. There was also a transport hub that could help foster development.

In this early phase of the People's Republic of China (PRC) life, the government poured vast amounts of resources into capital-intensive factories producing goods and metals. In these early years, China followed an import substitution strategy and structured its economy around the model of the Soviet Union. China followed this pathway for 30 years and created a Big Push setting (Brandt, Ma, & Debin, 2016). This Big Push strategy overwhelmed all else and governed the allocation of scarce resources. China adopted a command economy model, and resources were allocated under the plan. Market forces were eschewed in favour of state-led resource allocation.

Most of the investment in China went to heavy industry, more than 80% in this period, and consumption was squeezed. However, the PRC was able to restart economic growth after years of stagnation and depression associated with the war. The Chinese economy took off after 1949, and the Big Push strategy produced improved growth results for a period.

Missing the benefits of openness seemed to work against China in this phase. Specifically, while other East Asian countries such as Taiwan and Hong Kong could source cheap factor inputs from abroad, China did not have that option or rather closed off that option. The enhanced openness of these other Asian countries allowed them to absorb foreign technology and converge to international best practices faster. Indeed, by 1978, using the available data with 1960 as the base year, Hong Kong was considerably more economically advanced than China (See Fig. 2.1). This would have helped in part to convince the new Chinese leadership after Mao Zedong's death of the need to open the economy.

In the early years of the PRC, the surpluses the government realized from the firms under their control provided them with part of the resources to promote a Big Push industrialization effort (Brandt, Ma & Debin, 2016). However, while the Chinese followed the Soviet Union in many ways, there was one significant way they differed; specifically the ideological and social control which was especially tight in China (Naughton, 2007). During the reign of Mao Zedong, he maintained

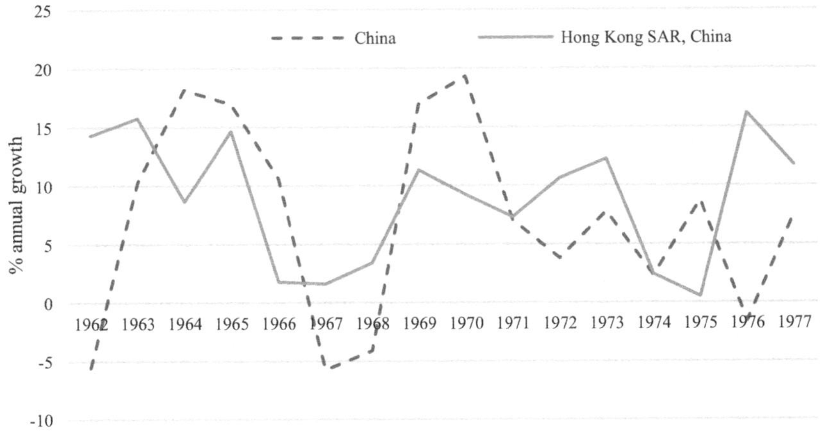

Fig. 2.1 GDP Growth (%), 1962–1977 (Source: WDI)

very strict and tight controls over the Chinese labour market and maintained control of worker movement and worker remuneration. Migration to urban areas was controlled. During the Cultural Revolution, Mao Zedong's regime sent many school leavers from the urban sphere (17 million approximately) to the rural areas of China to help boost rural output. In state-owned enterprises, employees were locked in with life-long employment, and there were cases where employment would move from parents to children. It became illegal for a firm to terminate a worker in this period in the Chinese economy.

In the first 3 years of the PRC, the economy progressed above that which was attained in wartime and during hyperinflation. Tight control of the budget and the money supply in China immediately after 1949 brought inflation under control. By 1952, the level of industry in China and agriculture was higher than before 1949. The Chinese government pushed forward with radical land reform and, between 1950 and 1952, redistributed 42% of China's arable land. In so doing, the Chinese authority gained widespread support among ordinary people. In the urban sphere, during these 3 years, the new government took over many of the factories and took control of those which they expropriated from the Japanese. In this early phase, many skilled people joined the line-up and provided strong support to the extent that industrial output increased.

According to Naughton (2007), during the 1950s, every aspect of the Soviet's Big Push strategy was copied, and the Chinese also imported Soviet industrial technology and organizational design. In the 1950s, there were two twin peaks of rapid change: 1953 and 1956. Investments ramped up quickly, and 156 industrial parks were built inland using techniques imported from the Soviet Union or Eastern Europe. The Soviets assisted the Chinese in many ways and about 6000 Soviet advisors, according to Naughton, came to China while many Chinese students (about 10,000) studied in the USSR. In the second peak of the transformation, dubbed the "high tide of socialism," Mao Zedong pushed hard for greater public ownership. Specifically, in 1955, Mao Zedong announced that he was displeased at how farmers became a part of agricultural cooperatives. The personal intervention of Mao helped, and while by the end of 1954, a mere 2% of farm households were controlled by the cooperatives, by 1956, it had grown to 98%. Some private ownership in the urban sphere, which remained up until this point, was ended, and by the end of 1956, China was a full-fledged socialist state. The socialist model had created changes in some places, and Naughton (2007, p. 68) noted, "Extraordinarily rapid economic growth had taken place, and industrial production expanded 17% annually between 1952 and 1957. Almost every sector of the economy was rehabilitated, and massive investments in education and training laid the groundwork for sustained future growth. It was a period of rapid social mobility, as farmers moved into the city and young people entered college. It was a period of dramatic progress, now looked back upon with nostalgia by many of those in China old enough to remember it. Having accumulated experience in its economic construction, China now seemed well on the way to defining its brand of socialism, which was more flexible and market responsive than the Soviet model."

By 1956, the PRC had transitioned from a capitalist economy to a command-type economy following the Soviet model. The Chairman of the Communist Party at this point (Mao Zedong) made a call to intellectuals to express their concern for the progress of China up to that point. On 27 February 1957, Mao in a speech before the Supreme State Conference, said, "let a hundred flowers bloom; let a hundred schools of thought contend." Many spoke out and the editor-in-chief of the Guangming Daily noted "… a party leading a nation is not the same as a party owning a nation: the public supports the party…." Consequently, Mao Zedong implemented the Anti-rightist campaign, which targeted those who spoke out in the Hundred Flowers campaign as well as their intellectual support and they were corralled and sent to labour camps.[56]

The Great Leap Forward (GLF) was built on an urge for faster economic growth, and it took a distinctly Chinese slant. The GLF triggered an accelerated push for economic growth in which resources were transferred from agriculture to the industrial sector. For a while, flawed statistical reporting made the GLF look impressive, and against a background of inflated data, the ruling elite made two sharp changes: they cut back on labour and land for agriculture, and secondly, they increased procurement for grain by the state. In combination, these two changes meant that less was produced, and more was taken out by the state, leaving an even smaller amount behind. Harvests declined, and food stocks fell. In 1960, a full-blown famine was declared in China. The Russians, alarmed by the Chinese approach, pulled their advisors, and a rift developed between the two economies. Recognizing the stress of the situation in early 1961, some 20 million workers were sent back to work in agriculture in the country. By 1964, some of the markets that were closed during the GLF were reopened so that an additional source of food could be brought on board from peasants to increase the food supply.

Mao's eccentricity continued, and after a brief pause following the GLF, he set on a pathway of the "Cultural Revolution" by promoting the Red Guards, which started with a group of students who wanted to overthrow the leadership of the Communist Party, leaving only Mao. The result was a disruption of the productive system and factional conflict.

As the disruptions from the Cultural Revolution subsided, the focus continued to be on economic construction in China. This was called the third front. As China focused on the third front, agriculture was not starved for resources, but efforts were maintained to boost the capital sector. Martial law was sometimes used. Society was partly militarized, and there were elements of an attempt to revive aspects of the GLF. It came with a heavy state involvement, and the market mechanism was ignored. This time, though, austerity was built into the program (Naughton, 2007). An increased amount of Chinese manpower was tied up in the development of China. In 1971, though, Richard Nixon visited China, and Zou Enlai took a role in pursuing a more moderate approach to economic relations with the capitalist world.[57] A big step was the establishment of 11 fertilizer plants designed by a Dutch US group as part of a decision to spend US$4.3 bn on importing industrial goods. As Zhou

Enlai's health faded, Mao brought in Deng Xiaoping in 1974, to support the transition.

In 1975, China embarked on a "rectification" of the policy errors from the Cultural Revolution. At this point, Deng, recognizing the challenges in China, noted, "At present, there are many good problems that we cannot solve without a great effort. We must be daring and resolute." Deng's return to the big stage of Chinese leadership did not last long, and he was again removed in 1976. indeed, the period 1974–1976 was one in which there was a paralysis of economic policymaking, and a deadlock emerged in the top leadership of the party. This was broken, though, in 1976, and the new leader, Hua Guofeng, initiated a 10-year plan with massive investments. However, things did not work out smoothly, as the investment plans that were set out were very unrealistic in many ways. Secondly, China's efforts to pay for some of the much-needed industrial equipment via the export of oil revenues ran into many obstacles. However, by the end of 1978, the Third Plenum made a break from the past and marked the return of Deng Xiaoping as the paramount leader. A host of new policies was adopted by the Chinese Communist Party (CCP) leaders.

2.5 Conclusion

This chapter provided a brief sketch of the great leaders and some of their economic contributions that helped to shape modern-day China. The nation's history of dynastic rule, particularly during the Tang and Song dynasties, laid a strong cultural foundation, while the struggles of the Qing Dynasty and subsequent revolutions highlighted the resilience of the Chinese people in the face of adversity. The end of the Qing Dynasty and the emergence of modern China has helped to unleash a rapidly growing Chinese economy. Indeed, at one point in time, Napoleon Bonaparte noted, "There lies a sleeping giant. Let him sleep. For when he wakes, he will shake the world," and indeed, the historical observation of this economy is a testament to this. China, as an emerging developing economy, has become an important global engine of growth and an industry leader. In reviewing China's remarkable economic rise, historical, political, and social factors have played crucial roles. From the establishment of the People's Republic of China in 1949 to the transformative reforms under Deng Xiaoping, each phase of development has been marked by unique challenges and responses that shaped the nation's trajectory. The legacy of socialism, coupled with strategic economic policies and a focus on modernization, has enabled China to become a formidable global player.

China's increasing presence in regions like the Caribbean illustrates its broader strategy of securing resources and expanding its influence globally. Investments in infrastructure and productive capacity in countries like Jamaica have led to mutual benefits, enhancing both economic growth in the Caribbean and providing China with critical raw materials to support its expanding economy.

Xi Jinping's leadership marks a pivotal moment in China's quest for global prominence. His vision, encapsulated in the concept of the "Chinese Dream," aims to rejuvenate the nation and assert its position on the world stage. The shift from Deng's "hide your strength, bide your time" approach to a more assertive stance reflects a confident China willing to confront challenges and reshape international norms. This transformation is not without risks, as tensions with established powers like the USA could escalate into broader geopolitical conflicts if not managed carefully.

Looking ahead, China's trajectory will be influenced by its ability to navigate the challenges of an interconnected world while fostering sustainable development. The need for ongoing reform, particularly in addressing socio-economic disparities and environmental concerns, remains critical for sustaining long-term growth. As China continues to position itself as a leader among developing nations, its relationships in the Caribbean and beyond will play an essential role in shaping the future of global economic governance. The delicate balance between assertiveness and cooperation will be key to ensuring that China can maintain its upward momentum while contributing to a more equitable and stable international system.

Notes

1. https://exceptionalcaribbean.com/2021/08/03/the-chinese-have-influenced-the-caribbean-in-a-powerful-way/.
2. https://sta.uwi.edu/uwitoday/archive/february_2023/article13.asp.
3. https://www.forbes.com/sites/earlcarr/2023/01/27/chinas-engagement-in-the-caribbean-and-the-united-states-response/?sh=1e35e5a7ac3f.

4. Testimony before the US-China Economic and Security Review Commission (2021). https://theglobalamericans.org/2022/01/why-might-taiwans-allies-in-latin-america-and-the-caribbean-soon-look-to-china/.
5. China is a non-borrowing member of the Caribbean Development Bank: https://www.caribank.org/countries-and-members/non-borrowing-members.
6. https://news.usni.org/2024/03/12/southcom-commander-warns-of-risk-of-chinese-investment-in-south-america-caribbean.
7. https://foreignaffairs.house.gov/china-snapshot-project-the-caribbean/.
8. https://jamaica-gleaner.com/article/lead-stories/20240531/jamaica-urged-take-advantage-chinas-us4b-development-fund.
9. https://www.theatlantic.com/international/archive/2020/06/china-west-portugal-macau-taiwan/612379/.
10. The Genesis of East Asia.
11. Paper Money in Early China.
12. Chen, Ting, and James Kai-sing Kung. 2019. *Why the Song Dynasty? The Rise of a Merchant Class And The Emergence Of Meritocracy In China*. Web.
13. https://www.washingtonpost.com/news/wonk/wp/2016/10/28/why-the-industrial-revolution-didnt-happen-in-china/. See also Edwards (2013) in a piece entitled "Song China and England" argued that the Song Dynasty experienced an Industrial Revolution several centuries before England.
14. https://www.weforum.org/agenda/2016/06/8-facts-about-chinas-economy/.
15. Agricultural Development in the Qing China.
16. http://news.Xinhuanet.com.
17. The White Lotus War: Rebellion and Suppression in hate Imperial China.
18. Rebellion Violence and Crime in Qing China 1722–1911.
19. What Does China Want? Between 1820 and 1839, the annual shipments of opium into China increased from 4000 to 40,000 chests (Greenberg 1951, p. 221).
20. Foreign Interference in Hong Kong.
21. Prior to the First Opium War trade relations between China and Europe took place via the Cohong. The Cohong refers to the guild

of Chinese merchants (or hongs) who operated the import–export monopoly in Canton (present day Guangzhou).

22. The Taiping Rebellion was triggered by a famine in the Guabgxi Province and the suppression of the peasants, e.g., protests by the Qing government.
23. https://www.history.com/topics/asian-history/taiping-rebellion.
24. http://yris.yira.org/global-issue/4210.
25. The Political Institutions of Modern China.
26. Encyclopaedia Small Silver Coins.
27. https://www.carnegiecouncil.org/education/1919/chinaprotests/_res/id=Attachments/index=0/May%204th%20Movement%20Excerpt%20and%20Questions.docx.
28. May Fourth Movement 1919.
29. https://www.pbs.org/wgbh/commandingheights/shared/minitext/prof_maozedong.html.
30. https://www.britannica.com/event/Cultural-Revolution.
31. Under Mao, the Chinese situation was tied to the Soviet bloc. This tie was broken in 1960 and until China was excluded from the UN and was hit with a complete US Embargo from 1950 to 71.
32. How the Maoist Revolution Wiped Out Drug Addiction in China.
33. In mid-1959, the Yellow River (or Huang Ho) flooded, and this resulted in many drownings and ruined crops. There was also serious drought in the Shaanxi, Hebei, Shandong, and Henan provinces. The coastal provinces of China in 1961 endured 11 major typhoons and again in 1961, the Northern provinces suffered months of drought (Du, Du and Lee, 2016 in Natural Disasters in China).
34. Writing on the period, historian Frank Dikotter (2010), in a book entitled Mao's Great Famine, noted, "Mao thought he could catapult his country past his competitors by herding villagers across the country into giant people-communes. In pursuit of a utopian paradise, everything was collectivized. People had their work, home, lands and belongings and their livelihoods taken from them.".
35. https://www.scmp.com/article/723956/revisiting-calamitous-time.
36. As part of this phase, Mao Zedong published a "Little Red Book" of quotations which was printed, and millions of copies were distributed throughout China. He shut down the schools and

called for youth support against other leaders for their bourgeois values. The population was urged to rid itself of the four Olds "Old Customs, Old Culture, Old Habits and Old Ideas.".

37. For Whom the Bell Tolls: The Political Legacy of China's Cultural Revolution (2017).
38. https://www.history.com/topics/asian-history/cultural-revolution.
39. www.history.com.
40. https://www.europarl.europa.eu/RegData/etudes/BRIE/2020/659407/EPRS_BRI(2020)659407_EN.pdf.
41. Deng Xiaoping: The Years in France.
42. https://www.britannica.com/event/Tiananmen-Square-incident.
43. Gu Mu was the Vice Premier.
44. Cited on https://tblanchardgh10.weebly.com/uploads/3/7/8/1/37814663/10.7_deng_xiaoping_and_tiananmen_square.pdf.
45. Deng searched for avenues to improve China's economic outlook after Mao's death. This solution, Deng argued, resided in competing with the world in technology and boosting economic growth. Deng introduced the four modernizations and, via the Open Door Policy, invited the world to help develop China.
46. Deng introduced the "household responsibility system." This system was started in 1979 and officially adopted in 1982. Under this system, farmers contract pieces of collective land and independently pursue their production activities which was highly successful (Xu, Huayu, The Long-Term Wealth and Economic Benefits of Property Rights).
47. Chinese Economy Under Mao Zedong and Deng Xiaoping.
48. https://www.journals.uchicago.edu/doi/10.1086/713935.
49. Higher Education Reform in China Today.
50. https://www.nytimes.com/2012/11/04/world/asia/chinas-xi-jinping-would-be-force-for-us-to-contend-with.html; https://www.reuters.com/article/us-china-congress-xi-idUSBRE8AE0BZ20121115.
51. https://www.aljazeera.com/news/2021/5/31/china-eases-birth-limit-allows-couple-to-have-3-children.
52. https://www.reuters.com/world/china/china-says-each-couple-can-have-three-children-change-policy-2021-05-31/
53. https://www.dw.com/en/xi-jinping-and-the-chinese-dream/a-43685630.

54. Xi's approach to the development of China has placed it on a risky trajectory. His perception that the CCP should guide the economy and his reining in of the private sector could potentially constrain China's future. Jude Blachette, August 2021, in the race to consolidate powers and to stave of Disasters notes, "Xi faces no genuine political rivals, has removed term limit on his tenure in office and has installed allies and loyalists in key positions. New research centres are dedicated to studying his writings and speeches, party officials publicly extol his wisdom and virtue, and party regulations and government planning documents increasingly claim to be based on "Xi Jinping Thought.".
55. The war of resistance against the Japanese 1937–1945 according to the China-Daily. The war of Resistance against Japanese Aggression caused 35 million deaths and US$600 bn in economic losses for China.
56. Karl (2010) "*Mao Zedong* and *China* in the *Twentieth-Century World*: A Concise History.".
57. The Chinese at this point was engaged in hostilities with the Soviets and they were fearful of a rising Japan. Nixon's visit to China helped to open communication, trade, and cultural exchanges. Oriental furniture became fashionable in the USA almost immediately. By visiting China, President Nixon helped to send a message of the legitimacy of Chinese leadership (Overhold 1973, "President's Nixon's Trip to China and its Consequences.").

CHAPTER 3

Basic Macroeconomic Overview of the Chinese Economy

3.1 Introduction

The historical observation, in general, is that China's economic growth since the 1950s has impacted the global economy in various ways. The sharp increase in its exports has helped lower some manufactured goods' prices on the global marketplace. The decline in prices in the importing countries helped to raise consumers' real income. When China exports low-cost intermediate goods, this can reduce the cost of production and increase firm-level profitability. However, at the same time, falling prices have an adverse effect on exports that are displaced (via a deterioration of the terms of trade and a loss of export markets). China's rapid economic growth has also boosted demand for many countries, creating multiple benefits for third countries. Furthermore, China tends to have a differentiated impact on the labour force of other countries whose labour markets are dominated by low-cost, low-skill, and less educated persons.

Zeng (2021) states that multinational corporations have heavily invested in China to reduce their production costs and capitalize on China's growing domestic market. The burgeoning middle class in China has generated increased demand for many goods. The International Trade Administration (2021) said, "Indeed, Chinese consumers play an increasingly important global role, now the world's largest market for a wide range of products from vehicles to air conditioners to video games." This has turned China into a global supply chain hub. Chinese companies have

R. Hosein et al., *China in the Caribbean*,
https://doi.org/10.1007/978-3-031-71985-1_3

increased the rate of adopting new technology and aim to nurture alternate sourcing, manufacturing, and transportation options. There is also the priority to allow for the localization and regionalization of supply chain relationships.

Therefore, it is no surprise that China has filed the most patents for inventions globally, and its spending on R&D has recently increased considerably. According to the World Intellectual Property Indicators 2020 report, China has led the world in the number of patent filings since 2011. In 2019, according to the World Intellectual Property Organization (WIPO), China filed 1.4 million patents, or 43.5% of the total patent applications for that year. China is a global leader in several technologies, including e-commerce artificial intelligence, fintech, high-speed trains, renewable energy, and electric cars (Vengelers, 2017). Xinhua (2024)[1] noted that China's research and development (R&D) expenditure exceeded US$458.5 bn in 2023, which was 8% higher than in 2022. McKinsey has ranked China among the top three investors in the world in fintech, virtual reality, autonomous vehicles, robotics, and big data. Indeed, China has invested in higher education and science as part of its economic development thrust.

The rapid growth of China is not without challenges, some of which are presented below. Consider that as the economy grows, the global geopolitical dynamics also change, given China's market presence, resulting in Sino-American trade disputes and accusations of China's cover-up of the COVID-19 virus (Bahi, 2021).[2] Specifically, the US Trade Representative enacted billions of dollars in duties after a Section 301 investigation by the USA found that China had engaged in unfair trade practices, including intellectual property theft.[3]This prompted a trade war, with China retaliating. Other challenges relate to the economy's structure and the internal nuances of debt and real estate.

Against this background, this chapter provides a sketch of the macroeconomic situation in China post-1978, although, where possible, data dating back to 1960 is presented once available. Therefore, the rest of the chapter will also include an overview of growth before it delves into some noteworthy specifics about the population and labour market. The magnitude of foreign direct investment inflows into China is also elaborated and a discussion on the available data is undertaken regarding the structure of output and poverty.

Some nuances of the modern digital economy will be presented, followed by a consideration of the debt situation and then concluding comments.

3.2 A Brief Overview of China's Economic Growth Performance

Real GDP growth in China averaged 8% in 1962–2023.[4] Prior to 1979, real GDP growth averaged 7.03%, and from 1979 to 2011, it averaged 9.8%. In the period 1991–2011, real economic growth in China averaged 10.5%, but since 2011, there has been a deceleration of economic growth, averaging 6.3% in the period 2012–2023 and 5.7% for 2016–2023. For 2024 growth is expected to be 4.6% with average annual growth for the period 2025 to 2029 being 3.6%.

In 1960, GDP in China stood at US$59.7 bn. It fell in 1961 and 1962 due in part to the impact of the Great Leap Forward and then again in 1967 and 1968 because of the Great Cultural Revolution. China also contracted in 1976 when Premier Zhou Enlai died, and the health of Mao Zedong declined. In July 1976, China also experienced the Tangshan earthquake, which resulted in extensive damage to railway infrastructure, fuel resources, and factories in various parts of China (Chen, 2005).[5]China experienced strong economic growth after 1976, and by 2023, its GDP stood at US$17.8 tn accounting for almost 17% of world GDP (Fig. 3.2).

After China joined the WTO in 2001, the economic growth rate accelerated and was only interrupted by the Global Financial Crisis of 2008. After 2008, supported by a massive stimulus package, growth resumed. The growth of the Chinese economy after 2012 is referred to as the "New Normal" (Kwan, 2014[6]; Tung 2016[7]). Observe from Fig. 3.1 that growth for the period 2013–2019 averaged 7% as compared to 10.6% for the 7 years before that. One factor that helped to spur economic growth was investment in infrastructure, which surged in the 1990s, including after 1997, when the Chinese government increased public investment to offset the impact of the Asian financial crisis (Naughton, 2007). After joining the WTO, investment continued to play a significant part in driving growth, and gross capital formation escalated from 33% in the 1990s to 39% between 2001 and 2008 and further to 45% between 2009 and 2014 as part of a fiscal response to the Global Financial Crisis (Jenkins, 2010, see Fig. 3.5). Since 2012, China's economic growth has slowed considerably, and this is, in part, on account of sluggish international trade since 2009. Even so, China accounted for about 15.3% of global economic activity from 2012 to 2023.

To enhance growth after 2008, China embarked on a stimulus package of RMB4 Trillion[8] and invested heavily in infrastructure and, since 2009, has invested in the industry rejuvenation plan (IRP) (Naughton, 2007; Fardoust, 2012). This plan covers ten sectors.[9]

China grew so quickly that by 2023 its share of world GDP soared to 17% (Fig. 3.2) compared to 4.3% in 1960. Its per capita GDP also escalated and, in 2023, was approximately 14,000% more than in 1960.

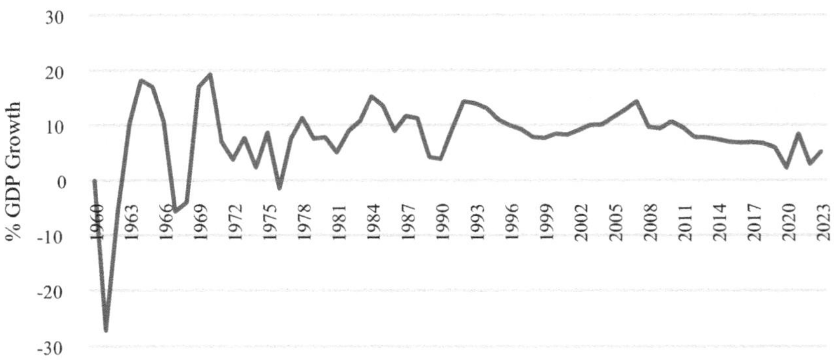

Fig. 3.1 Real GDP Growth China, 1961–2023 (Source: WDI)

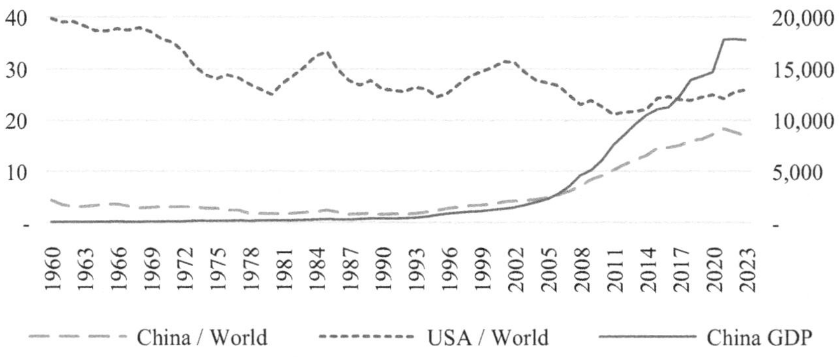

Fig. 3.2 China's relative growth performance 1960–2023 (Source: WDI)

Only a few countries in the history of humankind have managed this pace of economic growth (Ireland, Singapore and South Korea). Significantly, as shown in Figs. 3.3 and 3.4, high real GDP growth in China did not result in a rise in the inflation rate, which, for the time period 1987–2023, averaged 4.7%. In India, the corresponding inflation rate was 7.3%, and for Brazil, it was 310%.

In terms of overall labour productivity, Tian and Yu (2012) found that the total factor productivity (TFP) was only about 2% per annum

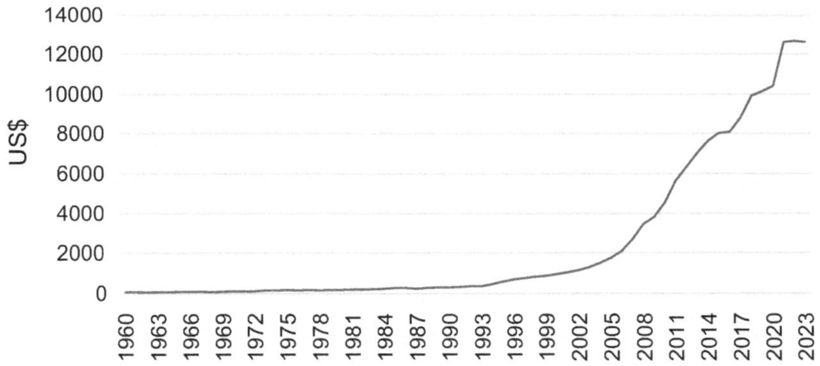

Fig. 3.3 China's GDP per capita (current US$) 1960–2023 (Source: WDI)

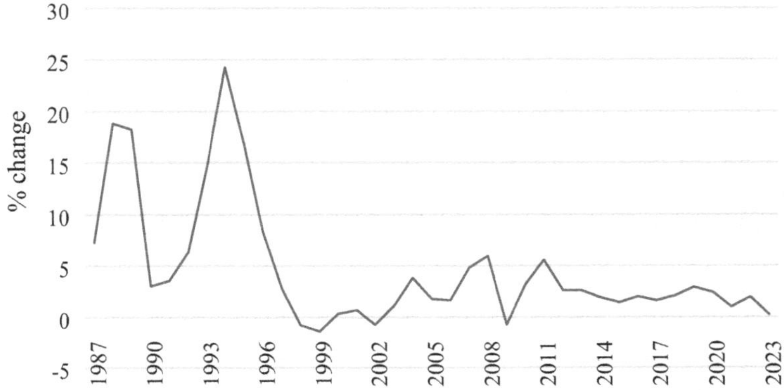

Fig. 3.4 China's inflation, consumer prices (annual %) 1987–2023 (Source: WDI)

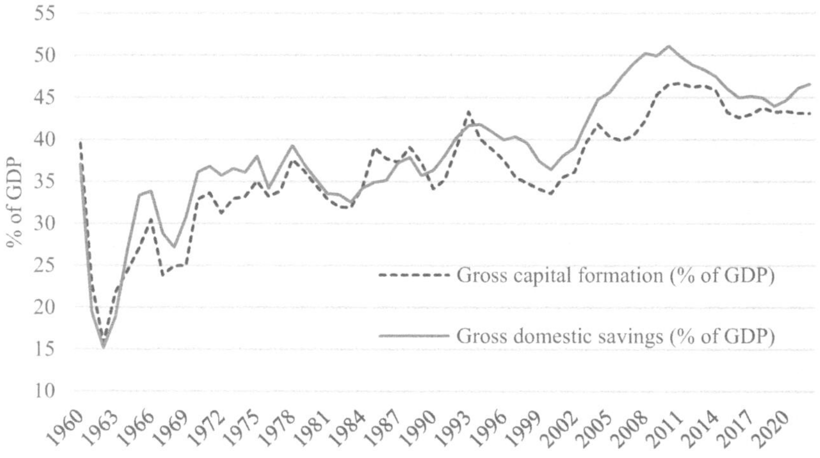

Fig. 3.5 China's trends in gross capital formation and gross domestic savings as a % of GDP, 1960–2022 (Source: WDI)

and, for the period 1978–2008, contributed only 20% to the economic growth of China.[10] In developed countries, this percentage is closer to 40%.[11] Since the global financial crisis, there has been a decline in China's TFP (WB, 2019).[12] The decline of China's TFP matters as it is already low and, according to the WB (2019), is about half of the level of the OECD economies, and thus, there is considerable room for China to increase its output by improving its TFP. The WB (2019) noted, "Firm-level data suggests that productivity growth has been slowing due to declining contributions from the entry of new firms and from decreasing contributions from within sector productivity changes" (p. xvii).

Nonetheless, the rapid growth of China is due to two main factors: large-scale capital investments financed by large-scale domestic savings and foreign direct investment (FDI). Economic reforms in China, after 1978, led to an increase in domestic savings as a percentage of GDP (Yang, 2019). An initial low level of capital endowment and a high return on the associated capital encouraged productivity gains; these reforms included the development of the non-state sector initiative during the 1980s, reform of the state-owned enterprises (SOEs) in the 1990s, and the ascension of China to the World Trade Organization. The significant level of savings supported a high level of investment (Naughton,

2007) (See Fig. 3.5).[13] The Chinese approach of high savings and high investments followed neoclassical logic.[14] The industrialization process also benefitted from an ample supply of labour linked to the rapid growth of China's population and the absorption of rural workers by the manufacturing sector (WB, 2019).

Many believe that China's growth has been mainly based on capital accumulation, and there are valid econometric exercises and discourses that confirm this view. However, it should be noted that a challenge confronting the Chinese economy is an increase in the country's incremental capital ratio (ICOR, measured as the ratio of investment to growth).[15] The high investment in infrastructure and real estate can explain a significant part of the increase in the country's ICOR. Chivakul (2015) noted that the real estate sector in China escalated from 4% of GDP in 1997 to 14% by 2016. The strong demand for housing was due to urbanization and changes in household formation as more small families proliferated. Land prices have also increased considerably. Before 2007, the UN (2019 p. 23) notes that the cost of land used for industrial purposes was US$70 per square meter, and by the end of 2017, this had almost doubled. There was also a need to upgrade housing. The rapid increase in household income and high savings helped to fuel the demand for the real estate sector. However, the housing boom was accompanied by escalating property prices and the Evergrande problem.[16]

Note, though, that while the ICOR in infrastructure and real estate is high, the ICOR in the business sector marginally deteriorated since the Global Financial Crisis of 2008. This may suggest that an improved credit allocation can help improve productivity and efficiency (WB, 2019).[17] Indeed, in China, there is too heavy a flow of credit to sectors with a high ICOR, which, in turn, affects long-term national productivity.

3.3 The Population and Labour Force and Chinese Wages

Figure 3.6 shows that China's population increased from 660 million people in 1960 to 1.4 billion people in 2023.

China was able to capitalize on the demographic transition to improve its position in the division of labour in the global space. China exploited its abundance of labour and its relatively low cost to enhance its comparative advantage in the production of processing and assemble-type activities, helping to insert China into the international production network.

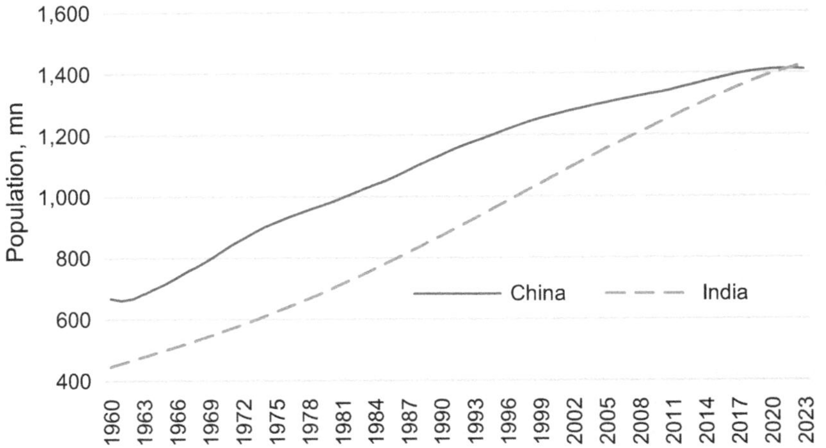

Fig. 3.6 Population (mn) 1960–2023, China and India (Source: WDI)

The UN (2022) notes that the benefits for China of "the Demographic dividend were felt especially after joining the WTO in 2001. Over the last decade, the Chinese business environment further improved, and the efficiency of labour resources increased, under the promotion of supply-side structural reform, high-quality development, and other strategies. Consequently, the positioning of China in the global value chain constantly improved."

Figures 3.7 and 3.8 show the segment of the population of China and India above 65 years and the corresponding population less than 14 years. Note that for China, there is, clearly, an increase in the number of people over 65 years and a decline in the number of people under 14 years after 1975. For India, while the number of people over 65 years has also increased, but there is also an increase in the number of people between 0 and 14 years especially if we compare 2023 with 1975. India will have a growing labour force for many more years.

Nulimaimaiti (2023)[18] explains that by 2050, more than 38% of China's population is also expected to be aged over 60, which raises concerns over the state pension fund, elderly care facilities, and medical services. Watkins (2022) explained that if the trend continues, the country's population will be 1.44 billion by 2029 before reaching an "unstoppable decline." The report indicated that China would go into

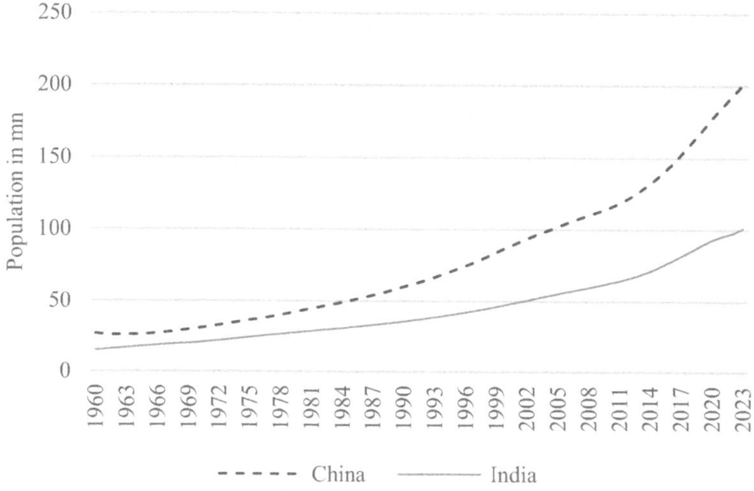

Fig. 3.7 Population (mn) 1960–2023, ages 65 and above, China and India (Source: WDI)

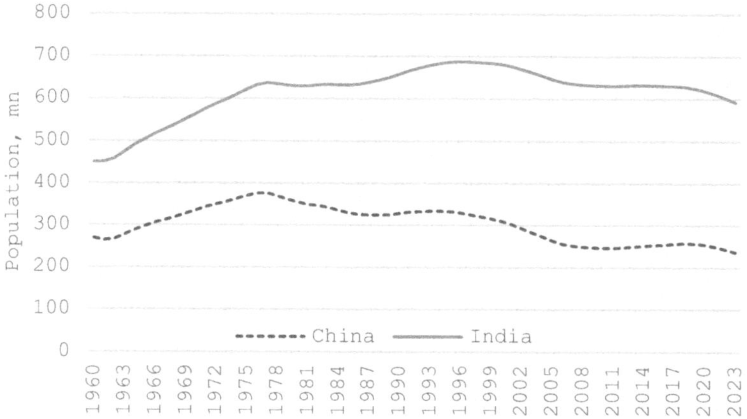

Fig. 3.8 Population (mn) 1960–2023, ages 0–14, China and India (Source: WDI)

an "era of negative growth of population" and warns that the population number will go back to the stages of the mid-1990s by the year 2065.

Indeed, Dixon and Gill (2021) noted that China has fewer young people and more elderly people than peer economies that reached upper middle-income status. China, thus, has more elderly people to support and will become an increasingly older society as more of the workforce reaches retirement age. This demographic shift will help to keep downward pressure on interest rates and asset returns (UN, 2019), and this can have an adverse impact on the long-term economic growth performance of China. (Note the UN 2019 indicated this although wages have been rising at about 5% per year.)

In urban China, labour was allocated by the Bureau of Labour and Personnel in direct accordance with the national plan. When workers were assigned, they not only received their salaries but also several benefits for health, housing, and other social amenities. The government set wages, and the wage-setting process kept differentials small (Freeman, 2014).[19] The household's registration system, *hukou*, kept people tied down to their place of origin and was designed to restrict rural–urban migration. After 1978, many of these restrictions remained in place, and State Owned Enterprises (SOEs) were not allowed to release workers. As reforms progressed in the Chinese economy, there was a substantial increase in farm employment in rural areas. However, wages were kept low, with productivity growth motivated principally by movement from low-productivity areas to higher productivity areas. As the demand for labour in urban areas expanded, it became easier for rural workers to work in urban areas without an urban *hukou*. Many rural workers moved to urban areas. A major turning point was a 1994 labour law, that allowed for the no-fault dismissal of workers if economic conditions necessitated it. With the passing of this law, millions of workers were shed, and urban unemployment rates increased. Freeman (2014) notes that at the turn of the century, the "iron rice bowl" used to allocate workers was effectively replaced by more market-led forces.[20]

According to data available from the World Bank (WB), China's labour force increased until about 2017 and thereafter showed clear signs of decreasing. In contrast, India's labour force is continuing to expand (Fig. 3.9).

China's labour force will decline in the future given the age distribution shown in Fig. 3.10 below. The WB's (2019), Innovative China notes that China's labour force is expected to shrink by 47 mn by 2030

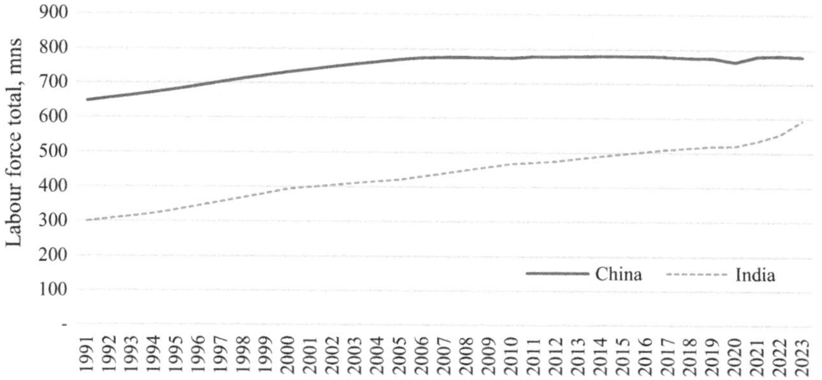

Fig. 3.9 Labour force, total mn, 1990–2023, China and India (Source: WDI)

(from 793 mn in 2010 to 746 mn in 2030). The UN has also indicated that in the 2030s, the Chinese labour force is expected to shrink by 1% per annum, and of course, this will adversely impact economic growth. The ageing of the population in China is such that by the year 2030 the proportion of the population that is older than 60 years will rise to 13.8% compared to 6.6% in 2010.

Further, note that the median age in China is 38.4 years compared to 28.4 in India. Both countries have a higher male population to female ratio: in India, there are 108.2 males to 100 females, and in China, there are 105.3 males to 100 females. India is three times as densely populated as China (464 persons per sq km in India as compared to 153 per sq km in China).

The combined realities of a shrinking and ageing labour force in China require that China improve its labour productivity by investing in human capital formation so that the economy can benefit from these workers throughout their lives (Fig. 3.10).

Indeed, a major factor that boosted the competitiveness of the Chinese industry has been relatively low wages. In 1978, when China embarked on opening the economy, the average level of urban wages was 3% that of the USA. Wages did not increase much until after 2000. Even more, Ceglowski and Golub (2007) have noted that unit labour costs, i.e., wages as a proportion of output per worker relative to the same ratio in the

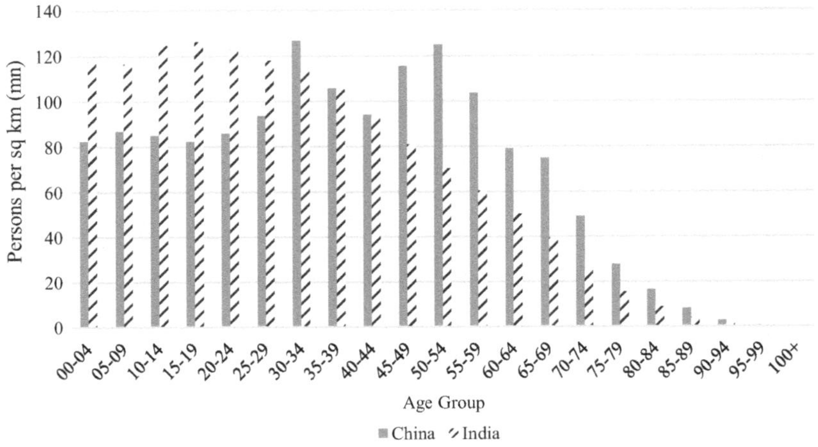

Fig. 3.10 Age Distribution of the Population, 2023, China and India (Source: WDI)

USA, decreased from above 70% in the 1980s to close to 30% in the mid-1990s. Note that after mid-2003, wages in China increased quickly, with both absolute unit labour costs and relative costs rising swiftly.

Several factors combined to keep the wages of unskilled Chinese workers low during the 1980s and 1990s. The first of these was that during these two decades, the working age population grew faster than the total population. Secondly, the *hukou* system was broken in many regards by the high level of rural-to-urban migration and, thirdly, the high level of layoffs from SOEs. In more recent times, as the high-growth rate of working age population declined, the inflows of rural workers eased, and labour shortages emerged, especially in the more industrialized areas. Significant strikes in 2004 and 2005 in Shenzhen resulted in minimum wage increases, spreading to other parts of China. Subsequently, Li et al. (2012) observed the "end of cheap Chinese labor."[21]

Note that China's capabilities are an important part of its innovation capabilities. Huld (2023)[22] explains that, on average, 85% of workers had a high school diploma, with 35% possessing a college degree, as compared to 47% for OECD economies (Fig. 3.11) which compares tertiary school enrollment in China to India.[23]

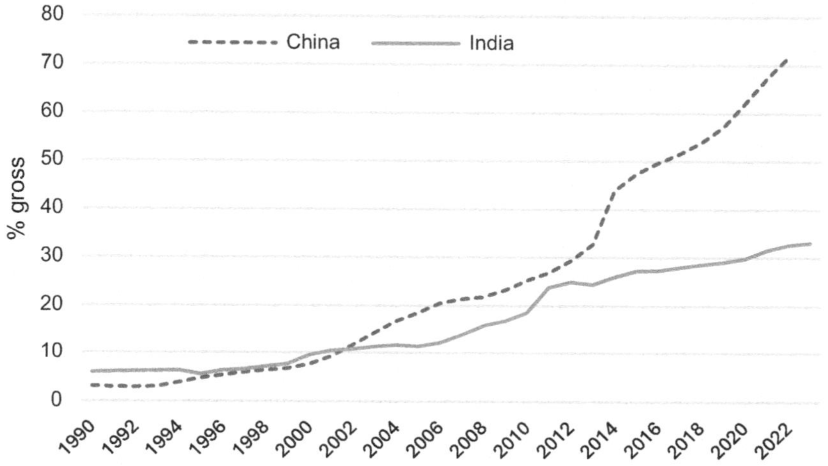

Fig. 3.11 School enrolment, tertiary 1960–2023, (% gross), China and India (Source: WDI)

3.4 FDI in China

China did not have many foreign loans prior to 1979, and even foreign aid was looked upon with suspicion by China's decision-makers. For example, after the disastrous earthquake of 1976, Chinese authorities even refused aid from the Red Cross. This attitude towards FDI changed in 1979 when Deng Xiaoping implemented much-needed economic reform and an open-door policy. Several factors pushed China in this direction, including a) the poor performance of China under its closed-door policy and b) the performance of the four Asian tigers. Qu (1997) stated that in pursuing FDI, China hoped to:

1. Access technology and expertise to upgrade existing structures and, thereby, improve efficiency.
2. Improve economic development outcomes.
3. Access foreign markets and improve export earnings.
4. Access managerial skills from foreign companies.

Three phases of reform of FDI policy after 1979 were identified by Fu (2000) and Zhang (1999); these are:

1. In the initial phase (1979–1985), several laws and regulations were used to attract foreign investors to China. As mentioned, four Special Economic Zones were created with special treatment for foreign investors in this phase.
2. The continuous development phase (1986–1991)—the government extended its open-door policy towards more provinces. It publicized the "Law in Enterprises Operated Exclusively with Foreign Capital" and "Provision on Encouraging Foreign Investment" in the mid-1980s, which was used to help encourage FDI and reduce uncertainty towards investments in China, which led to an increase in foreign capital, resulting in improved growth performance. The ban on foreigners from having joint ventures in China was lifted, and the open policy moved from coastal regions to the Western inland cities in the 1990s.
3. The high-growth phase (1992 onwards).

In 1995, China added a new policy measure to its FDI stance. Two documents were developed: Temporary Direction Guidelines for FDI and Industry Guidance Catalogue for FDI. The UN (2022) notes that the government of China classified FDI projects into five broad types: encouraging, restricting (limiting A, limiting B), prohibiting, and allowing. The government provided preferential treatment to the types of FDI classified under encouraging and limiting B, and these were mainly manufacturing projects (Fig. 3.12).

The open-door policy inserted by Deng Xiaoping advocated for Equal Trading Rights of all countries. At first, foreign investments were welcomed via jointly owned economic units; then, by 1986, China accepted wholly owned foreign enterprises, and in 1988, China accepted cooperative joint ventures. Up to one decade, after this policy was launched, FDI into China was relatively dormant, and the majority of FDI inflows consisted of Hong Kong and Taiwanese firms relocating their labour-intensive manufacturing activity in textiles, garments, footwear, and toys to China (Lardy, 1995). In 1986, when significant FDI regulations were lifted throughout China, the resulting impacts were a) reduced corporate tax rates for foreign firms and b) lifting of restrictions on profit remittances for foreign firms.

In 1992, Deng Xiaoping launched another phase of reforms, and with these reforms,[24]more foreign firms were allowed access to the domestic market, which helped increase manufacturing productivity (the surge in FDI also helped increase manufacturing sector output).

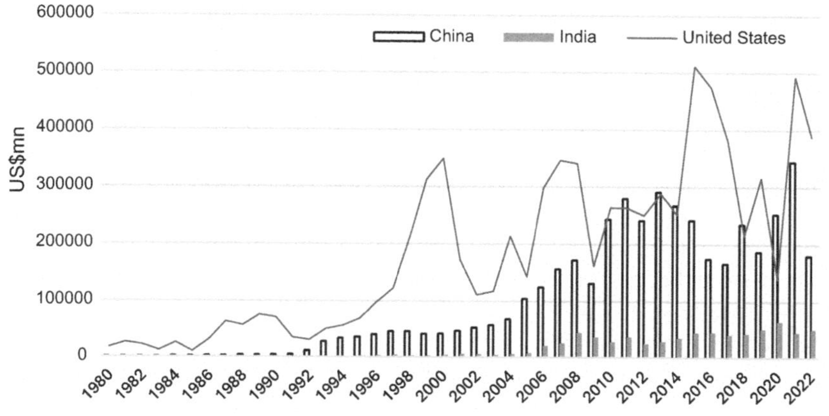

Fig. 3.12 Foreign direct investment, net inflows (BoP, current US$bn) 1980–2022, China, India, and USA (Source: WDI)

China also made a deep-rooted commitment to service liberalization in its services commitment to the WTO. This also encouraged a significant amount of FDI into service-oriented industries (Tseng & Zebregs, 2002).[25] Since then, thousands of multinational companies have invested in China, and Table 3.1 demonstrates that China received the second highest amount of FDI inflows globally in 2022.

Table 3.1 Top ranked FDI Destinations for (2022)

Rank	*Destination Country*	*US$bn*
1	USA	388.08
2	China	180.17
3	Singapore	140.84
4	Hong Kong	120.95
5	France	105.42
6	Brazil	91.5
7	Australia	67.12
8	Canada	53.71
9	Sweden	50.05
10	India	49.94

Source: Nayak (2023)[26]

The commencement of China's New Foreign Investment Law (FIL) on 1 January 2020 provided significant opportunities for foreign investors. These opportunities relate to increased flexibility in joint ventures. The FIL replaces previous laws and regulations that govern joint ventures, cooperative joint ventures, and wholly owned foreign enterprises. The FIL seeks to address concerns by foreign firms for a fairer, more competitive environment in China in which foreign investors, alongside their domestic partners, would be treated similarly.

It should be noted, though, that many of the products under the rubric "Made in China" are merely assembled in China! Regarding the iPhone, Kraemer, Linden, and Dedrick (2011), in Capturing Value in Global Networks, found that for Apple's iPhone manufactured in China, for example, 58.5% of profits went to Apple and another 2.4% went to other companies in the USA besides Apple. These researchers found that Chinese labour accounted for a mere 1.8%, and non-labour factor inputs from China accounted for 3.5%. For the iPad, Apple's profit was 30%.

The UN (2019) has noted that the increase in FDI to China helped to foster the transfer of technology to China. Of the 7 mn graduates in China per annum, according to the UN (2019), about 1.8 mn are trained in science and engineering, and this no doubt played a tremendous role in helping grow the manufacturing sector and the R&D activities in China.

3.5 Structure of Output and the Poverty Situation in China

Following Dixon and Gill (2021), this section looks at three economies when they transitioned from middle-income economies to high-income economies using GDP per capita in real PPP terms. These three economies are the USA, Japan,, and South Korea. The USA started its upper middle-income phase in 1923 and moved into the high-income phase in 1959. Japan moved into the upper middle-income phase in 1967 and graduated in 1978. The corresponding years for Korea are 1987 and 2001. Based on the available data, Dixon and Gill (2021) illustrate that China's high expected growth rate would take 15 years to progress from upper middle-income status to high-income status. This 15-year period is compared to 11 years for Japan, 14 for South Korea, and 36 for the USA.

As already mentioned, the first 30 years of the PRC were marked by several failures. At the same time, though, the country was able to establish a relatively strong and solid industrial foundation. China initially adopted an import substitution strategy, which, at the time, was the predominant approach to development used by developing countries, following in the mode of Prebisch and Singer (Rodrick, 1997) (Fig. 3.13).[27]

As the graph above would indicate though, China is an economy that is still transforming. As can be seen, agricultural output as a % of GDP is on the decline.

The government of China enabled the growth of industry relative to agriculture and services sectors. The strategy yielded fruit and as the Chinese economy grew, there was a clear change in the structure of production. Agriculture value added toppled from 35.1% in 1961 to 7.1% in 2023. Note though, that agriculture output in China has continued to increase and overall, China is now one of the world's largest producers of agricultural goods. Indeed, to this end, Ross (2023)[28] explains that China is one of the four largest food producers globally, alongside India, the USA, and Brazil.

In the same interval of time, industry value added as a percentage of total output escalated from 30.2% in 1961 to 47.6% in 2006, although thereafter, it declined, as per capita GDP increased, to 38.3% in 2023. (Note that industrial growth in China is strongly associated with the

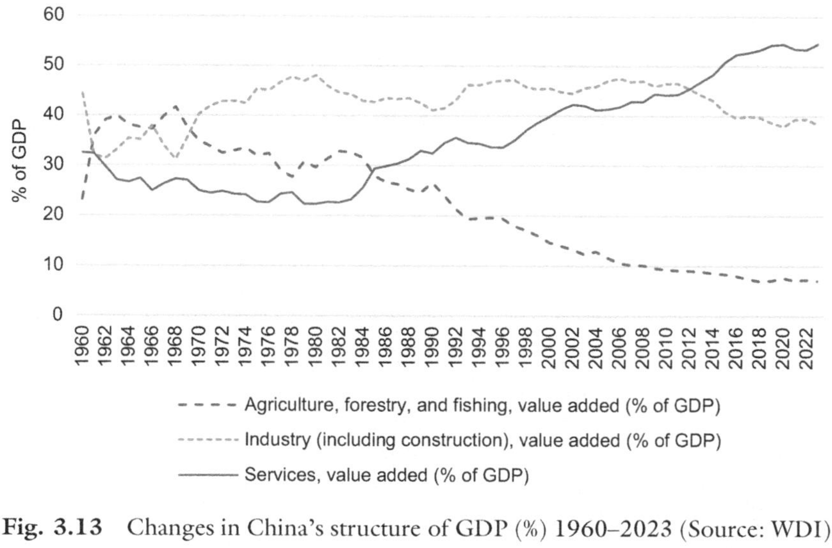

Fig. 3.13 Changes in China's structure of GDP (%) 1960–2023 (Source: WDI)

growth of China's merchandise exports in international trade.) Note also, that since 2010, China's industry value added as a percentage of GDP was the highest in the world. This is remarkable as, until 1978, industry in China was very tightly controlled, and investment was funded by the government.[29] Expansion prior to 1978 was motivated by the government, and the average enterprise size was very large (Maddison, 2007).

Understandably, an associated challenge of growing industry is greenhouse gas emissions. The Chinese economy has accounted for 60% of all additional greenhouse gas emissions since 2003 (Ferguson, 2020).[30] At the UN General Assembly on 22 September 2020, China added carbon neutrality to its plans for ecological conservation. China's CO_2 emission in 2020 accounted for 30.6% of global emissions, and China has been the largest emitter of carbon dioxide among all countries in the world since 2006. There has also been a greater focus on the environment and on the adoption of rules consistent with international patterns, as China has set a target of reducing carbon dioxide emissions by 18% and the energy intensity of its major industrial firms by 13.5% per unit of industrial value added by 2025.[31]

After 2007, though, the government of China reduced its management of the industrial sector, and there was a large expansion in industrial activity outside of the state domain. Thus, while in 1978 there were 265,000 collectives, by 1996, there were 1.6 mn, and in 2003, this escalated to 6.2 mn (Maddison, 2007). Maddison states that part of the reason these firms were successful is their freedom to respond to the market. Of course, the private sector also benefitted after 1978 from the massive inflow of FDI.

Although contracting from 32.3% in 1961 to 22.3% in 1979, the services sector expanded to 54.6% in 2023. Note that from 1952 to 1978, the services sector was squeezed and subjected to strong control levels. Maddison (2007) noted that between 1952 and 1978, there was a decline in the number of people engaged in retail outlets, catering establishments, and convenience trades from 9.5 mn to 6.1 mn, although the population increased by two-thirds in this same period. The number of these outlets crashed from 5.5 to 1.3 mn in the same period. After 1978, though, as with so many other types of activities in China, the constraints on the services sector were eased, and it grew very quickly. Services embodied in manufactured goods are an increasingly important aspect of the competitiveness of Chinese manufacturing. The service inputs into the manufacturing sector, such as design, marketing, and distribution costs. Barone et al. (2011) and Arnold et al. (2011) identify these service inputs as important to the global value chain. Note that the sectoral allocation of labour from agriculture to industry has been a major source of growth for China. However, as with the fall in labour, this reallocation will be a major source of growth for the future. China, according to the data provided by Dixon and Gill (2021), is now a service-oriented economy. Additionally, these researchers noted that China's agricultural sector is larger and its services sector smaller than the US, Japan, or Korea at the point in which these respective nations entered the upper middle-income group (using the WB classifications) as China has entered now. Employment by sector for these economies are shown in Tabke 3.2 below. (Note that China's share of global manufacturing increased almost six-fold between 1990 and 2020).

Dixon and Gill further note that if China wants to follow a pathway of economic activity similar to the listed comparator states and rebalance its structure of output as income grows, policymakers in China will have to find ways to reduce the size of its agricultural sector and increase the size of its services sector.

Another major challenge confronting the Chinese economy in the context of changing industrialization patterns is the rise in inequality. There has also been a rise in the disparity between per capita disposable incomes in rural and urban households in China. Weiping (2019), using a US$1.9 poverty line, showed that the number of people living in extreme poverty in China, declined from 88 to 1.5% in the period 1981–2013 (this represents 850 million people).[32] Dixon and Gill (2021) noted that the USA became a high-income economy in 1959 when the country adopted the meaning of poverty, which classified persons as poor if their daily

Table 3.2 Employment by sector (%) for selected economies

	USA		*Japan*		*Korea*		*China*	
	1923	*1959*	*1967*	*1978*	*1987*	*2001*	*2010*	*2025*
Services (%)	44.7	60.5	46.6	54.9	44.8	62.8	34.6	46.4
Industry (%)	31.9	31.2	32.1	31.4	34.2	27.2	28.7	28.2
Agriculture (%)	23.6	7.3	21.3	13.7	21.0	10.0	36.7	25.6

Source: Dixon and Gill (2021)

Table 3.3 Poverty headcount (% of persons below the poverty line) Official US poverty line $21.70

USA		*China*	
1923	55.6	2010	95
1959	22.4	2015	89.6

Source: Dixon and Gill (2011)

consumption was below US$21.7. At the start of its upper middle-income phase in 1923, 55.6% of the US population lived below this poverty line of US$21.7. As the Great Depression entered the economy, this increased to 78.1% in 1928 but declined to 22.4% by 1959. For China in 2015, this number stood at 89.6%, using this poverty line of US$21.70 (Table 3.3).

Further, as the Chinese economy grew, many of its firms became ranked in the Fortune Global 500. In 2020, for the first time ever, China had 133 firms in the top 500 (including Hong Kong and Taiwan), compared to 121 US companies. In 1980, there were no Chinese firms in the top 500 (See Table 3.4).

Table 3.4 Top 500 firms globally 1980, 2020

Rank	*Company (1980)*	*Revenues (1980) (US$Mn)*	*Rank*	*Company (2020)*	*Revenues (2020) (US$Mn)*
1	Exxon Mobil	79,106.5	1	Walmart	523,964
2	General Motors	66,311.2	2	Sinopec Group	407,009
3	Mobil	44,720.9	3	State Grid	383,906
4	Ford Motor	43,513.7	4	China National Petroleum	379,130
5	Texaco	38,350.4	5	Royal Dutch Shell	352,106
6	ChevronTexaco	29,947.6	6	Saudi Aramco	329,784
7	Gulf Oil	23,910.0	7	Volkswagen	282,760
8	Intl. Business Machines	22,862.8	8	BP	282,616
9	General Electric	22,460.6	9	Amazon	280,522
10	Amoco	18,610.3	10	Toyota Motor	275,288
11	ITT Industries	17,197.4	11	Exxon Mobil	264,938

(continued)

Table 3.4 (continued)

Rank	*Company (1980)*	*Revenues (1980) (US$Mn)*	*Rank*	*Company (2020)*	*Revenues (2020) (US$Mn)*
12	Atlantic Richfield	16,234.0	12	Apple	260,174
13	Shell Oil	14,431.2	13	CVS Health	256,776
14	US Steel	12,929.1	14	Berkshire Hathaway	254,616
15	Conoco	12,648.0	15	UnitedHealth Group	242,155
16	DuPont	12,571.8	16	McKesson	231,051
17	Chrysler	12,001.9	17	Glencore	215,111
18	Tenneco Automotive	11,209.0	18	China State Construction Engineering	205,839
19	AT&T Technologies	10,964.1	19	Samsung Electronics	197,705
20	Sunoco	10,666.0	20	Daimler	193,346
21	Occidental Petroleum	9554.8	21	Ping An Insurance	184,280
22	ConocoPhillips	9502.8	22	AT&T	181,193
23	Procter & Gamble	9329.3	23	AmerisourceBergen	179,589
24	Dow Chemical	9255.4	24	Industrial & Commercial Bank of China	177,069
25	Union Carbide	9176.5	25	Total	176,249
26	United Technologies	9053.4	26	Hon Hai Precision Industry	172,869
27	Navistar International	8392.0	27	Trafigura Group	171,474
28	Goodyear Tire & Rubber	8238.7	28	EXOR Group	162,754
29	Boeing	8131.0	29	Alphabet	161,857
30	Eastman Kodak	8028.2	30	China Construction Bank	158,884
31	LTV	7996.8	31	Ford Motor	155,900
32	BP America	7916.0	32	Cigna	153,566
33	Caterpillar	7613.2	33	Costco Wholesale	152,703
34	Unocal	7567.7	34	AXA	148,984
35	Beatrice	7468.4	35	Agricultural Bank of China	147,313
36	RCA	7454.6	36	Chevron	146,516
37	CBS	7332.0	37	Cardinal Health	145,534
38	Bethlehem Steel	7137.2	38	JPMorgan Chase	142,422

(continued)

Table 3.4 (continued)

Rank	*Company (1980)*	*Revenues (1980) (US$Mn)*	*Rank*	*Company (2020)*	*Revenues (2020) (US$Mn)*
39	Nabisco Group Holdings	7133.1	39	Honda Motor	137,332
40	Xerox	7027.0	40	General Motors	137,237
41	Amerada Hess	6769.9	41	Walgreens Boots Alliance	136,866
42	Esmark	6743.2	42	Mitsubishi	135,940
43	Marathon Oil	6680.6	43	Bank of China	135,091
44	Ashland	6473.9	44	Verizon Communications	131,868
45	Rockwell Automation	6466.1	45	China Life Insurance	131,244
46	Kraft	6432.9	46	Allianz	130,359
47	Citgo Petroleum	6276.5	47	Microsoft	125,843
48	Monsanto	6192.6	48	Marathon Petroleum	124,813
49	Altria Group	6144.1	49	Huawei Investment & Holding	124,316
50	General Foods	5472.5	50	China Railway Engineering Group	123,324

Source: Author compiled

3.6 Digital Economy

The UN (2022) pointed out that the digital economy in China contributed about 60% of its GDP growth in 2016 and became a significant driver of China's economic growth. Of note is that in 2016, China's digital economy was about one-third that of the US economy (32%) and accounting for 30% of Chinese GDP; its annual growth rate was about 19% or approximately three times the growth rate of the USA which stood at 6% (UN, 2022). Along this same pathway, the broadband speed in China increased more than three times in 2018 compared to 2015. According to data from the Worldwide Semi-Annual Big Data and Analytics Spending Guide (2023), the big data market in the USA climbed to US$14.7 bn in 2018, with China accounting for US$5.5 bn. Indeed, China is in the process of developing a technology Park in Beijing for approximately US$2.1 bn, and the government has also stated its intention of developing an AI industry which is expected to generate about US$60 bn in annual output by 2025 and by 2030 is touted to become a US$150 bn industry.

China has the highest number of internet users in the world. Further, online retail sales in China crossed US$1.3 tn in 2018. These sales accounted for 46.4% of global online retail sales, according to the UN (2022), and several large digital companies, such as Alibaba, have emerged in China. Alibaba was started in 1999 as an online business-business marketplace (B2B) and, by 2019, had its own B2B, B2C (business to consumer), and C2C (consumer to consumer) online retailing platform. Alibaba also established Alipay, which has its payment system and its own logistics system. Alibaba now provides cloud computing and consulting services related to big data (UN, 2022).

China's Artificial Intelligence capabilities are also changing the global landscape, especially with the release of platforms such as DeepSeek which was developed at a fraction of the costs of similar platforms originating in the US.

3.7 Debt

Consider Table 3.5, which shows the trends in debt indicators for China. These indicators point to the relatively strong position of the economy in terms of reserves, which at the end of 2023 accounted for approximately 143% of total external debt and is estimated to be 13.7% of GNI. Short-term debt, though, accounts for 53% of external debt in 2023, reaching a high of 62% in 2018. The total debt service as a proportion of GNI in 2023 is about 2%.

Table 3.5 China's Debt situation, 1981–2023

	Total reserves (% of total external debt)	*External debt stocks (% of GNI)*	*Short-term debt (% of total external debt)*	*Total debt service (% of GNI)*
1981	174.31	2.96	–	0.89
1990	62.34	15.28	16.85	1.95
2000	117.72	12.19	8.96	2.22
2005	290.85	12.59	51.87	1.21
2010	392.29	12.25	68.98	0.86

(continued)

Table 3.5 (continued)

	Total reserves (% of total external debt)	*External debt stocks (% of GNI)*	*Short-term debt (% of total external debt)*	*Total debt service (% of GNI)*
2015	255.31	12.12	61.65	1.15
2016	219.09	12.65	56.68	1.50
2017	189.82	13.86	60.46	1.68
2018	161.51	14.18	62.14	1.74
2019	152.44	14.85	57.01	1.94
2020	144.29	15.95	53.13	1.88
2021	125.83	15.40	53.09	1.91
2022	135.08	13.78	51.68	2.42
2023	142.53	13.7	53.19	2.18

Source: WDI

3.8 Conclusion

Mao Zedong emphasized, “Surpass the British and catch up with the Americans.” Deng Xiaoping emphasized “hide your strength, bide your time.” China’s strength, though, has become increasingly difficult to hide, and the current premier, Xi Jinping, not afraid to show it.[33]

At the fourth session of the 13th National People’s Congress, both the 14th Five-Year Plan (2021–25) and the Long-Range Objectives through the Year 2035 were approved. The 14th Five-Year Plan states that China would focus on a new development strategy of “dual circulation” in which domestic and foreign markets can boost each other but with the domestic market as the mainstay. In other words, in this new Five-Year Plan, China will be prioritizing domestic consumption although it maintains a strong degree of openness to trade and investment. Part of this switch from the “great international circulation” to the “domestic international dual circulation” is through a greater focus on domestic economic activity. China maintains a very strong manufacturing base. As shown in the body of the discussion above, China is the world’s largest manufacturer of goods and a principal hub for the international value chain. A careful look at China’s exports (done in the next chapter) will show that China is increasingly exporting medium-tech and high-tech exports. Even more, China has been adding more to exports domestically as supply chains have become deeper.

The Chinese economy, while expected to maintain growth, is projected to slow significantly in the coming years (Table 3.6). According to the World Economic Outlook (October 2024), average annual economic growth is expected to drop to around 3.8% from 2024 to 2029, a stark contrast to the impressive 9.4% average growth rate recorded between 1980 and 2019. Indeed, the bicycle symbol of the Chinese economy presented by the Economist in 2012 still resonates as relevant today as ever. "Even if it is a fading symbol of Chinese society, the bicycle remains a tempting metaphor for its economy. Bikes—especially when fully laden—are stable only so long as they keep moving. The same is sometimes said about China's economy. If it loses momentum, it will crash. And since growth is the only source of legitimacy for the ruling party, the economy would not be the only thing to wobble" (The Economist, May 26th, 2012; Special Report: China's Economy).

Several factors are responsible for China's rapid growth in the past, including the rapid structural transformation of the economy from agriculture to manufacturing, a high level of infrastructural investment, a demographic dividend, and a huge surplus pool of labour in the rural sector. The demographic divide key advantage for China, is also changing. The workforce is ageing, and the declining birth rate—exacerbated by previous policies like the One Child Policy—means there will be fewer workers available to drive economic growth. These shifts necessitate a fundamental change in economic strategy, pushing for a transition towards more sustainable growth models that emphasize innovation, consumption, and services rather than mere investment in infrastructure and manufacturing. Indeed, some of these old growth drivers are no longer producing results as in the past for various reasons, and to maintain momentum, China will need to embrace changes that adaptability in its economic structure, some of which were discussed in the preceding chapter.

Table 3.6 Projected Real GDP growth (Annual per cent change), 2024–2029

	2024	*2025*	*2026*	*2027*	*2028*	*2029*
China, People's Republic of	4.642	4.086	3.77	3.577	3.38	3.306

Source: World Economic Outlook, October 2024

Notes

1. https://english.www.gov.cn/news/202403/05/content_WS65e6ff4dc6d0868f4e8e4b66.html.
2. https://www.emerald.com/insight/content/doi/10.1108/REPS-10-2020-0153/full/html.
3. https://china.usembassy-china.org.cn/four-year-review-of-actions-taken-in-the-section-301-investigation/.
4. At the start of reform in 1978, the State and collectively owned firms accounted for all the workforce in China as well as all of the investments. Since then, there has been a decline in the State's share to less than 20% of the workforce and to less than 30% of GDP, given the trends in the market-oriented reforms in the economy, which has allowed the private sector to expand quickly (WB 2019, Innovative China).
5. https://academic.oup.com/book/41795/chapter-abstract/354502913?redirectedFrom=fulltext.
6. https://www.rieti.go.jp/en/china/14100301.html.
7. https://www.sciencedirect.com/science/article/abs/pii/S0024630116300310.
8. https://www.oecd.org/gov/budgeting/public%20governance%20issues%20in%20china.pdf.
9. These sectors are (a) automobile (b) iron and steel (c) construction (d) ship building (e) petrochemical (f) light industry (g) non- ferrous metal (h) equipment manufacturing (i) electronic information and (j) modern logistics.
10. Yang et al. (2019), though, outline some of the various problems with using the Solow residual, including the fact that it does not account for technological progress, which is embedded in capital acquisition. The authors catering to this embeddedness of technology estimated TFP growth found that in contrast to the previous studies, TFP was as much as 4.1% per annum, and its average contribution to GDP growth was 41.9%, much more in line with that of advanced economies.
11. The WB (2019) in Innovative China indicated that Enterprise growth can be broken down into several parts, including the entry of firms leaving the industry and improvements within firms. If new firms are more productive than old firms, then they would increase overall productivity. Similarly, the exit of firms that are

performing poorly will also help to raise productivity and reallocate resources from poorly performing firms to better performing firms. The liberalization of markets goes a long way in this regard.

12. Innovative China.
13. The WB 2019 in Innovative China noted, "The country's rapid accumulation of basic infrastructure is the envy of many developing countries" (p. 11). The Chinese Economy: Transitions and Growth.
14. In a recent study, Bai and others have questioned whether China has been over investing. Bai (2006) notes that while the return to capital in China fell in the 1990s, it has remained relatively high, indicating that there has been no over investment. In another study by Lu and others 2008, it was noted that while corporate profitability fell in the 1990s, it has since started to increase and on this basis, they have argued that investments have not been excessive. Note, though, that some researchers such as Rawski (2002) have found how investment returns, while others have found evidence of pervasive over investment.
15. The higher the index, the lesser the productivity of capital, and the lower the index the higher productivity of capital. This index is a measure of inefficiency for capital.
16. https://foreignpolicy.com/2021/09/29/chinas-property-sector-evergrande/.
17. Innovative China.
18. https://www.scmp.com/economy/economic-indicators/article/3231282/china-population-100-million-more-senior-citizens-expected-next-decade-ageing-crisis-enters-crucial.
19. A Labour Market with Chinese Characteristics.
20. See also He, Huang, Liu and Zheng (2017), "Breaking the 'Iron rice bowl': Evidence of precautionary savings from the Chinese State-Owned Enterprises Reform."
21. In 2013, China's monthly wages stood at US$600. This was almost three times as high as in countries like Indonesia or Vietnam (see Donaubauer and Dreger 2016, The End of Cheap Labour).
22. https://www.china-briefing.com/news/chinas-labor-force-data-trends-and-future-outlook/.
23. https://data.oecd.org/eduatt/population-with-tertiary-education.htm.

24. This round of reforms saw the Chinese government focused on transitioning state-owned enterprises into modern companies. https://www.britannica.com/place/China/Economic-policy-changes.
25. https://www.elibrary.imf.org/view/journals/003/2002/003/article-A001-en.xml.
26. https://www.visualcapitalist.com/cp/top-countries-foreign-direct-investment-flows/.
27. Globalization Social Conflict and Economic Growth.
28. https://www.investopedia.com/articles/investing/100615/4-countries-produce-most-food.asp.
29. At about 1950, China embarked on an ambitious industrialization program called the 156 projects. With support from the Soviet Union, China built about 150 projects and these projects help to lay a strong base for China's industrialization.
30. Indeed, prior to the Beijing Olympics in 2008, many polluting factories were forced to stop production to help ensure that the air quality improved. Indeed, at one point in 2013, a severe smog descended on Beijing with the level of particulate in the air being 30 times of what was noted as being safe by the WTO. China also suffers from serious water pollution and its rivers are highly polluted on account of discharge from untreated waste (Ferguson, 2020).
31. Note in the "New Normal" growth period post 2012, a greater emphasis was placed on the quality of economic growth, especially as regards environmental impacts (UN, 2020).
32. As reflected in the various comments prior, pulling millions of people out of poverty was associated other transformational indicators such as the decline in agricultural value added and an increase in services value added.
33. This brings to mind The History of the Peloponnesian War by Thucydides. Athens' rise was a necessary but not a sufficient condition to start a war; rather, it was pride and honour that fanned the flames of war.

CHAPTER 4

China's Trade and External Outreach

4.1 Introduction

The Chinese statistical system was premised on Soviet systems until the 1980s and there was a blackout of statistical information in the 1960s and 1970s. During that time, information was distorted for a variety of reasons. The statistical office in China was closed completely for the period 1968–72 (Huang, 1996).[1] This situation, though, improved significantly after 1978, and accounts became more transparent Maddison (2007).

In the 1950s, a significant aspect of China's trade was with the USSR and other communist economies of the time. This stance is partly in alignment with the Stalin–Mao agreements of February 1950, in which the USSR provided support to China both of a financial and technical nature. The importance of communist trade partners became even more accentuated as trade embargoes were imposed by various countries on China including the European countries, Japan, and the USA, mainly on account of the role of China in the North Korean war in helping to displace UN forces. While some countries lifted their embargos in 1957, the leading giant economy of the time, the USA, froze Chinese assets and maintained a total embargo on all transactions with China until 1971 (China and the US Trade Embargo, 1950–1972) The exports of China, Japan, South Korea, Taiwan, Germany, the UK and the USA are shown the the Table 4.1 below for various periods.[2]

R. Hosein et al., *China in the Caribbean*,
https://doi.org/10.1007/978-3-031-71985-1_4

Table 4.1 Volume of merchandise exports, seven countries, 1929–2023 (annual average compound growth rates)

	1929–52	*1952–78*	*1978–2008*	*2009–2023*
China	1.1	2.6	19	6.6
Japan	− 0.2	13.2	8	0.25
South Korea	− 13.1	26.1	13.3	3.5
Taiwan	1.7	16.6		
Germany	− 2.3	10	8.9	1.6
UK	1.6	4.6	8.2	3.7
USA	2.3	5.2	7.6	1.5

Source: Maddison (1995) and author updates

Foreign trade before 1978 was concentrated on the imports of capital and technology-related goods and was led by the state. The Soviets were helping China with its development in this phase and a significant number of imports. The Soviets had also offered to supply China with nuclear weapons but reneged in 1958 as Soviet-China relations soured. Mao was disappointed in Nikita Khrushchev, because he abandoned the strict traditions of Levin and Stalin.[3] In the late 1950s and 1960s, relations became very strained, and the split between the two nations was even marked by small-scale fighting in the Sino-Soviet border conflict in 1969 (Ringger, 2023[4]). Soviet loans were terminated, and technicians were withdrawn from China. China's isolation from the international trading sphere is evident in the fact that its export volume declined by 20% between 1959 and 1970. Even more, imports from other communist countries fell from 66% of the total import trade in 1959 to 17% in 1970.[5]

From about the mid-1970s, the political leadership within China moved away from the autarky setting, motivated by Mao, and embarked on the pathway of the Asian countries that benefitted from their open arrangements with the rest of the world. This meant there was a movement away from central control of foreign trade and payments.

Box 4.1. China's Emergence from International Isolation, 1949–2023

1949 Oct	People's Republic of China was created. Diplomatic recognition was achieved by Burma, India, and communist countries in 1949, as well as by Afghanistan, Denmark, Finland, Israel, Norway, Pakistan, and the UK in 1950
1950 Feb	The USSR agrees to provide financial and technical assistance—eventually \$1.4 billion in loans and 10,000 technicians. China recognizes the independence of Outer Mongolia and agrees to joint Soviet-Chinese operation of Manchurian railways, Soviet military bases in Port Arthur and Dairen, and Soviet mining enterprises in Sinkiang
June 25 1950	North Korea invades South Korea, penetrating deeply into Pusan
June 27 1950	The USA changes its neutral line on Taiwan and sends in the 7th Fleet
1950 Oct	China sends "volunteers" (eventually 700,000) to N. Korea to push back UN forces advancing towards the Chinese border on the Yalu River
1950 Oct	China retakes Tibet
1953 July	Korean armistice
1954	India cedes former British extraterritorial claims to Tibet
1958	China menaces Taiwan in the Quemoy and Matsu incidents. Khrushchev retracts offer of atomic aid
1959	Revolt in Tibet, Dalai Lama flees to India
1960	USSR withdraws Soviet experts and abandons unfinished projects
1962	Border clash with India over Aksai-chin road from Sinkiang to Tibet
1964	First Chinese atom bomb test, 1969 first hydrogen bomb test
1963–69	Border clashes with USSR in Manchuria. China questions the legitimacy of Soviet/Chinese boundaries in Manchuria and Sinkiang
1971 April	USA lifts trade embargo on China
1971 Oct	China entered the United Nations, and Taiwan was ousted
1972 Feb	President Nixon visits China
1972 Sep	Visit from Prime Minister Tanaka to normalize diplomatic relations with Japan
1973	USA and China establish de facto diplomatic relations
1978 Dec	The USA establishes formal diplomatic relations and de-recognizes Taiwan
1979 Feb–Mar	A border war with Vietnam after the expulsion of ethnic Chinese and Vietnamese destruction of the Khmer Rouge regime in Cambodia
1980	China became a member of the World Bank and IMF

(continued)

(continued)

1986	China joined the Asian Development Bank
1997	Hong Kong was restored to China
1999	Macao was restored to China
2001	China admitted to the World Trade Organization
2003	China became a financial creditor nation
2010	China became the largest shipbuilder globally
2013	China became a middle-income country
2020	China became the largest trading partner of more than 120 countries

Source: MacFarquhar and Fairbank (1987 and 1991), author updates

In many regards, before its open-door policy in 1978, China's trading regime may have been characterized as inward-looking and import-substituting. Imports, basically, only focused on essential raw materials and capital goods (Li and Jiang 2018 in a book by Garnet, Song, and Fang). An assessment of the trade reform and liberalization process in China lends itself to four easy classifications: a) changes before 1978, b) 1978–1991, c) 1992–2000 d) post-WTO ascension in 2001. In the period before 1978 (1949–1977), China was mostly a closed economy, and Box 4.1 provides some key milestones in China's emergence from international isolation.

Between 1978 and 1991, there was a focus on administrative decentralization of trade planning, the retention of foreign exchange, the foreign trade contract responsibility system, and the deployment of a realistic exchange rate that did not penalize exports. These interventions were aimed at improving the role of exports in China's economic development process. To encourage the localities and industrial departments to push towards development, the central government assigned them a greater degree of decision-making authority over the administration of exports. The National Foreign Trade Corporations (FTCs), which were established before 1978, had their monopolistic powers dismantled, and their provincial branches were facilitated into becoming independent financial operating entities (Li & Jian, 2018 in Garnet et al., 2018; Song & Zhou, 2022). Each province was now allowed to create its trading agencies and to engage in trade without guidance from the national authorities. The number of export trade companies due to this change increased to 1200 in 1986 compared to 12 in 1978 and escalated to 5075 in 1988 (Li & Jian 2018 in Garnet et al., 2018). By 2021, the General Administration of Customs of the People's Republic of China (2022[6]) reported that the country had 567,000 enterprises with export and import records, which was 36,000 more than the previous year.

The system of exclusive mandatory and advisory planning for foreign trade that existed before 1978 was replaced with combined mandatory and advisory planning. The export plan, which covered 100% of exports in 1978, was whittled down to cover only 15% of exports by 1991, i.e., the free market was given more sway. According to Lordy (1992), imports covered by the plan fell to 15% of total imports by 1992.

Some researchers referred to the export thrust of China in this period as a "protected export promotion system" (Koves & Marer, 1991[7]). This was the type of approach South Korea had used in its ELG strategy. China, however, continued a highly protective import regime.

In the third phase (1992–2000), China pushed the removal of tariffs. Specifically, by 1 January 1992, China reduced import tariffs on 225 products from an average level of 45% to an average level of 30%. Further import surcharges were abolished on 14 products. In December of 1992, China further lowered its tariffs on 3371 items by 7.3%. On 1 January 1994, China reduced tariffs by 8.8% on 2818 items. Tariffs were also reduced on 200 agricultural and industrial items by an average of 50%. In January 1993, all import licences were abolished (Li & Jian, 2018).

In the fourth phase (post-2001), China ascended to the WTO (in 2001). With WTO ascension and recognition of China as a trading partner by the global economy, China implemented its various commitments. (WTO accession deepened the integration of China into the global economy and helped to provide China with an improved and more predictable global market).[8] Tariffs decreased from 15.6% in 2001 to 9.7% in 2005. In January 2005, the tariff rates for all information and technology products were eliminated. China also phased out by 1 January 2005, all import licences, quotas, and specific bidding requirements. Strategically, China's ascension to the World Trade Organization in 2001 was a pivotal part of its strategy of integration into the global economy. China's reform took place over a 15-year period and consisted of several measures, including the reduction of tariffs and the removal of non-tariff barriers to trade.[9]

4.2 China's Export Trends

China's increasing participation in global trade has made a significant contribution to the functioning of the international trade machinery.[10] Within four decades, China moved from being a negligible player in world trade to the world's largest exporter and the world's largest importer of goods, both finished and unfinished. Trade is a positive sum game and so, as China grows, other countries realize opportunities to benefit from its massive low-cost labour force.

When Deng Xiaoping initiated the reform and opening up of China, he said, ***"Emancipate the mind, seek truth from fact and unite as one to face the future."*** The growth in China's exports and imports has been nothing short of phenomenal. Specifically, exports from China increased from a paltry US$2.6 bn in 1960 to US$3380 bn in 2023.[11] (See Table 4.2 compares China's merchandise export trends with that of other economies.

Table 4.2 Merchandise exports 1960–2023 (US$bn)

	China	*USA*	*France*	*Germany*	*Japan*	*Italy*	*UK*
1960	2.6	19.6	6.9	11.4	4.1	3.7	10.6
1970	2.3	43.2	18.1	34.2	19.3	13.2	19.4
1980	18.1	225.6	116.0	192.9	130.4	78.1	110.1
1990	62.1	393.6	216.6	421.1	287.6	170.3	185.2
2000	249.2	781.9	327.6	551.8	479.2	240.5	283.2
2010	1577.8	1278.5	523.8	1258.9	769.8	447.3	420.2
2011	1898.4	1482.5	596.5	1474.0	823.2	523.3	510.4
2012	2048.7	1545.7	568.7	1401.1	798.6	501.3	478.8
2013	2209.0	1579.6	581.0	1445.1	715.1	518.3	546.8
2014	2342.3	1620.5	581.4	1494.2	690.2	529.8	510.8
2015	2273.5	1502.6	506.3	1326.2	624.9	457.0	465.9
2016	2097.6	1451.0	501.2	1334.4	645.1	461.7	410.9
2017	2263.3	1546.3	535.3	1448.2	698.3	507.4	441.0
2018	2486.7	1664.0	582.2	1560.5	738.1	549.5	486.4
2019	2499.5	1643.2	571.0	1489.4	705.6	537.7	469.7
2020	2590.2	1431.6	488.4	1380.6	641.3	496.1	404.7
2021	3316.0	1754.3	585.0	1636.7	756.0	615.6	470.5
2022	3544.4	2065.2	620.5	1675.8	746.8	658.6	533.0
2023	3380.0	2019.5	648.5	1688.4	717.3	677.0	520.7

Source: WDI

Prior to 1978, China was a closed economy, and its exports were not substantive. The growth of exports averaged 7.8% per annum for the period 1961–1977. After 1977, there are three distinct periods in China's export-led growth performance. The first period is from 1978 to 2001 (Yang, 2009). In this period, the average annual growth of exports was 16.5% (with a minimum value of – 0.42% and a maximum value of 36.7%). This strong growth is on account of several factors, one among them being starting from the bottom of the barrel with another being an abundance of low-cost labour. (One source noted that employment in 1978 in village and township enterprises stood at 28.3 mn and increased dramatically to 130.9 mn in 2001 (See Angang, Linlin and Zhixiao, China's economic growth and poverty reduction)).

In 2001, China joined the WTO and, in so doing, reduced its tariffs considerably. The average growth of merchandise exports per annum from 2002 to 2008 was 27.3%. In 2007, merchandise exports crossed US$1 tn for the first time in China (see Table 4.3).

In the period, 2009–2023, the average annual growth rate of China's merchandise exports was 6.6% which was still higher than the world average of 3.4%.

China was able to heavily insert itself into various aspects of the global value chain. This insertion into the global valve chain was facilitated by large-scale infrastructural projects in various segments of the economy including energy, transport, and the power grid. The investment in transportation helped to smoothen labour flows from different parts of China to production points helped with the movement of other factors of production and lowered the cost of transport faced by the various enterprises.

China's export-led growth followed two streams of logic. In part, the ELG strategy followed a variant of the flying geese paradigm with China divided into three spheres: Eastern, Central, and Western. This "flying geese" perspective was written into the 7th Five-Year Plan from 1986 to 1990, starting with the Eastern region and followed by the Central then the Western region. The share of the central government's investment in the Eastern region was promoted and increased from 39.5% in 1953–78 to 53.5% in 1979–1991. The other aspect of the export-led growth strategy is one of a "great international circulation" which established processing trade as part of the strategy of economic development (Wang, 1988). This process started in Guangdong in the mid-1980s and was then escalated to the national level (Yao, 2010). During the last few

Table 4.3 Selected indicators of China's merchandise exports, 1992–2023

	China's exports as a % of GDP	*Growth of China's merchandise exports*	*Growth of world merchandise exports*
1992	19.90	18.12	7.24
1995	20.25	22.95	19.31
2000	20.57	27.84	12.84
2005	33.33	28.42	13.96
2006	35.21	27.17	15.41
2007	34.36	25.95	15.67
2008	31.14	17.23	15.24
2009	23.55	(16.01)	(22.30)
2010	25.92	31.30	21.80
2011	25.14	20.32	19.86
2012	24.01	7.92	0.93
2013	23.08	7.82	2.45
2014	22.36	6.03	0.20
2015	20.55	(2.94)	(12.90)
2016	18.67	(7.73)	(3.09)
2017	18.39	7.90	10.58
2018	17.95	9.87	10.19
2019	17.50	0.51	(2.74)
2020	17.20	3.67	(7.53)
2021	18.61	28.03	26.44
2022	19.82	6.89	11.64
2023	18.99	(4.64)	(4.55)

Source: WDI, WITS and author calculations

decades, the flying geese paradigm saw a relocation of certain types of export-oriented industries from Japan to the Asian Newly Industrialized countries of China. The flying geese model was first used by Akatmatsu (1962) with a focus on specific industries in specific countries. Jenkins (2019) noted that a triangular trade emerged among East Asia, China, and the West to the extent that *"instead of exporting finished products directly, the East Asian economies export parts and components to China, which in turn export finished products to the USA and Europe"* (Tang & Zhuy, 2008, p. 73; Ganlier et al., 2007, p. 56–68).

The growth of China's trade since it joined the WTO has been phenomenal. Yao (2008, 2009, and 2010) noted that some commentators are of the view that the reason for China's exceptional trade performance is because of the value of the yuan. This argument is premised on two factors: the yuan is severely undervalued, and as such, a devaluation will cause Sino-US trade to improve. The PIIE (2010) has found that the yuan is undervalued by 20% and argues that a 10% appreciation will cause China's current account surplus to be eroded by up to US$250 bn.

Secondly, apart from the exchange rate, two profound transformations have taken place in China that have helped it increase exports, these are:

1. Rapid pace of industrialization
2. The extraordinary demographic transition since the One Child Policy in 1979 (Yao, 2010).

The export industries benefit considerably from a supply of labour from the inland sources. In the 1980s, industrialization was carried out by the township and village enterprises (TVEs) scattered across urban and other areas. These TVEs are either owned in a collective way by the local residents or are mainly owned and controlled by the peasants. The collectively owned TVEs account for about two-thirds of the output of the TVEs (Fu & Balasubramanyam, 2003). Indeed, Fu and Balasubramanyam found that the TVEs are much more efficient as compared to similar SOEs. In later years, the industrialization process in China, according to Yao (2010), was driven more by exports. Tong (2008) noted that at one point, 90% of China's exports came from nine coastal cities and provinces.

The One Child Policy of the Chinese, according to some sources, avoided 400 mn births[12] since its introduction and consequently, there was a drastic increase in the working age ratio with less people to feed; families saved more money and poverty fell as living standards increased (Bloom et al., 2007, Huang, 2017,[13] Kane, 2019[14]).

The double transition in the context of the joining of the WTO helped China to flex its comparative advantage.

4.2.1 Direction of Exports and Composition of Exports

Figure 4.1 shows the trends in the exports of China to developed and developing countries. China's export share to high-income economies increased from 85.5% in 1992 but this fell to 55.5% in 2023. Clearly, then and as shown in the graph below there has been an increase in the share of low- and middle-income countries in the export share of China. This increased from 11.6% in 1992 to 37.2% in 2023.

Significantly, China's export performance is not one based on narrow comparative advantage and as Rodrik (2006) notes, China's overall export level: "is that of a country with an income per capita level three times higher than China's" (p. 4). In another study, Schott (2007) found that China's export bundle increasingly overlaps with that of some of the world's most developed economies and that this overlap is not on account of its factor endowments only.

Note that, as Table 4.4 shows, China's factor endowment base changed from 1970 to 2021, with a significant rise in its stock of educated people. As the factor endowment base changed, this fed into a change in the structure of production and exports.

The changing structure of production in the Chinese economy, which is increasingly towards manufacturing, resulted, in true Heckscher–Ohlin fashion, in a change in the structure of exports (Fig. 4.2).[15] Specifically, agricultural raw material exports decreased from 5.1% of total merchandise exports in 1985 to 0.36% in 2023. Similarly, in this same

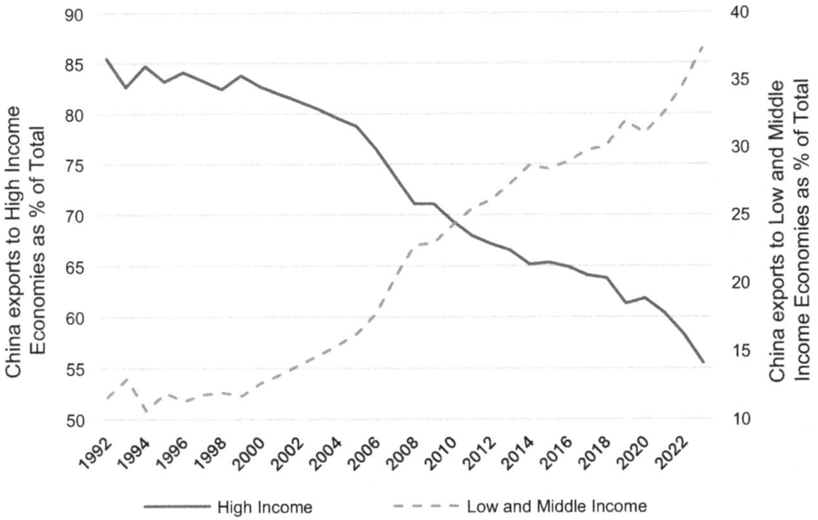

Fig. 4.1 China merchandise exports to high-income and low- and middle-income economies as a % of total trade 1992–2023 (Source: WITS)

Table 4.4 Trends in selected factor endowment indicators, 1970–2021

	1970	*1980*	*1990*	*2000*	*2010*	*2020*	*2021*
Agricultural land (% of land area)	39.8	45.5	53.8	55.6	56.1	55.5	55.5
Arable land (% of land area)	10.6	10.3	13.2	12.8	12.9	11.6	11.6
School enrolment, primary (% gross)	107.0	109.7	127.5	112.3	99.0	103.2	104.1
School enrolment, secondary (% gross)	27.5	43.2	36.7	60.1	88.2		
School enrolment, tertiary (% gross)	0.1	1.1	3.0	9.8	24.2	58.4	63.6

Source: WDI

period, and as Table 4.5 shows, food exports and the exports of ores and metals declined. Significantly, though, manufacturing exports escalated from 26.4% in 1985 to 92% in 2023, a dramatic increase in a short period.

The International Monetary Fund (IMF) has estimated that exports and investment linked to building fundable capacity accounted for about

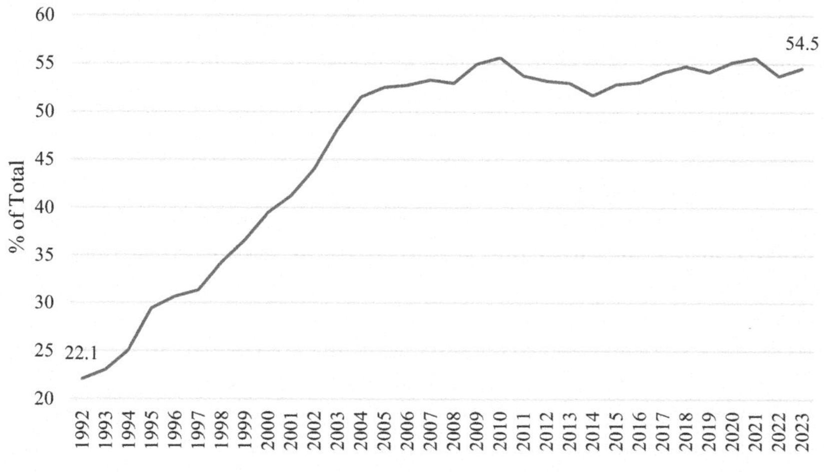

Fig. 4.2 Medium and high-tech exports (% manufactured exports), 1990–2023 (Source: WITS)

Table 4.5 China's distribution of merchandise exports by type (%) of total, 1985–2023

	Agricultural raw materials exports	*Food exports*	*Manufactures exports*	*Ores and metals exports*	*Merchandise exports % Exports of Goods and Services*
1985	5.12	12.57	26.43	1.52	97.11
1995	1.81	8.27	84.04	2.07	101.05
2005	0.53	3.23	91.92	1.79	98.53
2015	0.42	2.78	94.30	1.17	96.33
2016	0.44	3.16	93.72	1.13	95.44
2017	0.42	3.05	93.51	1.20	93.17
2018	0.42	2.91	93.24	1.33	93.80
2019	0.39	2.87	92.87	1.26	95.00
2020	0.33	2.69	93.54	1.12	94.56
2021	0.34	2.29	93.55	1.37	94.46
2022	0.38	2.30	92.65	1.51	96.71
2023	0.36	2.46	91.88	1.32	96.5

Source: WITS

60% of China's growth in the time period 2001–2008 which is considerably higher than in the G7 countries and in the rest of Asia (Guo & N'Diaye, 2009). External demand was an important part of China's manufacturing production but post-2008, this has remained sluggish (UN, 2019).

4.2.1.1 Export Sophistication

China has increasingly distinguished itself as an exporter of capital goods. As a start, note that many Chinese manufacturing goods exported are classified as medium and high-technology exports (Fig. 4.2). Specifically, the diagram below shows the trend in the proportion of medium and high-tech exports as a percentage of manufacturing exports increased from 22% in 1992 to 54% in 2023. This is a significant increase. Indeed, Robert Schott of the US Economic Policy Institute noted, *"everyone knows that we would lose jobs in labour intensive industries like textiles and apparel but we thought we could hold our own in the capital intensive high tech arena. The numbers we are seeing now put the lie to that hope – as China expands its share even in core industries such as autos and aerospace."*

Table 4.6 Export sophistication measures China to world, 2000–2022

Year	*Log of product sophistication (EXPY)*	*Log of GDP per capita, PPP*
2000	9.79	8.15
2010	9.91	9.09
2015	9.92	9.45
2019	9.94	9.69
2020	9.94	9.71
2021	9.95	9.78
2022	9.95	9.81

Source: WITS

4.2.1.2 A Note on Export Sophistication

The level of export sophistication of a country captures the productivity of the export basket of a country associated with its pattern of specialization. A country is considered a more sophisticated exporter if its export basket consists of goods with a higher level of specialization. A more sophisticated export basket results in a higher expected GDP per capita, which indicates a more sophisticated export portfolio.

In terms of export sophistication,[16] note that the index increased over the period 2000–2022 and does validate the observations from the previous Table 4.5. The trend in the index is indicative of increasing export sophistication of Chinese exports (Table 4.6). The index ranges from 0 to infinity[17] with higher values of EXPY indicating a more sophisticated export portfolio.

4.3 China's Import Trends

The diagram above shows that China's merchandise imports expanded from US$2.6 bn in 1960 to US$2556 bn in 2023 (Fig. 4.3). This phenomenal progression shows that China is not a mercantilist economy (Table 4.7).

Direction and Composition of Imports

China imported 80.8% of its total merchandise imports in 1961 from high-income economies, with the rest of the imports coming from low- and middle-income economies, of which 0.75% came from Latin America and the Caribbean (Table 4.7). By 2023, though, China was importing considerably more from low- and middle-income developing economies, with the share of imports from Latin America and the

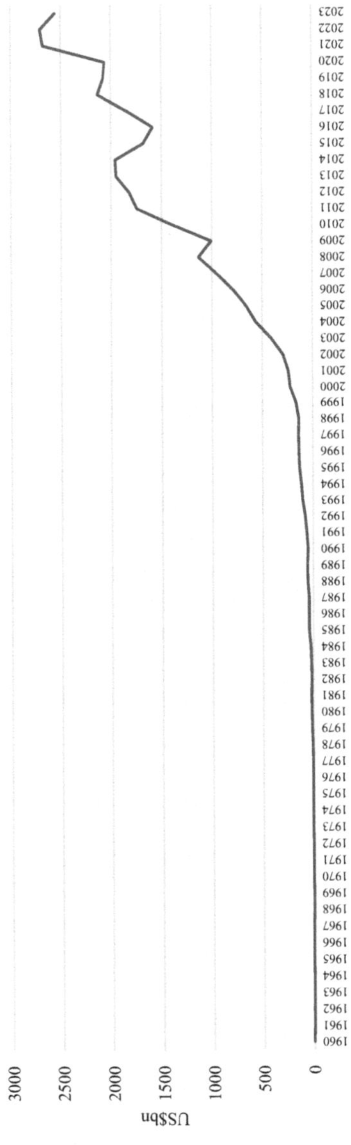

Fig. 4.3 China's merchandise imports, 1960–2023 (current US$bn) (Source: WDI)

Table 4.7 China's distribution of merchandise imports by market (%) of total, 1961–2023

	High-income economies (% of total merchandise imports)	*Low- and middle-income economies*					
		East Asia & Pacific (% of total merchandise imports)	*Europe & Central Asia (% of total merchandise imports)*	*Latin America & the Caribbean (% of total merchandise imports)*	*Middle East & North Africa (% of total merchandise imports)*	*South Asia (% of total merchandise imports)*	*Sub-Saharan Africa (% of total merchandise imports)*
1961	80.80	6.32	–	0.75	3.35	4.53	2.59
1978	74.96	4.69	0.04	4.77	1.60	0.96	1.01
1979	78.91	4.18	–	5.44	0.88	0.60	1.02
1980	82.16	3.95	0.16	3.30	1.46	1.27	0.85
1990	84.91	4.51	0.31	2.56	0.40	0.40	0.54
2000	60.30	7.87	4.27	2.19	1.40	0.99	18.58
2001	57.91	8.77	4.05	2.32	1.17	1.03	19.02
2002	57.36	9.67	3.68	3.08	1.40	1.26	20.99
2003	56.92	9.58	3.30	3.28	1.44	1.60	21.92
2004	54.64	9.87	3.61	3.34	1.95	1.77	23.68
2005	54.28	10.27	3.35	3.53	2.15	1.59	24.52
2006	53.41	10.72	3.43	4.28	2.22	1.83	26.23
2007	51.85	9.59	3.52	5.09	2.76	2.06	27.95
2008	54.78	9.94	3.65	5.02	2.54	1.65	26.87
2009	53.31	10.40	3.64	5.05	2.70	1.78	28.16
2010	51.39	10.59	4.35	5.21	3.11	1.61	30.19

(continued)

Table 4.7 (continued)

	High-income economies (% of total merchandise imports)	*Low- and middle-income economies*					
		East Asia & Pacific (% of total merchandise imports)	*Europe & Central Asia (% of total merchandise imports)*	*Latin America & the Caribbean (% of total merchandise imports)*	*Middle East & North Africa (% of total merchandise imports)*	*South Asia (% of total merchandise imports)*	*Sub-Saharan Africa (% of total merchandise imports)*
2011	49.66	10.42	4.69	5.23	3.12	1.35	30.77
2012	50.81	9.89	4.36	5.01	2.98	1.17	29.40
2013	51.49	10.32	4.09	4.99	3.05	1.11	29.55
2014	53.80	11.42	3.84	4.87	2.17	1.10	27.62
2015	53.96	12.21	3.66	5.20	1.91	1.02	27.61
2016	52.83	12.33	3.92	5.60	2.18	1.13	29.22
2017	50.44	12.35	4.38	6.05	2.68	1.13	31.00
2018	48.20	13.17	4.98	6.64	2.39	1.09	32.62
2019	48.36	14.23	5.03	6.91	1.57	1.25	32.41
2020	47.21	14.42	4.92	6.91	1.64	1.33	32.97
2021	43.66	14.87	6.15	6.88	2.06	0.87	35.00
2022	43.36	15.17	7.08	7.90	1.88	0.96	37.13
2023	60.30	7.87	4.27	2.19	1.40	0.99	18.58

Source: WDI

Caribbean increasing to 7% in 2022. This offers significant export opportunities for the region. This is critical, as it means all countries via the trade channel benefit economically (except probably South Asia) by the growth in China's merchandise imports.

As concerns the composition of merchandise imports, Table 4.8 shows the import of agricultural raw materials into China as a percentage of total imports fell from 7.72% in 1984 to 2.62 in 2023. Food imports as a proportion of total imports into China also declined from 9.03% in 1984 to 3.19% in 2006 but increased to 8.98% in 2023. Import of manufactures into China has gradually decreased, likely because of import substitution, where locally manufactured goods were substituted for imports (Dong & Xia, 2023[18]). Significantly, though, the imports of fuels as a percentage of merchandise imports increased from 0.51% in 1984 to 21% in 2023 and the import of ores and metals increased from 5.53% in 1984 to 14.6% in 2023. The rapid increase in demand for fuels and ores and metal imports can have significant spillover benefits for countries exporting these commodities. Details on how these price increases can benefit commodity-exporting CARICOM economies are provided in Chapter 3. China, as a rapidly growing economy, is a heavy consumer of fuel and ores, and this can have tremendous positive externality spillover benefits for other countries that export ores and fuel.

4.3.1 A New Trade Superpower or Simply the Case of an Undervalued Currency?

Figure 4.4 shows the trends in China's share of world exports and imports. In 1985, China accounted for a mere 1.72% of world exports and 1.22% of imports. By 2023, though, China's share of world imports was 11.2% and 10.35% of world exports. China has been able to run huge trade surpluses, especially with the USA and the EU.

Because of its rapid economic rise, China's growth has meant that its economic welfare influences that of other countries. With the USA, China boasted a trade surplus, which has contributed to the US current account deficit. The EU also has a large trade deficit with China, which stood at US$433 bn in 2023. The USA had a trade deficit of US$279 bn with China in 2023.

The large trade deficits with the EU and the USA sparked concerns with China's exchange rate policy. The RMB's value relative to the US dollar and the euro has triggered extensive discussion in the USA and in

Table 4.8 China's distribution of merchandise imports by type (%) of total, 1984–2023

	Agricultural raw materials imports	*Food imports*	*Fuel imports*	*Manufactures imports*	*Ores and metals imports*
1984	7.72	9.03	0.51	69.18	5.53
1985	5.81	4.10	0.41	52.25	3.90
1995	5.20	6.99	3.88	78.84	4.44
2000	4.81	4.14	9.47	74.84	5.95
2010	3.77	4.62	14.66	61.19	14.33
2011	4.27	4.65	17.01	56.28	14.74
2012	3.95	5.41	18.68	54.76	13.11
2013	3.72	5.50	17.58	54.67	12.70
2014	3.57	5.82	17.46	57.15	11.51
2015	3.70	6.66	12.93	60.98	10.18
2016	3.48	6.28	11.12	64.86	9.43
2017	3.94	6.61	14.59	59.76	11.30
2018	3.57	6.18	17.49	58.30	10.69
2019	2.99	6.65	16.61	59.95	11.18
2020	2.88	8.21	14.07	59.94	13.76
2021	2.65	8.12	16.06	55.58	15.25
2022	2.69	8.51	20.63	51.49	13.49
2023	2.62	8.98	21.03	48.64	14.59

Source: WITS

China. For many years, the USA called for an appreciation of the RMB in relation to the dollar on the presumption that this would improve the USA's exports to China and the US trade deficit. The USA has not been alone. In 2009, the then European Commission President (Jose Manuel Barroso) encouraged Beijing to revalue its currency as *"major imbalances because of trade or because of currencies can create problems in the future if they are not fully addressed."* Indeed, at one point, Barroso, speaking at a seminar in Beijing, noted, "*There is a risk that the economic emergence of China is seen as a threat. That is why we need to deal with the question responsibly to avoid protectionist measures which would be very difficult to contain.*"

One would expect that the rapid growth of China and the increase in its stock of reserves would have led to an appreciation of the Chinese currency. This would be the case if the Balassa–Samuelson effect held for China. The Balassa–Samuelson effect states that productivity differentials

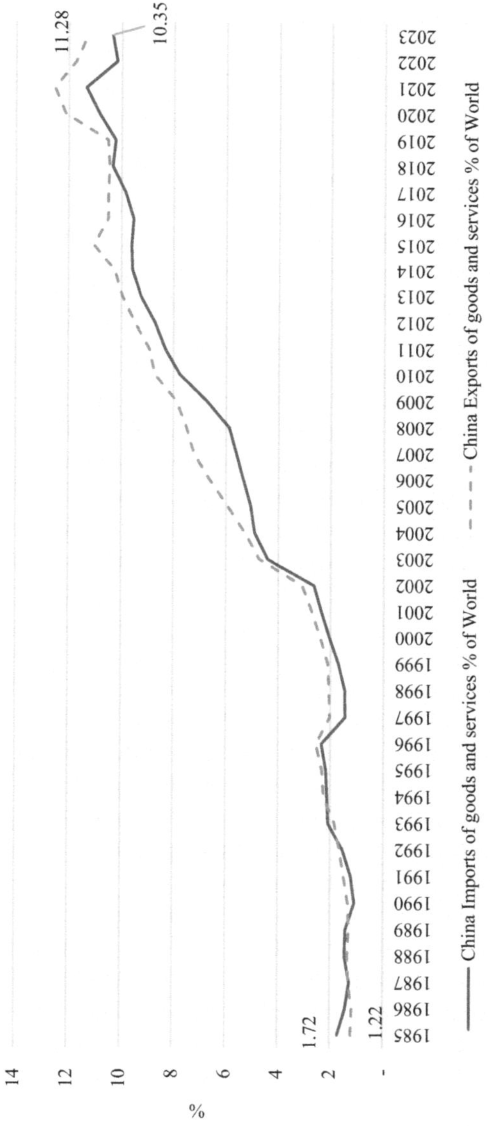

Fig. 4.4 As deep as it gets: there is a new superpower in the world (Source: WDI)

between the production of tradable goods in different countries help to explain observed differences in wages and infers that the currencies of those countries with higher productivity will appear undervalued in terms of exchange rates.

The data in Table 4.9 shows the GDP per capita of the Chinese economy relative to the US economy, and it also shows the RER between the USA and China. 1994 is used as the base year as the Chinese currency was unified in that year.[19] The Balassa–Samuelson (B/S) argument infers that per capita GDP in a country is highly correlated with labour productivity in its tradable sector. The income catch-up variable is China's per capita GDP as a proportion of the USA's, which increased over the period from 3% of real per capita GDP in 1994 to 19% by 2023. The nominal per capita GDP of China increased from 2% of the USA's level in 1994 to 15% by 2023. An upward movement in the ratio implies that the labour productivity of China's tradable sector is catching up with that of the USA. The B/S effect hypothesizes that as this ratio grows the real exchange rate between both countries should grow (Yao, 2010, p. 13). As the data in the diagram below shows, this only weakly occurred in the Chinese case (Fig. 4.5). One explanation for the weak performance of the B/S effect in China is posted by Yao (2010), as the yuan was overvalued in the period prior to 1978, and there were devaluations in the 1980s and 1990s. Wang and Yao (2009) argue that there are two avenues for the B/S effect to occur. One is a nominal appreciation of the currency and the other is an increase in the price of non-tradable goods. Because for long periods of time post-1994, China used a crawling peg, then the appreciation of the nominal exchange rate did not occur. The increase in the price of the NT good occurs through an increase in the wage rate. An increase in productivity of the tradable sector typically triggers an increase in wages therein, which then spills over to other sectors. However, in the case of China, the massive inflow of workers from the rural sector helped to keep wages subdued and weakened the growth of prices in the non-tradable sector.[20] In 1998, the Chinese government targeted 8.28 yuan (which is the base unit of the RMB) per dollar. This rate remained constant until June 2005. In July 2005, on account of pressure from the USA and other trading partners, China appreciated its currency 2.1% against a basket of currencies used until July 2008, when it halted the appreciation on account of the effects of the global crisis on China's exports. It allowed the RMB to appreciate again after June 2010 and from July 2005 to June 2015, the RMB appreciated 35.3%

against the US dollar. After 11 August 2015, China announced that the daily RMB would become more "market oriented." Between 2015 and November 2022, the Chinese currency devalued overall 13.5% against the US dollar. This devaluation continued through the end of 2023 but began to improve in 2024.

China is planning to increase its trade volume from US$4.65 tn in 2020 to US$5.1 tn in 2025 as indicated in the 14th Five-Year Plan. According to this plan, China will import high-quality consumer goods. As it stands, China's main trading partners are the Association of Southeast Asian Nations (ASEAN), the European Union, the USA, and Japan. These four together account for more than 50% of China's exports and imports. The new plan also seeks to actively trade with emerging markets in Asia, Africa, and Latin America and so Caribbean countries would do well to take note.

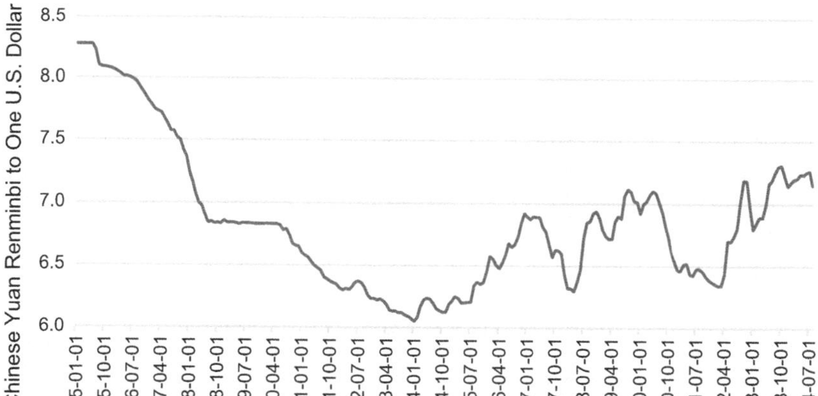

Fig. 4.5 Chinese yuan renminbi to US dollar spot exchange rate, Chinese yuan renminbi to one US dollar, monthly, not seasonally adjusted (Source: Federal Reserve Bank[21])

Table 4.9 Real exchange rate calculation China and the USA

	China		*USA*		*RER China and the USA*
	GDP per capita (constant 2015 US$)	*GDP per capita (current US$)*	*GDP per capita (constant 2015 US$)*	*GDP per capita (current US$)*	
1994	1385	473	41,107	27,695	100
1995	1520	610	41,711	28,691	117
2000	2194	959	48,616	36,330	115
2005	3391	1753	52,650	44,123	114
2010	5647	4550	52,821	48,651	140
2011	6153	5614	53,259	50,066	150
2012	6592	6301	54,080	51,784	155
2013	7056	7020	54,844	53,410	159
2014	7533	7636	55,818	55,304	161
2015	8016	8016	57,040	57,040	161
2016	8517	8094	57,659	58,207	152
2017	9053	8817	58,703	60,322	149
2018	9619	9905	60,127	63,201	152
2019	10,156	10,144	61,331	65,548	147
2020	10,358	10,409	59,395	64,317	149
2021	11,223	12,618	62,741	71,056	153
2022	11,560	12,663	63,721	77,247	139
2023	12,174	12,614	65,020	81,695	127

Source: WDI and own computations

4.4 China and Tourism

Interesse (2023)[22] explains that on average the expenditure per Chinese user for outbound travel for the first half of 2023 increased by 24% as compared to that of 2019 with the top 10 most popular destinations being, Hong Kong, Macao, Japan, Thailand, France, South Korea, Australia, Canada, UK, and Singapore. Even so, Bersola (2023)[23] notes that "the number of Chinese citizens traveling overseas is projected to reach 228 million annually by 2030, compared to 170 million in 2019." This reflects that China will become one of the largest tourism markets in the world in the medium-term period (Table 4.10).

Table 4.10 China outbound tourism (1992–2023)

	Outbound travellers (millions)	*Outbound spending (US$ billions)*
1992	3	3
1995	5	4
2000	11	13
2001	12	14
2002	17	15
2003	21	15
2004	29	19
2005	35	22
2006	35	24
2007	41	30
2008	46	36
2009	47	44
2010	57	–
2015	117	–
2020	20	–
2021	26	–
2023	87	–

Source: Marano et al. (2006), Zhang (2006), and UNWTO World Tourism Barometer (April 2010), and author compiled

4.5 Chinese Foreign Direct Investment (FDI) Outflows

The outward FDI of a country partly helps to reflect the economic strength of a country and helps to play a crucial role in the country's economic development. As China has integrated into the global economy its outward FDI accelerated.

In recent years, the world economy has benefited from an increase in the amount of FDI outflow from China. Prior to 2000, as the data shows, China's OFDI was not prolific, and the government exercised a measure of control over outward FDI both at the level of private firms and SOEs. This policy approach, however, was amended with the introduction of the "Zou-Chu-Qu" strategy (which, literally, means Going Global) that was announced in 2000 by Premier Zhu Rongji in a report to the National People's Congress. In its 10th Five-Year Plan, policymakers made Going Global one of its main thrusts to help the Chinese to better integrate into the global system. The Go Global Strategy was again stressed in the Eleventh Plan.

Several factors have contributed to FDI's outward orientation, including the changing relationship between the government and SOEs and the Chinese people's dissatisfaction with the way China has managed its reserves. The offshore renminbi centres, and the BRI are ways for China to expand its renminbi centres.

Specifically, a major driving force of China's OFDI has been its massive reserves, which it has accumulated since 1990, as shown in Table 4.11.

Significant benefits have accrued to the countries benefitting from overseas Chinese outward FDI, as receiving countries did not only benefit from FDI but also from technology transfers. The UN (2019, p. 40) noted that there has been no significant study of Chinese investments abroad. While Gui-Diby et al. (2015) explains that there are minimal linkages with the rest of the economy when construction-related investments are considered. The authors also estimated that Chinese investment

Table 4.11 Indicators of China's outward FDI, 1977–2023

	Total reserves (includes gold, current US$bn)	*Foreign direct investment, net outflows (BoP, current US$bn)*
1977	4.5	
1980	10.1	
1985	16.9	0.7
1990	34.5	0.8
1995	80.3	2.0
2000	171.8	4.6
2005	831.4	13.7
2010	2913.7	57.9
2011	3254.7	48.4
2012	3387.5	64.9
2013	3880.4	72.9
2014	3900.0	123.1
2015	3405.3	174.4
2016	3097.7	216.4
2017	3235.7	138.3
2018	3168.2	143.0
2019	3222.9	136.9
2020	3357.2	109.9
2021	3427.9	178.8
2022	3306.8	149.7
2023	3449.5	-

Source: WDI

does not contribute to the recipient economy's economic improvement, and this may probably be because of a limited amount of technological spillovers.

Specifically, China's outward FDI expanded from nil in 1979, at which point China embarked on its Open Door Policy, to US$913 mn in 1991. Liberalization of Chinese investment laws in 1992 helped China's OFDI escalate to US$4 bn (in 1992 Deng Xiaoping visited South China to reaffirm China's commitment to its Open Door Policy given the problems associated with Tiananmen Square). By 2016, China's OFDI peaked at US$216.4 bn with total OFDI flows for the period 2014–2022 amounting to US$1370.5 bn. Hang and Sum (1994) found that during the 1990s there was a financing of OFDI by Chinese investors. Although natural resources were still a factor in the late 1990s, other factors such as acquiring foreign technology and management skills also played a role. Deng (2004) noted that in addition to the motives identified by Lui (1999), two additional motives were to gain strategic assets, e.g., brands and marketing networks, as well as to facilitate diversification. As China pursued energy resources abroad, the term "energy diplomacy" was coined which was defined as "diplomatic activities designed to increase a nation's access to resources and its energy security."

Yongqin and Julan (2014) found that China's outward FDI were influenced by six-dimensional indicators; these include language, political stability, violence level, government efficiency, regulatory quality, rule of low level, and corruption control of the host country. Li (2019) found that the geographical distance between countries, the strength of the host country, and the efficiency of the labour market as well as the level of technological readiness were important determining factors of China's influence on countries in the BRI.

Chinese reserves were mainly invested in US government debt and have been generating very low returns and consequently, but segments of the Chinese economy expressed discontent (Zhu, 2018, Going Global 2). After the events of 2008, many Chinese nationals were of the view that it would make more sense to invest those reserves abroad in other types of assets and as a partial consequence, there was a rapid increase in the amount of FDI from China flowing abroad (Yongqin & Julan, 2014; Zhu, 2018).

China's transnational corporations emerged out of a carefully directed and executed strategy of the Chinese government, where the first generation of TNCs were state-owned enterprises Zhan (2017). Since the

1970s, though, these companies have strengthened their international presence and have expanded their scope beyond the borders of East Asia. The second generation of Chinese TNCs emerged during the early 1990s in manufacturing with some degree of revealed comparative advantage in electronics and information communication technology. China's cumulative level of FDI abroad between 2008 and 2022 totaled US$1759.3.1 bn.

Note, though, that China's outward FDI is slowing. This outward FDI peaked in 2016 and since then, has continued to decline. Part of the reason for the slump is that the "Guiding Opinions on Further Directing and Regulating the Direction of Overseas Investment" outlined a blacklisting of several sectors for outward FDI (Moody's, 2019). Moody's also noted that part of the decline is an increased awareness of the risks, and "this awareness of the risks stem from lessons, sometimes difficult ones, companies are learning...."

4.5.1 What Sectors Benefit from Chinese Outward FDI Target?

Chinese FDI targets a wide range of overseas destinations. For example, China invests in farmland that helps the development of its food production sector. In Zambia, Chinese investments target the mining sector. In Lao's People's Democratic Republic, the Chinese directly invest in rubber plantations. Note, though, that while some countries were hungry for Chinese FDI in the past, others have started to perceive that Chinese FDI in their high-tech areas can affect their role at the frontier of these technologies (Huang et al. 2019[24]). Thus, the USA has tightened its screening of Chinese investors, and the American Congress passed the Export Control Reform Act of 2018, which makes it more challenging to export key technologies to countries like China. In November 2018, the Commerce Department published 45 examples of emerging technologies, including face and voice recognition. Some notable blocked transactions include those by the Committee for Financial Investment in the US (CFIUS) which hindered Broadcom's attempt to acquire Qualcomm Alibaba from retaining money gram. The US Commerce Department also put on a blacklist for Chinese Companies that make microchips and supercomputers.

The Chinese government has also placed restrictions on outbound investments in areas such as real estate, hospitality, sports, and entertainment, and these, until recently, were major drivers of China's acquisitions abroad.[25]

Zhang (2019) in "Research on the Impact of FDI on Chinese Trade Structure Optimization" found a close relationship between OFDI and domestic trade export with FDI helping to expand the scale of overall export trade but it also helps to promote the upgrade of the domestic trade structure. OFDI helped to increase exports of intermediate goods, capital goods, and technological goods out of China.

4.6 China's Outward Orientation: Go Global and Other Strategies

4.6.1 Go Global Strategy

The Going Global strategy was initiated in 1999 and encouraged Chinese firms to take advantage of increases in world trade by investing abroad. As an ideological and economic premise, Going Global helps to reflect domestic goals, moving from an investment to an innovation-driven economy and helping the country to become more of a global actor (Haourm, 2016[26]; WEF, 2024[27]). Under Deng Xiaoping, the reforms proposed had two main elements: yin jin lai (bringing in) and zou chu qu (going out). At the start of the reforms, China focused on yin jin lai—i.e., bringing in FDI—and tried to benefit from the associated externality spillovers, given that it was backward in the sense of entrepreneurial talent and technology.

The first phase of China's reforms tapered off around 1990, and while the country continued to attract vast amounts of FDI, policy makers commenced the implementation of zou chu qu: going out, i.e., investing more abroad. The going out strategy worked very well, and indeed, 2015 was a milestone year as for the first time, China's ODI passed FDI.

During the first aspect of the going out project, China concentrated on making deep investments in the developing world in trade, energy, and infrastructure. A significant amount of the going global activities was spent on reaching out to resource rich countries.

In Going Global 1.0, the focus was on a variety of objectives, including China's global image, competing with other powers, and vying for diplomatic space (Zhu, 2013). As concerns Going Global 2.0 (2005-present), the rationale is different from the previous Global 1.0, which focuses more on conventional reasons for investment as well as political reasons. The first few years of Going Global 1.0 (1990–2005) coincided with China's 2001 admission to the WTO and in the period 2002–2012, provided a framework to seek out resources and access to markets offshore. With President Xi Jinping's ascension to power in March 2013, there was a determined attempt to crack down on corruption. President Jinping promised to crack down on both "tigers and flies." However, by the time the anti-corruption campaign was launched in 2012, it was clear the Going Global program was in trouble.[28] Many projects did not even break and they were plagued by economic issues in some cases and governance issues in other cases. Corruption was rampant in many of the Chinese investments abroad, as was rent-seeking (see Andrew (2004), "The intensification of corruption in China" and Johnton and Hao (1995) for an earlier account).

Going Global 2 emerged to encourage Chinese firms to invest abroad with a greater degree of responsibility so as not to tarnish China's image. Further, many of its construction, manufacturing, and energy-based firms are shifting their production abroad as they try to grapple with overcapacity.[29] Some of the key industries that have to deal with overcapacity are traditional industries like steel and cement but in lower end manufacturing industries as well.[30] The European Chamber of Commerce in China (2016) noted that the scale of overcapacity in China became separated from the real market demand, and its production was more than twice that of the next four biggest producers: Japan, India, the USA, and Russia. They indicated that 60% of the aluminium production in China is associated with a negative cash flow. This same source cites data from China's National Bureau of Statistics and the US Geological Survey, indicating that in 2011 and 2012, China consumed as much cement as the USA during the entire twentieth century (Ana Swanson, Washington Post, 2015). Going Global 2 provides the guiding framework for these firms to go abroad, without hurting the image of China.

4.6.2 Belt and Road Initiative (BRI)

China's BRI is the largest transcontinental infrastructural development project ever undertaken in any part of the world. In 2013, Xi Jinping launched the One Belt, One Road Initiative to help expand China's global reach and initiative. In 2015, Beijing changed the name to the

Belt and Road Initiative. China's Belt and Road Initiative is a geopolitical expression of its Going Global 2.0 initiative (Table 4.12).

China is focusing on BRI as part of its strategy to realize a greater degree of trade integration, connectivity of infrastructure, and the coordination of policy via cross-border investment as well as supply chain cooperation, according to the UN (2019, p43). Indeed, at the BRI Forum held in 2017, China committed US$124 bn to the global trade project. China has estimated that opening the corridors along the BRI and growing digital economies would lead to an expansion of trade. Nedopil (2024[31]) reports that the Chinese, via its BRI through financial investments and contractual cooperation for 2023 with some 149 countries, culminated in more than 200 deals worth US92.4 bn, which is 18% higher than in 2022.

With the Belt and Road Initiative, a wide range of projects are undertaken in energy, ICT, manufacturing, and transportation, and all of these projects seek to integrate China's supply capacity. These projects help expand Chinese firms' reach abroad and provide employment for Chinese nationals. Some of the projects also help China to expand its military reach in the region. A good example is the Gwadar Port in Pakistan, as it gives China access to the Indian Ocean for two key reasons: (a) strategic commercial reasons and (b) a deep-water port for its navy.

State-owned firms back the Belt and Road Initiative: the China Silk Road Fund, and supplemented by the China Development Bank and the Export–Import Bank of China. Many of the strategic investments are state-sponsored, and the intention is to advance China's economic and foreign policy goals. A handful of state firms are involved in the foreign projects, and they include China Harbour, CRRC Changchun Railway Vehicles, State Grid, China Three Gorges, and the shipping entity, the

Table 4.12 Going Global 1.0 and 2.0

Going Global 1.0	Going Global 2.0
Solving resource security	Ensuring return on investment
Buying whole value chains	Stimulating global demand
Buying majority stakes	Switching to portfolio investment
Seeking local political patronage	Avoiding dividing political elites
Projecting the China model	Blending with local operators

Source: Author compiled

China COSCO Shipping Corporation Ltd (Xinhua, 2024[32]; Huang et al., 2021[33]).

UN 2019, p. 41, notes that by promoting a free flow of capital, goods, and services, the BRI can help prompt a higher level of investment, trade, and tourism. The same source argues that the BRI could improve productivity as it can help foster an improvement in economic diversification, transport networks, and energy security.

4.6.3 *Is BRI Debt Diplomacy?*

Some commentators have said in the past, *"there are two ways to enslave a country: one is by the sword and the other is by debt"* (American statesman, John Adams (US President from 1797 to 1801)).[34] Some commentators consider China to be pursuing "debt trap diplomacy," i.e., luring poor developing countries into pursuing unsustainable loans, and when they cannot repay, Beijing will seize the associated assets (Table 4.13). In so doing, China can extend its military or economic reach. Two potential examples from the literature are outlined below and relate to Sri Lanka and Malaysia.

4.6.3.1 Sri Lanka

The two most cited controversial cases are Sri Lanka and Malaysia as "victims" of China's debt diplomacy. However, according to the study by Jones and Hameiri (2020), the governments of these two countries

Table 4.13 Various countries' debt to China, 2023

Country	*Debt to China (US$bn)*
Pakistan	26.6
Angola	21.0
Sri Lanka	8.9
Ethiopia	6.8
Kenya	6.7
Zambia	6.1
Bangladesh	6.1
Laos	5.3
Egypt	5.2
Nigeria	4.3

Source: https://www.visualcapitalist.com/ranked-the-top-20-countries-in-debt-to-china/

initiated the most controversial BRI projects to pursue their domestic agendas. The debt problems in these countries arose mainly from their local elites. China, in turn, has faced considerable negative publicity in these two countries. The idea to build the Hambantota Port project originated with the parliamentarian D. Rajapaksa of Sri Lanka. In 2001, one of the sons of this parliamentarian, Mahinda, commissioned a feasibility study for such a port, and this study indicated that the location of the port needed to be more suitable (Wijenayake, 2017). Even so, this port was included in the government's plans as recorded in the document "Regaining Sri Lanka Development Strategy." In 2004, Mahinda Rajapaksa became PM and commissioned another feasibility study, but the project's cost deterred the ambitions of Sri Lanka. Unfazed, a 3rd feasibility study was undertaken in 2006 using a Danish firm named Ramboll and found that the first phase of the port would be commercially viable (Rithmire & Li, 2019, p. 8). The project was then championed by the Sri Lankan Ports Authority (SLPA), and it was green-lighted in 2007. At this point, the government sought international backers.

Although costly, the PM went ahead with Chinese support as it allowed him to direct resources towards his home base and also in areas where the opposition party was making strides (US Embassy, 2007, "Sri Lanka: President State Visit to China Focus on Port project and other Infrastructure Aid"). As is usual in many developing countries, these projects also helped to provide fodder for a network of corrupt people (Kelegama, 2017, p. 441). In one place, it was noted that the company responsible for the construction of the port funnelled US$7.6 mn towards the affiliates of Mahinda Rajapaksa to help strengthen his 2015 bid to be re-elected.

The application for funding by Sri Lanka was supported by the "China Harbour Engineering Group" (CHEG), which was already doing work in Sri Lanka in the aftermath of the 2004 tsunami. The CHEG successfully lobbied the then government to transform the existing port plan in favour of a megaproject. By 2014, the debt-driven program of Rajapaksa was collapsing. One source noted that the "regime's mismanagement, authoritarianism and corruption which were major electoral issues in 2015, resulting in Rajapaka losing the presidential elections." The new president turned to the IMF and agreed to a US$1.5 bn stabilization package, which commenced in June 2016. One source notes that "the government's desire to offload the port and other loss-making ventures like the Hambantota airport—seems instead to reflect the terms of Sri Lanka's IMF Bailout."

In an article titled "China's Belt and Road Initiative: Hambantota Port An Example of China's Debt Diplomacy by Andre Wheeler 2020," it was noted that by the end of 2015, Sri Lankan debt was of such a nature that between 2019 and 2023, US$17 bn would be required to pay for loans from abroad that were maturing. Debt stood at US$55 bn and reserves at US$8.3 mn. China only accounted for 10% of Sri Lanka's debt, so it is a bit harsh to speak of debt diplomacy.

It is also said that China charges a high nominal rate of interest on its loans so as to entrap countries. However, Wheeler (2020) notes that China typically charges 2% on a loan with a typical repayment period of 20 years as well as a grace period that extends to a further 5–12 years. The Hambantota Port benefitted from US$1.3 bn between 2007 and 2014, and only US$357 mn of this total was obtained at the commercial rate of 6%, with the rest of the US$1.3 bn obtained at 2% (Jones & Hameiri, 2020). The loan repayments that were to be made by Sri Lanka to China's Exim Bank accounted for only 5% of Sri Lanka's foreign debt payment—so to speak of debt diplomacy in the case of this port is false.

The port turned out to be uncommercial and it generated massive surplus capacity as well as losses for the SLPA. As at April 2024 Sri Lanka's debt to China was US$8.9 bn.

4.6.3.2 Malaysia

Malaysia's United Malays National Organization (UMNO) was the main ruling party of Malaysia from 1957 to 2018. This party embraced the BRI and, in 2015, signed an MOU in the process, agreeing to several controversial projects. Alifah Zainuddin, in "What happened to China's BRI projects in Malaysia," noted that "despite the slew of BRI mega projects deals signed over the first five years of the Initiative, most have either been canceled or come to a standstill…." It was felt that China's assistance to Malaysia was linked to its interest in the Straits of Malacca. 80% of Chinese oil imports pass through the Strait of Malacca as it is the shortest distance between the Middle East and Europe. About 16 million BOE and 3.2 million barrels of LNG were transported daily through the strait in 2016. It is a highly important sealine for the Chinese economy. In 2003, President Hu Jintao referred to it as the Malacca Dilemma. For many years, China has angled for a railway land bridge to circumvent the straits.

In 2018, the Pakatan Harapan coalition won the elections and accused China of ensnaring Malaysia into a debt trap so that it could seize some of Malaysia's strategic assets. The new party, led by Mahathir Mohamad, started to push back against China.

However, in a detailed analysis of the facts, Jones and Hameiri (2020) found that this was not true and that many of the projects with which China is involved were driven by the commercial economic and political imperatives of Malaysia. Indeed, even the IMF (2018) indicated that Malaysia's public debt is manageable. Malaysia suspended only four of the BRI projects, while others were allowed to continue, yet others re-enacted, although they had been previously suspended. Jones and Hameri argued that the position of Malaysia with respect to China reflected both the needs of Malaysia but also greed. Malaysia, they argued, courted Chinese funding to try and maintain their domestic economic growth. They saw it as an ideal starting point from which they could feed the construction sector as it was important from a political point of view since it employed an important part of the political support for the UMNO via government-linked companies (GLCs). Gomez et al. (2018) argued that these GLCs receive lucrative contracts and project costs are inflated so that "kickbacks" for electoral purposes could also be so obtained.

However, Jones and Hameiri are clear in stating that the construction sector was not the source of the debt crisis in Malaysia but rather, the main aspect of the debt problem was that 1MDB (Malaysia's state-owned investment fund) "*borrowed vast sums of money through questionable deals, funnelling much of it back to Malaysia for political operations, with some RM 30 billion (US$7 billion) missing or misappropriated.*" In 2016, in the backdrop of all of this, Prime Minister Najib Razak pushed heavily for Chinese support for the construction of 2 megaprojects, the East Coast Rail Link (ECRL) and the two gas pipelines. Some new loans would be siphoned off to bail out the heavily indebted 1MBD.[35] Therefore, the deal was started in Malaysia by their PM and not the Chinese. To be fair, the Chinese insisted on commercial terms as well as sovereign guarantees so that their investment would be protected. Thus, against the backdrop of this, the new government led by PH pushed back against the Chinese support.

Jones and Hameiri (2020) contend, "recipient governments must take greater responsibility for the evaluation of potential projects to ensure their viability and sustainability. They must also develop their ability to bargain with Chinese partners to make certain that local people benefit from the BRI."

In an August 2020 piece, however, Jones and Hameiri noted, "*the BRI does not follow a top-down plan, but emerges piecemeal, through diverse bilateral interactions, with outcomes being shaped by interests, agendas and governance problems on both sides*." These researchers argued that to avoid any possible debt default in the future, benefiting governments must take more responsibility for evaluating their projects to ensure their viability and financial sustainability. Recipient governments should also develop their capacity to negotiate with the Chinese.

4.6.4 *Made in China*

Another major initiative of the Chinese government, launched in 2015, was the "Made in China" MIC 2025. This is the signature project of Xi Jinping's input, reflecting how important it is viewed. The MIC 2025 follows the style of Japan, South Korea, Singapore,, and Taiwan in moving beyond low-tech, labour-intensive manufacturing. Through MIC 2025, "China hopes to successfully overcome the middle-income trap and reduce its reliance on foreign technology." Zenglein and Holzman (2019). This initiative aims at increasing the competitiveness of Chinese industries and making China a dominant global manufacturer of several companies. The program intends to utilize government subsidies, bring together state-owned enterprises, and pressure intellectuals. This broad industrial plan focuses on boosting China's position in the global manufacturing chain, enhancing the process of leaping into emerging technologies, and reducing the reliance on foreign firms. The MIC 2025 pushes technological advancement and innovation as a basis for growth and productivity. The MIC calls for breakthroughs in 10 sectors, these are:

1. New generation information technology
2. Higher end computerized machines and robots
3. Aerospace
4. Maritime equipment and high-tech ships
5. Advanced railway transportation equipment
6. New energy and energy-saving vehicles
7. Energy equipment
8. Agricultural machines

9. New materials
10. Biopharma and high-tech medical devices.

China is seeking to update its economy from one that is merely an assembly plant for many foreign firms to one that is more adept at improving the product. Indeed, the MIC 2025 document notes, "China's manufacturing sector is large but not strong." The plan has targets, including by 2025, to boost manufacturing quality innovation and labour productivity to obtain an advanced level of technology, reduce the level of energy and resource consumption, and develop internationally competitive firms as well as internationally competitive industrial sectors. The plan also aims, by 2035, to reach parity with the global industry at an intermediate level and to make innovations and breakthroughs. It also targets leading some specific industries and setting global standards.

By 2049, which coincides with 100 years of the PRC's formation, China aims to lead global manufacturing and innovation and be competitive in advanced technologies and industrial systems (Zenglein & Holzman, 2019).

To implement MIC 2025, China plans the following approach:

1. China will use tax preferences to encourage foreign firms to shift their production and R&D to China. It will also install measures for foreign technological spillovers and use Chinese suppliers for key component supplies.
2. China will use forced joint ventures and partnerships to progress in various sectors. Because China is a major market, it leverages this to push for joint ventures and technology transfers to boost its indigenous capabilities.
3. Chinese government guidance funds (GGF) will channel state funds to Chinese companies to pursue R&D and other overseas acquisitions. The Made in China 2025 Congress report notes that by March 2018, some US$426 bn in government guidance funds had been implemented.

The Chinese officials believe the plan is transparent and non-discriminating. Indeed, one source notes, "*MIC 2025 aims to leverage the power of the state to alter competitive dynamics in global markets in industries core to economic competitiveness. By targeting and channelling capital to specific technologies and industries, MIC 2025 risks precipitating market inefficiencies and overcapacity globally.*"

4.7 Conclusion

This chapter reviewed China's external outreach, especially from the perspective of trade, investment, and tourism, as these are the main avenues through which it will directly influence CARICOM. The chapter illustrated the enormous surge in the export and import trade of China. It established that China is increasingly dependent on the global economy for its supply of fuel as well as ores and metal exports. The chapter also illustrates a surge in the amount of outgoing transits from China and the sharp increase in its outward investment.

The Chinese economy is set to become the largest economy in the world by 2030. As China grows, other economies can benefit as a rising tide lifts all boats. In this regard, tremendous opportunities are available to all countries, including those from CARICOM.

The chapter also presented a cautionary note, as many countries are becoming increasingly indebted to China. Sri Lanka and Malaysia are experiencing challenges with Chinese debt in different forms.

As external demand slows and China approaches the technological frontier, productivity growth will slow. At the same time, as China's income has grown, it has facilitated a rise in consumption, which has helped to spur demand-side activity since 2014 both at home and abroad.

China is also entering a new phase of economic activity founded on structural transformation, with consumption and services playing a bigger role. In the past, government-led stimulus activity has helped boost China's economic growth. This has, however, led to excessive credit growth that has, in turn, led to a rapid increase in debt. China will have to watch the developments in its debt as the UN 2009 has identified that the efficiency of investment in China is deteriorating, and the surge in credit and debt has led to a growing complexity in the balance sheets of banks, which can aggravate banking sector vulnerability (Chen & Kang, 2018).

As China reforms, this can have significant global and regional impacts, including on CARICOM through several channels, including import, export, prices, foreign direct investments, grants, and the movement of people. As the incomes of Chinese people increase, there will likely be a rise in the share of services consumed. CARICOM and associated regional institutions can nuance identified opportunities for non-traditional, deepened integration with China.

Notes

1. The Statistical Agency in China's Bureaucratic System: A Comparison with the Former Soviet Union. Yasheng Huang, Communist and Post-Communist Studies. Vol. 29, No. 1 (March 1996), pp. 59–75 (17 pages).
2. Chen, Xin-Zhu J. (2006).
3. In February 1956, The People's Daily, which is China's flagship newspaper, published a lengthy response to a speech made by Nikita Khrushchev in 1956. In that speech, Khrushchev adopted "de Stalinist perspective." The People Daily article was unsigned but responded by referring to Stalin as an "Outstanding Marxist-Leninist fighter" and opposed Khrushchev's attack on Stalin.
4. https://scholarsarchive.byu.edu/cgi/viewcontent.cgi?article=1328&context=sigma.
5. In the time period 1961–1974, before China's open door policy, its economic growth averaged 5.1% with the more open economies of Hong Kong, Singapore, and South Korea averaging 8.9%, 9.1%, and 10.1%, respectively.
6. http://english.customs.gov.cn/Statics/63ef2d4b-d9f8-411e-8424-34a08b11e3fd.html.
7. A system of promoting exports through incentives while protecting domestic producers.
8. The structural reforms associated with the ascension to the WTO helped the country in part to benefit from high TFP growth.
9. China's unweighted average tariff declined from 55.6% in 1982 to 12.7 in 2002. The standard deviation in 2002 was 9.1%.
10. The phenomenon of global production sharing has taken on, in recent times, a new dimension, with the emergence of China and India as the "Workshops of the World.".
11. This section provides an overview of how the exports of China has changed since 1960. In subsequent chapters a greater decomposition of this change in exports is undertaken. Later in this book we would look at how export structure of China changed, the extent of diversification of Chinese exports and the associated change in

skill intensity. It would also provide a decomposition of the export growth of China.

12. See Zeng and Heskett (2016), "The effects of China's Universal two-child policy.".
13. https://wol.iza.org/articles/how-does-the-one-child-policy-impact-social-and-economic-outcomes/long.
14. https://www.ncbi.nlm.nih.gov/pmc/articles/PMC1116810/.
15. See Freund and Ozden (2006).
16. The export sophistication index is drawn from WITS.
17. Page 39 Trade Outcomes Indicators User Manual.
18. https://www.bbvaresearch.com/en/publicaciones/china-structural-change-of-the-trade-forced-imports-substitution-industrialization/.
19. Prior to 1994, the Chinese currency was inconvertible in some regards as there were multiple exchange rates (there was an official rate and floating swap rates for new exports of manufacturers in different parts of China); there were exchange controls on current and capital account transactions and in general, exports and imports had to be processed through trading companies. In 1994, exchange controls were abolished on current account transactions and a new consolidated official rate at yuan 8.7 per dollar was established.
20. Although the Hukou system was in place, it was not rigidly followed on account of the rapid increase in economic growth in China and labour shortages in urban spaces. In some cases, rural to urban migrants have been able to purchase urban hukous.
21. https://fred.stlouisfed.org/series/DEXCHUS.
22. https://www.china-briefing.com/news/chinas-tourism-in-2023-outlook-trends-and-opportunities/.
23. https://www.moodiedavittreport.com/outbound-travel-from-china-set-to-reach-228-million-a-year-by-2030-says-new-report/.
24. https://www.bbvaresearch.com/en/publicaciones/china-five-facts-about-outward-direct-investment-and-their-implication-for-future-trend/.
25. HNA, Wanda, Fosun, and Anbang were collectively responsible for in excess of 25% of Chinese deals targeting assets in the EU and North America.
26. https://www.imd.org/research-knowledge/economics/articles/why-china-is-on-the-way-to-being-A-global-innovator/.

27. https://www.weforum.org/agenda/2024/06/why-china-is-making-innovation-the-new-engine-of-growth/.
28. In 2012, a campaign was launched against corruption at the end of the 18th National Congress of the CCP in 2012. It was the largest anticorruption effort in China's history. It was part of Xi Jinping's plan to simultaneously crack down on "tigers and flies," i.e., high-level officials and civil servants. More than 100,000 people have been indicted so far (Economists, 2015, Robber Barons, Beware).
29. In 2009, the former deputy of China's State Administration of Taxation, Xu Shanda, submitted a Marshall Plan to the Ministry of Commerce labelled the "Chinese Marshall Plan." This plan, in the context of the global financial crisis, provided guidelines as to how China could create demand through a strategy involving China's vast amount of foreign reserves to provide loans to developing countries who then, in turn, could contract large Chinese enterprises for support with infrastructure and construction. This vision helped to create the roadmap for the OBOR initiative.
30. These industries received preferential financial support from state banks, which allowed them to overproduce even when global demand fell. As a result, China made very small adjustments to its overcapacity, allowing global prices to fall for these commodities.
31. https://www.griffith.edu.au/__data/assets/pdf_file/0033/1910697/Nedopil-2024-China-Belt-Road-Initiative-Investment-report.pdf.
32. https://english.news.cn/20241008/e460bb752210417aa73ae9cf8b78384c/c.html.
33. https://www.mdpi.com/2071-1050/13/4/2144.
34. https://asia.nikkei.com/Politics/Brahma-Chellaney-China-is-ensnaring-vulnerable-states-in-debt-traps.
35. IMDB borrowed enormous amounts of money and was part of a huge scandal that involved bribery, money laundering, and corruption which started in 2009. Malaysia PM in 2015, Najib Razak, was accused of channelling approximately US$700 mn into his personal banking accounts from the IMDB. Najib Razak lost the elections in 2018 and the new PM Mahathir Mohammed reopened the investigations which were closed under Najib Razak. Razak was found guilty on several charges and was sentenced to 12 years imprisonment.

CHAPTER 5

Framework for Understanding Trade

5.1 Introduction

This chapter assesses the extent to which CARICOM economies have had their pattern of trade specialization altered on account of the rapid expansion in the trade of China in the last 30 years. The next section will discuss the direct trade complementary effect, after which the export potential and product diversification situation will be assessed. The extensive and intensive margins of T&T trade with China are then presented, followed by a discussion on the product concentration index. The case of Australia's trade with China will be reviewed as a situation of strategic dependence, after which the chapter will conclude.

In 1990, two of the largest economies in the world, India and China, accounted for 2.008 bn people. By 2023, this accelerated to 2.84 bn people, i.e., 35.4% of the world's population lived in China or India. The growing significance of these two (2) economies on the global front has raised considerable discussion and even concern among other countries. Table 5.1 indicates the size of these economies. In 2023, both economies were highly open, with trade as a proportion of GDP being 37.3% for China and 45.6% for India. In 2023, China's exports accounted for 11.3% of world exports. Indeed, as evidenced by the average growth rate from 1980 to 2023, which was 9.1% and 6%, respectively, China and India are global engines of growth.

R. Hosein et al., *China in the Caribbean*,
https://doi.org/10.1007/978-3-031-71985-1_5

Table 5.1 China and India in the Global Economy: How Giant Economies Grow, 1990, 2019, 2023

	China	*India*
Population 1990 (bn)	1.135	0.873
Population 2019 (bn)	1.397	1.366
Population 2023 (bn)	1.41	1.43
Share of World GDP 1990	1.59	1.41
Share of World GDP 2019	17.38	3.10
Share of World GDP 2023	17	3.4
Share of world exports 1990	1.14	0.53
Share of world exports 2019	12.03	2.09
Share of world exports 2023	11.3	2.5
Average growth 1980–1990	9.8	5.6
Average growth 1980–2023	9.1	6
Trade/GDP 1990	24.3	15.5
Trade/GDP 2023	37.3	45.6
Expected real GDP growth (%) 2024–2029	3.8	6.5

Source: WDI

Phenomenally, China's share of world GDP escalated from 1.59% in 1990 to 17% in 2023; in the same period, India's share of world GDP improved from 1.41 to 3.4%. In the medium-term period through 2024–2029, India, though, is expected to grow faster than China (an average of around 6.5% real GDP growth as compared to 3.8% for China). China, as an emerging economy in the global sphere, has implications for global and sector-specific demand, given the sheer size of its market. For this reason, the authors believe that it is prudent to isolate China's impact on the CARICOM region in terms of its trade and development impact, both directly and indirectly.

These direct and indirect effects can, in turn, be competitive effects or complementary effects (Shafaeddin, 2004; Kaplinsky et al., 2006), a matrix of which is shown in Table 5.2.

This chapter assesses in detail the first of the four permutations set out above in Table 5.2 while the other three permutations are discussed in the following three chapters.

Table 5.2 Direct and indirect effects of trade with China

	Direct	*Indirect*
Complementary	A—CARICOM sells more to China	C—CARICOM commodity exporting countries indirectly benefit as China bids up the prices of commodities exported from the CARICOM
Competitive	B—Deindustrialization, deagriculturalization, and other forms of displacement from China	D—Competition to CARICOM exporters by China in third markets

Source: Jenkins (2008)

5.2 Direct Trade Complementary Effect

1. Share and Level of Exports

As China grows, it provides market export opportunities for every other economy, including those of the Caribbean. In this regard, the data in Table 5.3 shows that exports by CARICOM countries to China represent only a small proportion of their total exports, although between 2000 and 2015 (data for subsequent years is a bit patchy), the export shares of most CARICOM economies to China increased.

From another dimension, Table 5.4 shows that exports to China from CARICOM member states between 2005 and 2023 increased for Antigua and Barbuda, Barbados, Belize, Guyana, St. Lucia, and Suriname.

Thus, in distinct ways, there has been an increase in exports by CARICOM countries to China.

Digging deeper, note that for the period 2000–2023, i.e., the period after China's ascension to the WTO, there was a low level or, at best, moderate degree of correlation between the exports of the listed CARICOM countries to China and China's imports from the world (Table 5.5). Note that the exports of Guyana, Jamaica, and Suriname have a high degree of correlation with China's imports for the period 2000–2023.

Table 5.3 Share of exports to China in the total exports of CARICOM countries, 2000–2023 (%)

	2000	*2015*	*2021*	*2022*	*2023*
Antigua and Barbuda		0.61			59
Bahamas, The		0.08			
Belize		0.05	0.02	0.08	0.01
Barbados	0.09	4.40	1.93	0.08	0.46
Dominica					
Grenada	–	0.01	1.01	–	0.0
Guyana	0.20	1.35	0.39	2.97	0.5
Jamaica	0.51	2.06	1.20		0.5
St. Kitts and Nevis	–	0.40			
St. Lucia	–	0.93			
Suriname	0.36	0.70	1.22	1.21	0.1
Trinidad and Tobago	0.02	0.33	4.03		
St. Vincent and the Grenadines		0.00			

Source: WITS and author calculations

Table 5.4 Exports by each CARICOM country to China, 2005–2023 (000 US$)

	2005	*2015*	*2021*	*2022*	*2023*
Antigua and Barbuda	0.6	32.0			2833.04
Bahamas, The		268.1			
Belize	22.9	163.3	39.9	181.5	30.17
Barbados	770.5	12,476.2	4339.9	189.1	1113.7
Grenada	0.0	1.7	227.1	0.0	5.104
Guyana	4578.8	15,646.2	9998.3	632,657.32	39,450.76
Jamaica	107,406.1	28,537.8	13,949.4		7559.18
St. Lucia	10.0	679.2			1466.77
Suriname	1427.7	12,864.8	25,812.6	26,759.9	
Trinidad and Tobago	3818.8	43,468.4	174,508.9	219.1	
St. Vincent and the Grenadines	40.7	0.3			

Source: WITS and author calculations

Table 5.5 Correlation scores in exports and GDP growth for selected CARICOM members with China

	Barbados	*Guyana*	*Jamaica*	*Suriname*	*Trinidad and Tobago*
CARICOM Exports correlation with China Imports					
2000–2023	0.49	0.63	0.68	0.98	0.76
CARICOM growth correlation with China Growth					
2000–2023	0.12	− 0.66	0.23	0.65	0.58

Source: Author calculated

2. Top 25 Goods Exported from CARICOM to China

In assessing the extent of the direct trade complementary effects, it is important to consider the composition of exports. As can be seen from Table 5.6, the top 25 commodities exported by CARICOM to China in 2023 were mainly "raw materials."

Policymakers should consider engaging the embassy of China more intensely for interventions such as trade fairs and exporter networking forums to increase the amount of export trade from the region. Embassies generally include a trade desk that collaborates with various business associations and other trade-related entities to deepen the trade presence of the home economy in host countries. Indeed, Rose (2005) found that foreign postings abroad add 6–10% additional exports to a country's profile. This is because foreign offices can assist in making connections for and on behalf of traders to deepen relations between economies. Ciuriak and Kinjo (2006)[1] expanded this line of reasoning by noting that an amicable diplomatic relationship between countries can be trade facilitating, as it can, in principle, reduce costs of international trade through political capital, addressing challenges immediately in terms of advocacy and bilateral irritants if and when they emerge. To this end also diplomatic relations encourage trade integration between economies (Whitten et al., 2020[2]).

The following section investigates where further export potential lies for CARICOM economies to China.

Table 5.6 Top 25 exports from CARICOM to China, 2020–2023 US$000

Code	*Product description*	*2000*	*2005*	*2010*	*2015*	*2023*
333	Petrol./bitum. oil, crude				203,876.2	610,251.3
512	Alcohols/phenols/derivs		8948.7		150,743.3	209,950.8
247	Wood in rough/squared	649.4	3364.6	13,477.8	35,326.1	24,060.6
343	Natural gas		8557.9	39,189.8	1230.5	7915.4
248	Wood simply worked	250.2	5185.9	4389.9	2936.7	7098.7
634	Veneer/plywood/etc		4,12.6	7592.5	6056.7	6767.5
287	Base metal ore/conc nes		6919.4	991.8	0.1	5890.4
034	Fish,live/frsh/chld/froz	1.2	157.0	1171.6	5806.6	4877.0
285	Aluminium ores/concs/etc	6067.4	17.4	24,461.5	32,971.2	4052.4
071	Coffee/coffee substitute		256.4	482.6	1543.9	2520.3
282	Ferrous waste/scrap	15.7	3324.4	4657.4	4022.8	2354.0
579	Plastic waste/scrap	47.0	459.5	349.8	3384.2	1603.7
288	Nf base metal waste nes	9.0	1592.4	749.9	594.4	1025.8
036	Crustaceans molluscs etc	0.0		270.3	119.0	700.6
112	Alcoholic beverages	84.9	3.4	–	25.9	238.8
351	Electric current					132.3
334	Heavy petrol/bitum oils			982.7		108.5
291	Crude animal mterial nes		0.3	0.0	237.7	105.2
899	Misc manuf articles nes	–	1780.6	12,331.9	2002.7	102.4
692	Metal store/transpt cont			5.6		52.0
098	Edible products n.e.s		34.7	–	274.8	41.6
781	Passenger cars etc					40.0
058	Fruit presvd/fruit preps		4.7	–	19.2	37.2
035	Fish,dried/salted/smoked		11.6	33.6	1.8	32.4
422	Fixed veg oils not soft					29.5

Source: WITS

5.3 Export Potential and Product Diversification Between China and CARICOM

The export potential index (EPI) helps to identify products with a high degree of export potential and diversification opportunities in a particular market (Decreux & Spies, 2006).[3]

A country's capacity to supply an existing product is premised on projected market shares. Its capacity to diversify into new products hinges on an understanding of product space Hausmann and Klinger (2007), Hausmann et al. (2007), and Hidalgo et al. (2007). This understanding of product space establishes a link between products based on an assessment of how frequently these products are part of the export basket of countries. The authors show that productive capabilities impact the modes of production, which, over time, become structural to the sector or industry. Further, Coniglio et al. (2017)[4] explained that while some new products are linked to initial production baskets, others are not, which, over time, contributes to changing an economy's comparative advantage structure.

Table 5.7 lists the top 25 commodities with export potential for TT, used here as a representative member of the CARICOM, in the Chinese market. These commodities include methanol alcohol, with an export potential of US$200 mn, and anhydrous ammonia, with an export potential of US$25 mn.[5] Notice that the commodities with the highest export potential are those commodities that can improve or expand domestic sectors in China. For example, Megan (2021)[6] explains that medical manufacturing, rail transport, hotels, and online commercial shopping services are among the fastest growing sectors in China for 2021.

In considering T&T's export potential to the Chinese market, we also reflect on the trend in product diversification over the period 2001–2022. Table 5.8 shows that over time, the number of products (sectors) exported to China by TT increased from 2010 to 2015 but subsequently declined to 13 by 2023; this trend was likely due to the impact of the COVID-19 pandemic.

Table 5.7 T&T Export potential in the Chinese Market, 2024

Product code	*Product Description*	*Export potential (TTO-CHN) Trade value $ mn*	*Actual export (TTO-CHN) Trade value $ mn*	*Total TTO Exports (TTO-Wrd) Trade value $ mn*	*Total China imports (CHN-WRD) Trade value $ mn*
290,511	Methanol "methyl Alcohol	185	223	1600.00	3100.00
720,310	Reduced Iron Ore	60	2.6	712.00	552.00
281,410	Anhydrous Ammonia	22	3.3	2100.00	267
29XXXb	Other Organic Chemicals	0.821	–	58	3200.00
38XXXX	Miscellaneous chemical products	0.641	0	16	5800.00
0303Xa	Fish nes, whole, Frozen	0.523	0.0032	4	2200.00
2202XX	Non-alcoholic beverages	0.505	–	28	545
210,690	Food Preparations	0.45	–	15	3200
220,210	Water, Sweetened	0.426	–	59	136
220,300	Beer made from malt	0.409	0	10	663
200,819	Nuts & other seeds, prepared or preserved, nes	0.378	0	7.2	469
190,410	Prepared foods from roasting cereals	0.303	0	18	161
854,449	Electric conductors < = 1000 V, without connectors	0.268	0	12	1200
190,531	Sweet biscuits	0.259	0	17	255

Product code	*Product Description*	*Export potential (TTO-CHN) Trade value $ mn*	*Actual export (TTO-CHN) Trade value $ mn*	*Total TTO Exports (TTO-Wrd) Trade value $ mn*	*Total China imports (CHN-WRD) Trade value $ mn*
340,250	Surface-active & washing preparations for retail, N.e.s	0.176	0	12	403
470,710	Waste & scrap of paper(-board), unbleached	0.161	0	3.2	610
190,590	Bread, pastry	0.156	0	24	483
760,200	Waste & scrap of aluminium	0.148	0.026	3.9	1700
210,390	Preparations for sauces, n.e.s	0.144	0.064	33	152
391,732	Flexible tubes of plastics, without fittings	0.143	0	4.1	326
722,830	Bars & rods of alloy steel, hot-rolled, n.e.s	0.138	0	5.8	339
310,210	Urea	0.126	0.113	264	40
180,631	Chocolate & cocoa preparations, in blocks < = 2 kg, filled	0.126	0	14	79
190,532	Waffles & wafers	0.118	0	5	200
151,319	Coconut oil & fractions processed	0.116	0	4.4	278

Source: ITC 2024

Table 5.8 T&T HH product index to China and World markets 2001–2022

Year	*China*		*World*	
	HH product index	*Number of products*	*HH product index*	*Number of products*
2001	0.4319	11	0.1212	2848
2005	0.2492	22	0.1732	2756
2010	0.1729	33	0.1489	2320
2015	0.3602	46	0.1256	2536
2021	0.9938	29	0.1075	2699
2022	0.9109	13	0.1751	1843

Source: WITS

5.4 Extensive and Intensive Margins of T&T Exports to China 2010–2015

Export growth can be separated into two components, i.e., an increase in exports of existing products (intensive margin) and an increase in exports of new products and markets (extensive margins). Uribe-Etxeberria and Silvente (2012) noted that understanding how export changes are decomposed is important in identifying nuances for addressing competitiveness, specifically in terms of what drives export growth at either level (extensive or intensive) and how this growth translates into benefits for the home economy. Specifically, the author also considered the question of what factors result in a shift from an export sector considered part of the export margin at the start of the period to being included in the intensive margin in subsequent periods.

This decomposition of the intensive and extensive margin can, therefore, be separated into the following:

Intensive Margin

(1) Increase of existing products in established markets
(2) Decrease in existing products in established markets
(3) Extinction of exports of products in established markets.

Extensive Margin

(4) Introduction of new products in new markets
(5) Introduction of new products in established markets
(6) Introduction of existing products in new markets
(7) Product diversification in established markets.[7]

These indices are obtained from the UNCOMTRADE and are specific to an exporting economy. As such, the details presented below are between T&T and China and map the latter's export profile from 2010 to 2022[8] using HS 2007 (nomenclature) for all HS 6-digit commodities (Table 5.9).

In the case of China for the intensive margin, there was a 108% increase in exports of existing products; this, the first component of what constitutes intensive margin, is known as the export variation and reflects an increase in exports of existing products in existing markets (Besedes & Prusa, 2007). The second indicator of – 5.79% refers to the decline in existing exports or the decline in existing product margins. The – 2.28% extinction of exports of products is known as the "product death margin" (Kuncic, 2013). The measure of intensive margin, therefore, reflects that more existing products are exported with fewer failures and can, therefore, be considered as the sustainable aspect of exports, as it represents an established market presence (Amurgo-Pacheco & Pierola, 2007).

For the broad category of extensive margin, the second and fourth sub-index reflect that there was no real increase in exports to established markets of new products and a 0.05% product diversification, respectively;

Table 5.9 T&T Export growth decomposition to China for the period 2010–2022

Category description	*Export growth decomposition*
Increase of existing products in established markets	108.02
Decrease in existing products in established markets	– 5.79
Extinction of exports of products in established markets	– 2.28
Introduction of new products in new markets	0.00
Introduction of new products in established markets	0.00
Introduction of existing products in new markets	0.00
Product diversification in established markets	0.05

Source: WITS

this means that there was a marginal increase in the number of products sold, implying that the profile of export basket expanded.

5.4.1 *Export Growth Decomposition 2001–2019 from China to CARICOM*

Table 5.10 shows the intensive and extensive market for China to CARICOM over three periods, 2001–2019, 2010–2019, and 2010–2023. Observe that the nature of export growth for China is biased towards an intensive trade margin; this implies that there was an increase in exports of existing products from China to CARICOM.

5.4.1.1 *Number of Zeroes*

Table 5.11 indicates the number of "zeroes" or sectors not exported to the world using HS 6-digit data. In other words, it represents the commodities under the HS classification system that are not exported by these countries. The maximum number of commodities exported worldwide is 5038 based on HS 6-digit data (WITS, 2021). As expected, China has fewer zeroes than smaller countries like those in the CARICOM. China's zeroes increased from 261 in 1992 to 318 in 2023. This may

Table 5.10 Export growth decomposition of China to the CARICOM market (various periods)

	2001–2019	*2010–2019*	*2010–2023*
Increase of existing products in established markets	101.35	582.48	139.08
Decrease in existing products in established markets	− 1.02	− 282.86	− 65.98
Extinction of exports of products in established markets	− 0.51	− 373.52	− 8.09
Introduction of new products in new markets	0	0	0.00
Introduction of new products in established markets	0.12	5.51	0.00
Introduction of existing products in new markets	0	0	0.00
Product diversification in established markets	0.06	168.38	34.99

Source: WITS

be due to deepening specialization in some product groups more suited to the country's changing comparative advantage in terms of production factors. Not surprisingly, in the context of their limited factor endowment, the number of zeroes remains relatively high for Caribbean countries.

Data on the number of zeroes above shows that there has been a decrease in the number of zeros associated with exports from China to CARICOM (See Fig. 5.1). This indicates that there has been an increased number of exported HS-classified commodities to the CARICOM region (Table 5.12).

The number of zeroes (sectors not traded) that are present between CARICOM countries and their exports to China remained relatively high over the period 2000–2023. If we focus on the snapshot years 2001 (when China gained WTO ascension) and 2019 (to avoid COVID-induced distortions), then for the listed CARICOM member states except for Barbados, the number of zeroes fell, indicating that the listed CARICOM member state exported more to China in the stated time

Table 5.11 Number of Zeroes using HS 6-digit data selected countries to the world 1991–2023

	China	*Barbados*	*Guyana*	*Jamaica*	*St Lucia*	*Suriname*	*Trinidad and Tobago*
1991	Na	Na	Na	4339	Na	Na	3929
1992	261	Na	Na	4302	4721	Na	3909
2000	241	4121	4135	4387	4753	4595	2369
2005	295	3760	4164	4183	4598	4454	2337
2010	585	3803	4313	4054	4076	4258	3579
2011	596	3865	4335	4137	4072	4189	3194
2012	625	3806	4423	4156	4221	4106	2814
2013	616	3818	4504	4189	4026	4551	3267
2014	612	3894	4389	4276	3976	4494	3396
2015	606	3977	4474	4314	3983	4907	3383
2016	292	3848	4366	4156	3417	4900	2388
2017	292	3861	4086	4130	3590	4904	2363
2018	287	3847	4193	3471	3633	4926	2310
2019	282	3445	3660	3340	3580	4843	2282
2020	311	3664	3661	3389	3703	4838	2376
2021	308	3542	3672	3524	5038	4283	2339
2022	332	3587	3700	5038	5038	4240	–
2023	318	3660	3367	3550	–	4756	–

Source: WITS

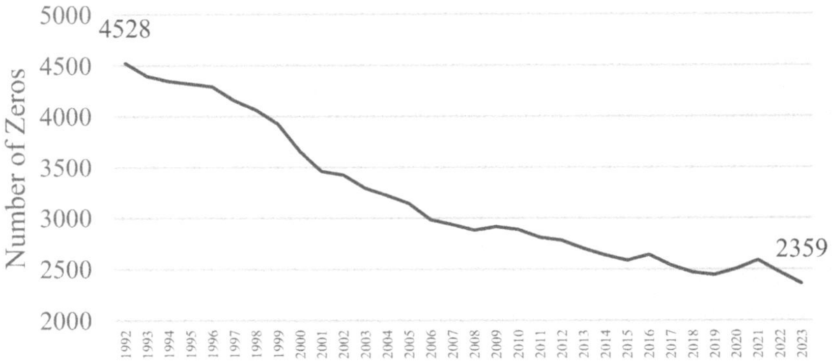

Fig. 5.1 Number of zeroes using HS 6-digit data from China to CARICOM 1992–2023 (Source: WITS)

Table 5.12 Number of zeroes to China from CARICOM countries using HS 6-digit data, 2000–2023

	Barbados	*Guyana*	*Jamaica*	*St Lucia*	*Suriname*	*Trinidad and Tobago*
2000	5031	5032	5033	Na	5036	5029
2005	5009	5017	5014	5036	5004	5016
2010	5013	5012	4995	4787	5022	5010
2011	4999	5020	5010	4988	5016	5009
2012	4995	5016	5010	4972	5007	5005
2013	4991	5022	5006	5033	5025	5020
2014	4998	5010	5000	5032	5027	5019
2015	5019	5017	5008	5001	5030	5018
2016	4986	5013	5008	4890	5029	5016
2017	4989	5003	5007	4907	5024	5020
2018	4979	5013	4978	5034	5027	5001
2019	5014	4998	5004	5024	5021	5016
2020	5024	5016	5010	–	5026	5024
2021	5025	5000	5018	–	5019	5028
2022	5031	4988	5018	–	5019	–
2023	5027	4983	5001	–	5008	

Source: WITS

interval overall, though the export basket of goods to China is very limited.

5.4.1.2 Export Duration 2001–2022

This indicator represents the number of new product-partner relationships with trade values of more than US$10,000.[9] It represents the extent to which these relationships change over time, assuming a specific starting point or year, and can be considered as a measure of persistence or survival (Phiri et al., 2021).[10] For the given start year, the number and percentage of surviving relationships in each succeeding year until the selected end date is reported. Sustaining trade relationships with a particular trade partner contributes to maintaining an economy's intensive margin of exports, and this has been shown to have more long-term growth benefits than extensive margins (Otamurodov et al., 2016).[11] Consider Table 5.13, which shows the export duration of selected partners to the CARICOM market, which, over the period 2005–2023, has been declining, indicating that the region is becoming increasingly marginalized as an export destination for traditional and non-traditional trade partners.

Table 5.13 Export Duration of Selected Markets with CARICOM, 2001–2023

Year	*China*		*India*		*UK*		*USA*	
	Start year 2005–414 number of export Relationships by the end of year	*Share (%)*	*Start year 2005–83 number of export Relationships by the end of year*	*Share (%)*	*Start year 2005–380 number of export Relationships by the end of year*	*Share (%)*	*Start year 2005–1648 number of export Relationships by the end of year*	*Share (%)*
2005	414	100	83	100	380	100	1648	100
2010	473	114	71	86	278	73	1868	113
2011	462	112	72	87	289	76	1901	115
2012	478	115	75	90	267	70	1866	113
2013	491	119	77	93	272	72	1838	112
2014	488	118	71	86	289	76	1831	111
2015	499	121	74	89	270	71	1819	110
2016	487	118	84	101	286	75	1806	110

(continued)

Table 5.13 (continued)

Year	*China*		*India*		*UK*		*USA*	
	Start year 2005–414 number of export Relationships by the end of year	*Share (%)*	*Start year 2005–83 number of export Relationships by the end of year*	*Share (%)*	*Start year 2005–380 number of export Relationships by the end of year*	*Share (%)*	*Start year 2005–1648 number of export Relationships by the end of year*	*Share (%)*
2017	463	112	75	90	261	69	1798	109
2018	470	114	75	90	270	71	1824	111
2019	488	118	78	94	276	73	1763	107
2020	474	114	73	88	253	67	1666	101
2021	506	122	71	86	252	66	1730	105
2022	506	122	79	95	281	74	1850	112
2023	548	132	77	93	294	77	1821	110

Source: WITS

5.5 Herfindahl–Hirschman Product Concentration Index (HH)

The index measures the spread of trade across an exporter's product profile. For a country with few exports, the index tends to 1. A high HH indicates that there is likely to be greater vulnerability to trade shocks as it reflects a situation of a concentrated export basket. As the index tends to 0, the country's export profile is characterized as more diversified. Table 5.14 shows that the number of products exported by China to the CARICOM market increased between 2001 and 2023, which resulted in the decline of the HH index.

The data below shows the number of products the listed CARICOM state exports to China between 1991 and 2022 at the 6-digit level (Table 5.15).

Regarding China, Barbados exported 5 products at the 6-digit level to China in 2000, but this increased to 49 in 2018 before dipping to 7 in 2022. Similar patterns exist in Guyana and Jamaica. The number of products exported by St. Lucia has been very volatile, from 1 in 2005 to 190 in 2010. The export performance of T&T and Suriname to China has been disappointing compared to the other countries.

Table 5.14 HH Product Index for China with World and CARICOM, 2001–2023

	HH Product Index	*Number of Products*
World		
2001	0.0039	4945
2005	0.0075	4891
2010	0.0082	4571
2015	0.0080	4543
2019	0.0103	4545
2020	0.0112	4522
2021	0.0098	4522
2022	0.0097	4497
2023	0.0095	4512
CARICOM		
2001	0.0184	1595
2005	0.1002	1920
2010	0.2150	2195
2015	0.0881	2504
2019	0.0091	2651
2020	0.0065	2589
2021	0.0095	2507
2022	0.0087	2629
2023	0.0077	2742

Source: WITS

Table 5.15 CARICOM export product lines to China, 2000–2022

	Barbados	*Guyana*	*Jamaica*	*St Lucia*	*Suriname*	*Trinidad and Tobago*
CARICOM countries export of product lines to China						
2000	5	5	3		2	2
2001	9	3	3	2	4	11
2005	25	14	20	1	25	4
2010	19	15	35	190	11	20
2011	32	12	20	43	16	17
2012	39	12	22	42	23	13
2013	40	11	25	4	7	13
2014	35	16	29	7	5	21
2015	16	9	23	31	5	15

(continued)

Table 5.15 (continued)

	Barbados	*Guyana*	*Jamaica*	*St Lucia*	*Suriname*	*Trinidad and Tobago*
2016	40	13	24	94	4	15
2017	44	23	23	91	8	17
2018	49	15	41	4	7	21
2019	20	28	36	14	17	22
2020	14	22	38	–	12	14
2021	13	38	20	–	19	10
2022	7	50	20	–	19	–

Source: WITS

5.6 Is the Devil in the Detail? A Closer Look at China and Australia Trade Ties

Dependence on one or two countries can create problems of its own, especially during times of geopolitical tension or in the face of a global pandemic. This is a critical lesson for policymakers in the region, as over-dependence on a single trade partner can result in economic vulnerabilities if trade is hampered in any way. A noteworthy example of this point is the relationship at present between Australia and China, which is at an all-time low, although Clarke et al. (2023)[12] and Interesse (2023)[13] did indicate that some strides have been considered to thaw the relationship. While China is imposing sanctions, Australia is calling for more dialogue (Hurst et al., 2020),[14] (Wood, 2021).[15] Australia is seeking to reduce its dependence on China and, as such, is seeking to diversify its trade and investment supply chain (Table 5.16, 5.17, 5.18). Bell and Collinson (2025) reflect that the China Australia relationship will be characterized by "uncertainties" in 2025.

Consider Table 5.19, which shows the trade between Australia and China from 2000 to 2022. Over the defined period, exports to China as a proportion of total exports increased from 5.5% to 37.4% in 2020, then declines to 25% in 2022. Imports from China increased from 7.8 to 28.8% of total imports in 2020 before declining to 27.1% in 2022. In 2015, Australia and China formed an FTA, but from 2015 to 2016, the relationship between the two countries became strained because of worsening economic relations. China imposed restrictions akin to sanctions on imports from Australia for commodities such as coal, copper ore, concentrate, beef, barley, wine, and timber, and with growing tensions,

Table 5.16 Major events in Australia-China relations

Apr	*Australia*	*Called for independent investigation into COVID-19*
May	China	Suspended imports of certain Australian meats on the grounds of technical issues such as product labelling and quarantine
	China	Imposed additional customs duties of more than 80% on Australia barley
Jun	China	Called for refraining from travel to Australia
Jul	Australia	Enabled Hong Kong citizens in Australia to apply for permanent residency
	Australia	Sent a letter to the United Nations rejecting China's sovereignty over the South China Sea
Aug	Australia	Sale of the Australian dairy business by Kirin Holdings to China's Mengniu Dairy was scrapped
Sep	China	Strengthened import quarantine on Australian wheat
Oct	China	Instructed domestic textile manufacturers to cease using Australian cotton. Suspended imports of Australian timber
Nov	China	Head of the press division of the Foreign Ministry tweeted a fabricated image of an Australian soldier holding a knife against a child
	China	Chinese Embassy to Australia handed over to the Australian media a document of 14 disputes regarding Australia's actions and views
	China	Strengthened quarantine of Australian lobsters, effectively banning imports
	China	Made a provisional decision to impose an anti-dumping customs duty of up to more than 200% on Australian wine
	China	Suspended unloading of Australian coal
Dec	Australia	Filed a case to the WTO claiming that China's additional tariffs on Australian barley are unreasonable
	Australia	Established Foreign Acquisitions and Takeovers Act strictly reviewing investments from overseas from the perspective of national security
	Australia	Enabled agreements made by local governments to be scrapped by the national government if found to be against national interests

Source: Okano (2021)

the possibility of future expansions in these types of interventions, is anticipated as Bell and Collinson (2025), discuss.

By April 2016, Australia rejected the sale of a large stock farm to a Chinese company because of national interest (Taylor, 2016). In July of that same year, Australia demanded that China accept South China Sea arbitration, rejecting Chinese sovereignty. In August, Australia halted the sale of a public power company to a Chinese government-owned

Table 5.17 Major events in Australia-China relations in recent years

2014	Nov	President Xi speaks in the Australian parliament, upgrading the two countries relations to a comprehensive strategic partnership and agreeing to conclude FTA
2015	Oct	Northern Territory government leases port in the region to a Chinese company for 99 years
	Dec	Australia-China FTA takes effect
		Launch of AIIB (with Australia participating as an original member)
2016	Feb	Australia publishes Defence White Paper
	Apr	Australia rejects sale of large stock farm to a Chinese company
	Jul	Australia demands that China accept South China Sea arbitration, rejecting China's sovereignty
	Aug	Australia halts sale of public power company to a Chinese government-owned company
2017	From mid-year	In Australia concerns increased about the spread of the influence of the Chinese Communist Party on Australian society
	Nov	Australia publishes Foreign Policy, White Paper
	Dec	Australia submits bill to stop interference in domestic politics by foreign governments and foreign nationals
2018	Feb	Suspension of exchange projects between Australia and China emerges
	Aug	Australian government decided to exclude Huawei from 5G
2019	Jan	Delays in customs clearance of Australian coal in multiple Chinese ports emerge
	Sep	Prime Minister Morrison comments that China is a newly developed economy rather than a developing economy (receiving favourable treatment under the WTO schemes and such) in relation to trade friction between the USA and China
	Nov	Prime Minister Morrison and Premier Li meet in Bangkok (the last summit meeting as of now)
2020	Apr	Relations markedly deteriorate due to Australia's comments about an independent investigation into COVID-19

Source: Okano (2021)

company (the sale was blocked because it was contrary to national interest) (BBC, (2016), Barrette and Kaye (2016)).

Part of the dilemma is that Australia has become very dependent on China. By the end of 2023, 32% of Australian merchandise exports went to China, and 25% of its imports came from China (See Table 5.19). The point here is that diversification, in terms of market, is critical to reducing dependence on a single trade partner; indeed, this is a lesson

Table 5.18 Main incidents of investment by Chinese companies being halted or rejected by the Australian government

	Area of investment	*Overview of incident*
2016	Agriculture	Halted acquisition of S. Kidman stock farm by a Chinese company
	Electric power	Halted sale of public power company Ausgrid to State Grid Corporation of China and Hong Kong company
2020	Beverages	Did not approve sale of Australian dairy business by Kirin Holdings to a Chinese company
	Construction	Planned to reject the acquisition of major general construction company Probuild by Chinese government-owned China State Construction Engineering
2021	Electric power	Rejected contract to engineer, procure, and construct (EPC) gas-fired power plant in New South Wales by a Chinese government-owned company

Source: Okano (2021)

Table 5.19 Australia-China Trade ties US$000, 2000–2023

	Australia exports to China and World US$bn			*Australia imports from China and World US$bn*		
	China	*World*	*Exports to China/ Exports to the World*	*China*	*World*	*Imports from China/ Imports from the World*
2000	3.47	63.77	5.45	5.57	71.27	7.81
2005	12.30	106.01	11.60	17.34	124.79	13.90
2010	53.74	212.11	25.34	38.00	200.79	18.93
2015	61.01	187.79	32.49	46.29	199.33	23.22
2020	92.62	247.16	37.47	60.21	209.57	28.73
2021	116.82	342.04	34.15	72.86	260.98	27.92
2022	102.35	410.25	24.95	83.73	308.78	27.12
2023	120.22	369.24	32.56	71.82	287.22	25.01

Source: WITS

for Caribbean economies in engaging trade with a large partner such as China.

5.7 Assessing Dependence

Dependency is characterized by reliance on a foreign supplier for imports without necessarily involving critical risks to national security. However, strategic dependency goes further, involving specific categories of goods crucial for national infrastructure, economic stability, or security. Rogers (2020) defines strategic dependence as a level of dependence by country A on country B that allows country B to impact the overall availability of the goods in country A. Three measures used by Rogers (2020) to assess strategic import dependence are:

1. More than 50% of A's imports in sector i must come from country B.
2. A must be a net importer.
3. B accounts for more than 30% of global trade in commodity i.

After performing the three tests, it is important to assess both the scope and impact of each to differentiate between dependency and strategic dependency. Strategic dependency thus implies a vulnerability that could constrain a country's ability to maintain its development, which is important to CARICOM countries, but also essential services or production in times of crisis, whether due to economic, geopolitical, or supply chain disruptions.

Taken together, these criteria in (i), (ii), and (iii) show the trade conditions under which country A can be constrained by country B. The dependency of CARICOM economies on China was calculated for 2019 and 2023. The three tests listed above reveal whether the country relies on imports for the specified category of goods, with the majority coming from China. The more reliant the country is, on China for supplies, the more challenges it will face in securing alternative supplies if trade barriers with China emerge.

Table 5.20 shows that Guyana and Jamaica lessened the number of sectors dependent on China between 2019 and 2023, with an increase in number of sectors dependent on China, in St Lucia, Suriname, and Trinidad and Tobago.

For 2023 Barbados, Jamaica, and St. Lucia are the least dependent on China. Barbados has zero industries that meet all three conditions, and Jamaica depends only on China for silk products. St. Lucia depends on China for 3 sectors (man-made fibres, footwear, and headgear).

Table 5.20 Dependence of selected CARICOM economies on China (2019, 2023)

	Barbados	*Guyana*	*Jamaica*	*St. Lucia*	*Suriname*	*Trinidad*
HS2 (2019)	0	8	2	1	2	8
HS2 (2023)	0	5	1	3	5	10

Source: Author computed

Guyana depends on China for leather articles, other vegetable textiles, special woven fabrics, Umbrellas, sun umbrellas, walking sticks, seat sticks, whips, riding crops and parts thereof, toys, games, and sports requisites. Suriname depends on China for silk, man-made staple fibres, special woven fabrics, umbrellas, sun umbrellas, walking sticks, seat sticks, whips, riding crops and parts thereof, and costume preparations with feathers.

Trinidad and Tobago is the most exposed and is overall dependent on China in ten (10) industries: articles of leather, cork products, man-made filaments, special woven fabrics, textile fabrics, knitted clothing, not knitted clothing, worn textiles and rags, footwear, umbrellas, furniture, and toys.

5.8 Conclusion

This chapter analyses how the rapid growth of Chinese trade over the past few decades has reshaped the trade patterns of CARICOM economies. The chapter outlines both the direct and indirect effects of trade with China, categorized as either competitive or complementary. CARICOM's exports to China, though still a small fraction of total exports, have shown some growth, particularly in the raw materials sector.

The export potential and diversification of CARICOM products were also presented. The export potential index (EPI) is employed to identify products with high export opportunities, revealing that Trinidad and Tobago has significant potential for commodities like methanol and anhydrous ammonia. A decline in product diversification from 2015 to 2023 was noted, attributed to factors like the COVID-19 pandemic. The chapter further examined the trade margins of Trinidad and Tobago (T&T) with China and evaluated product concentration indices. The findings indicating a substantial increase in existing product exports but a minimal introduction of new products. The discussion reflected on

China's direct trade and complementary effect on the CARICOM region. This effect is evidenced by an increase in regional exports to China. The details above do indicate that in the last 10 years, that there has been an increase in the amount of trade and exports from CARICOM to China. This increase has prompted concerns among other nations, including CARICOM countries, about dependency on Chinese trade. To this end, the chapter examined Australia's current strained relationship with China as a cautionary case study for CARICOM economies regarding over-dependence on a single trade partner. The assessment of dependency reveals that Trinidad and Tobago is particularly vulnerable due to reliance on China for ten industries, while Barbados, Jamaica, and St. Lucia maintain lower levels of dependency.

The positive trends in terms of increased regional exports to China auger well for the region as market presence deepens in this large economy, but regional policymakers must remain vigilant in terms of maintaining this presence and not diverting trade from other markets with potential positive spillover effects. The chapter concluded with a call for CARICOM economies to diversify their trade relationships to mitigate risks associated with reliance on China.

Notes

1. https://www.researchgate.net/publication/228121567_The_Role_of_Embassies_and_Consulates_in_Promoting_Trade_Does_Economic_Freedom_in_the_Host_Economy_Matter.
2. https://jshippingandtrade.springeropen.com/articles/10.1186/s41072-020-00076-w.
3. The EPI is useful as it can assist countries to understand in which product areas to increase their exports to new markets or to existing markets https://umbraco.exportpotential.intracen.org/media/1089/epa-methodology_141216.pdf.
4. https://www.researchgate.net/publication/316488536_The_pattern_of_structural_change_testing_the_Product_Space_framework.
5. Data for other CARICOM economies at the time of the study is unavailable.
6. https://chinasuccessstories.com/top-8-fastest-growing-industries-in-china-2021/.

7. For example, a home country exports a specific commodity, x to a partner A, and another commodity, y to partner B in the base year. In the final year, the home country begins to also export y to partner A, thereby diversifying its trade profile. In this case, the existing product(s) were exported to at least one partner in the base year and established market(s) are those to which the home country exported at least one product to in the base year.
8. 2015, in this case, is used as the final year, given that T&T trade data is only available up to 2015.
9. http://wits.worldbank.org/WITS/WITS/TradeIndicatorsHelp/TradeOutcomes_Help.htm.
10. https://www.mdpi.com/2077-0472/11/1/73/pdf.
11. http://www.ecoforumjournal.ro/index.php/eco/article/view/394.
12. https://thediplomat.com/2023/04/where-are-australia-china-relations-headed/.
13. https://www.china-briefing.com/news/china-australia-trade-relations-growing-stronger/.
14. https://www.theguardian.com/australia-news/2020/dec/03/morrison-asks-for-dialogue-with-beijing-as-other-countries-pledge-support-for-australia.
15. https://www.9news.com.au/national/china-suspends-economic-dialogue-agreement-with-australia/7a72ff6f-8bdc-4d34-91a2-49ee819efac6.

CHAPTER 6

Direct but Competitive Effect

6.1 Introduction

In the previous chapter, the possible direct and indirect impacts of the growing presence of China as a global trade giant were presented, focusing on China's direct and complementary effect on the CARICOM region. In this chapter, we present China's direct but competitive impact on CARICOM. This chapter will include a discussion on the trade trends of China (imports and exports), a discourse on the potential deindustrialization impact of China's trade patterns, the welfare impact of a prospective partial scope agreement with China, and CARICOM's changing specialization pattern over time. This chapter will then conclude. Consider the Table 6.1 which situates China relative to the US and India. One observes that in 2023, in China exports as a proportion of GDP accounts for 20% as compared to 22% for India and 11% for the USA.

6.2 Trends in Imports (and Exports) of China and Other Large Economies

China's rapid growth and greater economic openness since 1978 led to the country emerging as an important player in the global economy (Chapter 3, Fig. 3.1). China's GDP growth has averaged 9.25% over the period 1978–2021 and was ranked as the world's second-largest economy

R. Hosein et al., *China in the Caribbean*,
https://doi.org/10.1007/978-3-031-71985-1_6

Table 6.1 Trends in Exports, Imports, and GDP for China, India, and USA, 2000–2023

	Exports of goods and services (BoP, current US$bn)			*GDP (current USbn$)*			*Exports/GDP*		
	China	*India*	*USA*	*China*	*India*	*USA*	*China*	*India*	*USA*
2000	190.0	59.9	1083.0	1211.35	468.39	10,252.35	15.7	12.8	10.6
2005	773.3	154.6	1291.5	2285.97	820.38	13,036.64	33.8	18.8	9.9
2006	991.7	193.3	1464.0	2752.13	940.26	13,814.61	36.0	20.6	10.6
2007	1258.1	240.1	1660.8	3550.34	1216.74	14,451.86	35.4	19.7	11.5
2008	1497.9	305.1	1849.6	4594.31	1198.90	14,712.84	32.6	25.4	12.6
2009	1262.7	260.8	1592.8	5101.70	1341.89	14,448.93	24.8	19.4	11.0
2010	1656.4	348.0	1872.3	6087.16	1675.62	14,992.05	27.2	20.8	12.5
2011	2008.9	446.4	2143.6	7551.50	1823.05	15,542.58	26.6	24.5	13.8
2012	2175.1	443.8	2247.5	8532.23	1827.64	16,197.01	25.5	24.3	13.9
2013	2355.6	468.3	2313.1	9570.41	1856.72	16,784.85	24.6	25.2	13.8
2014	2462.9	485.6	2392.6	10,475.68	2039.13	17,527.16	23.5	23.8	13.7
2015	2360.2	428.6	2280.0	11,061.55	2103.59	18,238.30	21.3	20.4	12.5
2016	2197.9	430.4	2238.3	11,233.28	2294.80	18,745.08	19.6	18.8	11.9
2017	2429.3	489.4	2390.8	12,310.41	2651.47	19,542.98	19.7	18.5	12.2
2018	2651.0	537.0	2538.6	13,894.82	2701.11	20,611.86	19.1	19.9	12.3
2019	2631.0	546.0	2528.4	14,279.94	2870.50	21,433.22	18.4	19.0	11.8
2020	2738.9	484.7	2160.1	14,687.7	2674.9	21,323.0	18.6	18.1	10.1
2021	3555.2	643.1	2567.0	17,820.5	3167.3	23,594.0	20.0	20.3	10.9
2022	3719.3	767.6	3018.5	17,881.8	3353.5	25,744.1	20.8	22.9	11.7
2023	3511.2	773.2	3051.8	17,794.8	3549.9	27,360.9	19.7	21.8	11.2

Source: WDI

in 2023, at market exchange rates (IMF, 2023). This rapid expansion in the value and structure of exports has prompted research into the export threat to other countries across the globe.

China's exports have expanded rapidly over time and by 2023, China was perched as one of the world's largest exporters. Indeed, China's exports increased from US$190 billion in 2000 to US$3.5 trillion in 2023. This compares to an increase in US exports from US$1.083 trillion in 2000 to US$3.01 trillion in 2023. China's exports were so rapid that from 15.7% per cent of GDP in 2000, it climbed to 19.7% in 2023. For the USA, exports of goods and services as a % of GDP stood at 10.6% in 2000 and, by 2012, escalated to 13.9%, although by 2023, it declined to 11.2%.

As Table 6.2 shows, the biggest export market destination for Chinese goods is the USA. The USA accounted for 14.8% of total Chinese exports in 2023, and Hong Kong came in second, accounting for 8.1% of Chinese exports.

Table 6.2 China's main export markets, 2023

	2023 US$bn	*2023%*
USA	501.22	14.8
Hong Kong, China	274.52	8.1
Japan	157.50	4.7
Korea, Rep	148.98	4.4
Vietnam	137.61	4.1
India	117.68	3.5
Russian Federation	110.94	3.3
Germany	100.57	3.0
Netherlands	100.20	3.0
Malaysia	87.37	2.6
Mexico	81.46	2.4
UK	77.91	2.3
Singapore	76.95	2.3
Thailand	75.73	2.2
Australia	73.81	2.2
Other Asia, nes	68.51	2.0
Indonesia	65.20	1.9
Brazil	59.11	1.7
United Arab Emirates	55.68	1.6
Philippines	52.40	1.6

Source: WITS

Consider Table 6.3, which shows that CARICOM imported US$1.74 bn from China in 2021, as compared to US$158.25 mn in 2000. By the end of 2023, regional imports from China amount to approximately US$1.8 bn. The clear indication, then, is that CARICOM is obtaining increasingly more imports from China.

Table 6.3 shows that the import from China by every CARICOM member state increased in the indicated period. For some states like Belize, Barbados, Guyana, Jamaica, Suriname, and Trinidad and Tobago, the increase in imports from China was relatively sharp between 2000 and 2023. An increase in the growth of imports from China can affect CARICOM countries in two ways. (Where data is available for 2023, it is included). Where these imports compete with domestic production, they can adversely affect domestic production and perhaps even sprout some kind of deindustrialization. At the same time, cheaper goods from China can help lower domestic prices and improve consumer surplus. This will be elaborated a little later in this chapter.

In 2000, CARICOM's imports totaled US$12.6 bn, which escalated to US$23 bn by 2019. In 2019, China accounted for US$1.77 bn and was the region's third-largest import partner, compared to its 12th in 2000. By 2023, imports from all sources declined to US$19.32 bn, of which China accounted for US$1.777 bn as the second-largest import source (Table 6.4).

Table 6.5 takes the discussion one step further and provides a detailed look at what is imported from China using 3-digit (rev 3) SITC data. As is clear from Table 6.5, all of CARICOM's top imports from China fall in the classification of sitc 5, sitc 6, sitc 7, or sitc 8, indicating that CARICOM mainly imports manufactured goods from China.

Table 6.6 pushes the information from Table 6.5 one further step forward and shows the import of machinery and transport equipment by each member state from China as a proportion of their world imports of the same commodity. For Antigua, imports of machinery and transport equipment from China increased from 0.24% in 2000 to 6.5% in 2021 before declining to 4.66% in 2023. For Guyana and Jamaica, the proportion of imports from China increased from 3.84% and 1.05% to 16.4% and 16%, respectively. In the case of Belize, the ratio moved from 0.42 to 15.99%; in the case of Barbados, it increased from 0.94 to 6.1% in 2023. For Trinidad and Tobago, the share of machinery and transport equipment that came from China increased from 0.72 to 12.36% between 2000 and 2022.

Table 6.3 Imports from China 2000–2022 (US$mn)

	2000	*2005*	*2010*	*2015*	*2020*	*2021*	*2022*	*2023*
Antigua and Barbuda	0.8	4.81	42.14	20.52				27.73
Bahamas, The	0.84	0.4		25.9	34.02			
Belize	3.21	16.79	74.54	100.83	113.1	168.74	242.16	229.52
Barbados	16.15	49.1	57.8	91.44	39.21	67.25	94.96	75.92
Dominica	0.71	3.58	8.93					
Grenada	1.41	10.84	13.62	10.45	14.55	11.54	17.66	24.50
Guyana	16.96	31.52	83.9	113.5	213.24	279.21	339.86	644.79
Jamaica	46.02	141.75	242.9	409	392.08	463.89		607.68
St. Kitts and Nevis	0.21	1.68	3.06	7.34				
St. Lucia	8.11	10.28	11.54	11.16	31.99			
Montserrat	0.03	0.28		0.33	0.35		0.16	
Suriname	11.33	52.75	100.76	103.86	124.6	117.76	173.78	166.58
Trinidad and Tobago	51.45	167.99	373.26	659.25	490.65	605.67		
St. Vincent and the Grenadines	1.01	6.56	20.18	18.18	20.06	24.4		
CARICOM	158.25	498.33	1032.62	1571.75	1473.85	1738.45	868.58	1777.38

Source: WITS and author calculations

Table 6.4 CARICOM top 20 import partners, 2000, 2019, 2021, and 2023

CARICOM Imports from World US$000s 2000		*CARICOM Imports from World US$000s 2019*		*CARICOM Imports from World US$000 2021*		*CARICOM Imports from World US$000s 2022*		*CARICOM Imports from World US$000s 2023*	
World	*12,640,504.1*	*World*	*22,995,574.6*	*World*	*20,829,546.1*	*World*	*14,542,579.1*	*World*	*19,324,620.0*
USA	6,093,006.1	USA	8,867,708.5	USA	7,116,998.7	BHS	5,152,927.9	USA	7,154,794.0
TTO	895,878.2	TTO	1,782,109.9	CHN	1,738,454.6	USA	3,332,406.8	CHN	1,777,381.0
VEN	883,520.0	CHN	1,770,207.3	SGP	1,691,338.7	TTO	1,208,707.2	TTO	1,630,185.0
JPN	517,626.7	SGP	1,021,678.4	TTO	1,012,097.7	CHN	868,576.1	JPN	669,195.3
GBR	489,340.0	JPN	758,148.1	BRA	941,076.2	NLD	442,121.3	BRA	649,633.7
CAN	340,365.5	NLD	704,445.8	MEX	717,393.7	JPN	272,852.4	NLD	555,933.4
COL	299,941.4	BRA	597,106.0	JPN	516,291.1	GBR	253,952.3	GBR	520,594.9
MEX	268,189.8	GBR	555,158.6	NLD	482,846.1	MEX	229,365.9	MEX	429,885.3
NLD	233,899.7	MEX	465,320.6	CAN	479,562.2	SUR	158,400.2	COL	371,046.6
BRA	190,854.8	CAN	447,756.6	GBR	442,520.8	PAN	140,666.6	TUR	276,155.9
DEU	159,369.9	COL	426,894.4	TUR	383,853.4	TUR	129,591.6	CAN	273,666.7
CHN	158,214.4	DEU	326,453.2	DEU	312,061.4	BRA	129,412.6	IND	257,449.1
ANT	153,303.5	TUR	278,604.9	COL	284,617.0	CAN	124,979.8	PAN	251,536.3
GAB	123,974.8	THA	272,033.9	IND	284,132.6	GTM	122,662.1	DEU	249,733.6
FRA	115,015.6	IND	225,528.9	GTM	222,913.3	IND	114,037.7	BHS	237,115.4
ITA	110,550.8	PAN	190,404.5	DREP	218,775.5	HKG	100,224.2	DOM	228,144.8
BRB	106,040.2	ITA	184,103.6	AUS	218,107.3	CYM	98,732.7	ESP	220,234.6
GUY	79,717.2	KOR	180,970.8	THA	201,145.3	JAM	93,264.3	GTM	218,871.6

Source: WITS

Table 6.5 Top 20 imports of CARICOM from China 2015–2023 US000$

Rank	*SITC Rev 3 Code*	*Description*	*2015*	*2020*	*2021*	*2022*	*2023*
1	723	Civil engineering plant	31,490.9	29,698.0	50,692.2	72,322.4	133,072.8
2	782	Goods/service vehicles	12,609.6	30,395.1	23,227.7	42,695.2	87,859.0
3	893	Articles nes of plastics	54,374.9	74,870.3	86,307.3	127,691.3	75,151.4
4	691	Iron/stl/alum structures	26,413.3	37,561.2	59,632.8	55,674.8	60,971.1
5	625	Rubber tyres/treads	64,494.2	56,646.6	60,127.8	84,922.0	59,474.3
6	851	Footwear	56,697.0	37,304.4	49,842.3	79,761.3	49,701.7
7	821	Furniture/stuff furnishg	48,319.4	45,317.7	57,222.5	65,832.3	49,225.2
8	741	Indust heat/cool equipmt	36,380.9	51,884.9	47,812.1	64,824.8	43,126.2
9	778	Electrical equipment nes	27,315.1	28,423.8	36,495.2	49,629.4	36,487.5
10	679	Iron/steel pipe/tube/etc	48,165.7	29,315.7	30,527.6	52,849.0	35,985.2
11	775	Domestic equipment	33,265.0	49,731.6	57,603.4	59,513.7	35,388.6
12	728	Special indust machn nes	6306.9	10,458.8	15,810.2	18,486.5	31,125.4
13	845	Articles of apparel nes	21,217.8	22,968.8	28,957.9	39,833.5	30,269.9
14	676	Iron/steel bars/rods/etc	89,560.1	6939.4	11,013.9	18,840.9	30,144.5
15	764	Telecomms equipment nes	127,248.0	47,658.7	53,842.5	57,368.8	28,664.8
16	771	Elect power transm equip	13,433.4	7239.3	8445.7	11,732.3	28,413.3
17	699	Base metal manufac nes	25,510.3	37,383.2	37,126.3	54,990.5	27,742.3
18	744	Mechanical handling equi	9242.1	14,384.1	16,053.9	22,724.9	26,646.8
19	831	Trunks and cases	27,318.0	17,915.3	19,187.9	29,781.7	26,505.5
20	773	Electrical distrib equip	14,801.9	12,646.2	18,760.3	29,860.7	23,861.7

Source: WITS and author calculations

Table 6.6 Imports of machinery and transport equipment by each CARICOM member state from China as a % of the World imports of the same, 2000–2023

	2000	*2005*	*2010*	*2019*	*2021*	*2022*	*2023*
ATG	0.24	0.71	31.00	5.31	6.50	4.28	4.66
BHS	0.00	0.00		0.48		2.99	
BLZ	0.42	3.68	4.29	12.05	14.23	14.66	15.99
BRB	0.94	3.13	5.61	11.49	5.99	7.71	6.1
DMA	0.14	1.12	8.73		8.74		
GRD	0.24	3.18	8.45	3.32	2.85	5.34	5.97
GUY	3.84	6.45	6.77	4.20	4.69	16.86	16.39
JAM	1.05	3.49	9.06	13.17	16.32	16.03	16.03
KNA	0.06	0.34	0.77				
LCA	1.95	1.39	2.86	10.26			
MSR	0.05	2.67		6.00		0.99	
SUR	2.55	4.51	7.64	8.41	6.26	6.73	10.31
TTO	0.72	2.53	7.46	11.51	11.49	12.36	
VCT	0.27	2.48	5.16	10.82	11.66		
CARICOM	0.90	2.65	6.95	8.47	9.18	11.64	13.95

Source: WITS

6.3 Are Chinese Imports Sprouting Deindustrialization Within CARICOM?

The direct effects of imports from China are unclear and require some scrutiny. On one hand, Chinese imports crowd out domestic markets by lowering local production and, in so doing, could adversely affect employment and consumption. On the other hand, if the increase in Chinese imports diverts imports away from other countries, instead of lowering domestic production, this can introduce lower-priced products to the market that could boost consumption. This section explores the impact of Chinese industrialization on the industrialization process within CARICOM in general and, because of data availability, specifically on the Trinidad and Tobago economy.

Wood and Mayer (2010) have argued that the entry of China into the world market has affected the economic structure of many of its partner economies. China, with its massive stock of low-cost labour was able to produce and specialize in the production of low-cost, labour-intensive manufactured goods and imported goods that it needed but in which it did not have a comparative advantage. The expansion of China's exports and the increase in demand for primary products altered the relative prices on world markets (Kaplinsky, 2006, Mayer & Fajarnes, 2008). Consequently, there was a shift in the demand functions for low-intensive manufacturers and an associated increase in demand for raw materials used in these types of production functions. Indeed, the magnitude of demand by China as a large developing economy would have the impact of increasing the prices of these primary products on the international market.

Acemoglu, Autor, Dorn, and Hanson (2014) noted that employment growth was unimpressive even before the Great Recession in the USA. Indeed, these researchers note that between 2000 and 2007, some considerable gains were made in the US economy in the 1990s, with major losses in US manufacturing employment. These researchers explored the contribution of the rise of import competition from China on sluggish US employment growth. The study found that the increase in US imports from China, which grew rapidly after 2000, was a significant factor behind the reduction in US manufacturing employment through input–output linkages and other general equilibrium effects and played a significant role in suppressing US job growth. In this study, these researchers applied industrial-level and local labour market-level approaches to help them determine the size of employment losses in those manufacturing sectors that are directly exposed to Chinese import competition. This study also examined employment effects on indirectly exposed upstream and downstream industries. The central result found by these researchers suggests job losses were fairly high, ranging between 2 and 2.4 mn on account of the rising import substitution from China in the period 1999–2011.

Pierce and Schott (2016) investigated the steep decline in US employment to a policy called Permanent Normal Trade Relations (PNTR) status with China. The introduction of PNTR with the Chinese by the USA allowed Chinese producers to enter the US market and expand. The researchers found that this Chinese penetration helped to reduce US manufacturing employment by coaxing US producers to invest in more capital-intensive goods or skill-intensive goods.

Note, though, that China's industrial progress resulted in a loss of comparative advantage on production lines in countries such as Japan and South Korea but had a positive impact on East Asian and ASEAN members, as these economies benefited from spillovers from China in terms of trade and technology (see Feenstra & Sasahara, 2018).

Amann, Lau, and Nixson (2009) have shown that the improved growth of China's main exports, particularly in the clothing and textile industries, has triggered a negative impact on other countries in Asia that produce the same type of goods. These researchers used a gravity model and found that the threat of China's exports of textiles to other Asian countries was greater than its exports of clothing, implying that China's potential as an exporter of clothing and textiles was greater than its existing export levels and therefore a threat to other clothing producers. These researchers also found that higher-income Asian countries fared better than their lower-income counterparts. The authors noted that this was because the higher-income Asian economies specialized in aspects of the textile and clothing industries, and these were less exposed to Chinese competition.

Giovannetti and Sanfilippo (2009) investigated how Chinese exports affected African goods. These researchers identified that trade is one of the key channels through which Chinese economic growth impacts various economies in the global economy, including developing economies. This paper focused on African manufacturing production and identified that African exports had been favoured in the past by preferential treatment. This study focused on the period 1995–2005 and found significant evidence of a displacement effect at different levels of Chinese goods on African manufacturing goods. This indicates that Chinese goods are being substituted for African goods in specific regional markets. While this deepens China-Africa trade relations, the loss of market share can negatively impact African producers.

Autor, Dorn, and Hanson (2013) analysed the impact of a greater degree of Chinese competition on the employment situation in the USA between 1990 and 2007. They found that transfer payments increased due to unemployment, instability, and other payments in trade, exposing labour market vulnerabilities in the USA. The study concluded that Chinese competition negatively impacted labour market outcomes in the USA.

Bernard, Jensen, and Schott (2002) examined the relationship between import competition from low-wage countries and the impact on the reallocation of US manufacturing, focusing on the period 1977–1997. This research paper found that both employment and output goods are lower in those plants that face higher levels of low-wage competition in the industry in which they exist. The study found that manufacturers reallocated over time in the USA towards industries that are more capital- and skill-intensive. This study found that growth performance between industries in different countries is driven by increased plant failure rates and the slower growth of surviving plants. Within industries, it was found that low-wage competition had the strongest effect on those that were least capital and skill-intensive. Those plants that survived switched into more capital and skill-intensive sectors where there was lower-wage competition. The authors concluded, *"Together these results support the view that US manufacturing is moving away from comparative disadvantage activities and towards comparative advantage industries* via *exit, growth and industry switching."*

Hanson and Robertson (2008) examine China's growth's impact on developing countries specializing in manufacturing. This study focused on ten developing countries where the manufacturing sector represented over 75% of their merchandise exports. The listed countries are Hungary, Malaysia, Mexico, Pakistan, the Philippines, Poland, Romania, Sri Lanka, Thailand, and Turkey. These researchers used a gravity model of trade. In this model, they decomposed bilateral trade into several components, including those associated with demand conditions in the importing country, those associated with supply conditions in the exporting country, and bilateral trade costs. Hanson and Robertson found that the impact of China was, at best, only a modest negative shock.

Wood and Mayer (2009) attempted to measure the effects of China's opening up to the world, on other developing countries, especially the balance between the labour-intensive manufacturing and primary production. These researchers applied Heckscher–Ohlin's theory, treating the opening up of China as a shift in the world average factor endowment, which, in turn, changed the relative endowments of all countries and, hence, their associated comparative advantage. The study found that (subject to a variety of qualifications) China's opening led to a lowering of the ratio of labour-intensive manufactured goods to primary output by as much as 7–10% and the associated ratio of exports by 10–15%. Note that these were average effects in the study. This paper also compared the impact of China with actual changes in the relevant ratios in various countries using a difference-by-difference methodology. Using 33 developing countries, these researchers found that there was a decline in the ratio of labour-intensive manufacturing to primary production during the 1990s for both output and for exports. Note, though, that when a block of 70 developing countries was employed, the average export ratio tended to rise, contrary to what good practice HO theory would suggest. The researchers then made a finer delineation of the developing countries into regions, and they found that the impact of China was clearest on the East Asian bloc of countries with a similar sectoral structure and similar factor endowments to China. The study found that in other regions besides those in East Asia, region specific influences tended to impact on the outcome of a rise or fall in the labour-intensive ratio of manufacturing goods to primary production.

Bloom, Draca, and Van Reenen (2015) looked at the impact of Chinese imports on innovation, IT, and productivity on trade-induced technical change using panel data across 12 European countries for the period 1996–2007. This paper found that the absolute volume of innovation increases within the firms that are most affected by the import of Chinese goods. In this study, Bloom et al. (2015) corrected for endogeneity by removing all of the product-specific quotas after China joined the World Trade Organization in 2001. Chinese import competition, it was found later, increased technical change within firms and encouraged a reallocation of employment between firms in favour of more technologically advanced firms. These within and between effects were relatively similar in magnitude and accounted for 14% of European technology upgrading in the period 2000–2007. The study also found that rising Chinese import competition is associated with declining employment and the share of unskilled workers.

Similarly, Iacovone (2009) investigated the impact of Chinese exports on the Mexican market using data from 1994 to 2004. The study found that sales of smaller plants and of marginal products are likely to be forced out of the market. Large plants, however, were more likely to expand and grow. This "creative destruction" they found operated not only at the firm level but also at the product level.

In Ethiopia, the footwear sector was overwhelmed by Chinese imports. Gebre-Egziabher (2009) noted that imports of footwear from China overwhelmed the Ethiopian market. The Chinese imports threatened the sector's competitiveness. Using firm-level data, this study found that the impact of Chinese imports involved downsizing, bankruptcy, loss of assets, and informalizing of activities. Ethiopian firms responded by improving their designs and lowering prices.

Paz (2019) in a study on the "*Impact of the China Shock on the Manufacturing Labour Market in Brazil*," investigated the impact of a large exposure to China on the Brazilian economy. The study used data for the period 2000–2012 to assess the impact of trade on the manufacturing sector. The study found that import penetration deepened from 3 to 20% from China during this period. This study used household survey data and found that an increase in import penetration from China or the ROTW lowered the employment level, the wage rate, and the inter-industry premium.

6.3.1 Wages and Export Prices of China

Navarro (2006) in explaining "the China price" noted that one of the stunning attributes about China is that "for the first time we have a huge, poor country that can compete with very low wages and in high-tech. Combine the two, America has a problem." To investigate the low-wage suggestion and use the minimum wage as a guide, note that wages in China are lower than minimum wages in several CARICOM economies, as shown in Table 6.7.

It is a fact, though, that the wage advantage of a small country disappears over time as it experiences economic growth. The short-run downward pressure on wages within a country, though, can be maintained if the country has a huge rural population or reserve army of workers. In this regard, note that China's policy of urbanization is aimed at moving hundreds of millions of workers from rural areas to urban areas (Yue et al., 2022, China Labour Bulletin, 2023).[2] According to the world development indicators, China's rural population in 2023 will be around 500 million, while the total population of the USA will be about 55 million;

Table 6.7 Minimum wage in selected economies

	Annual Minimum wage US$	*As a % of China*	*As a % of India*	*Date started*
Antigua and Barbuda	6317	145.7	825.4	1 November 2014
Bahamas	10,920	251.9	1426.9	15 August 2015
Barbados	6500	150.0	849.3	1 March 2012
Belize	3861	89.1	504.5	26 March 2012
Dominica	3081	71.1	402.6	1 June 2008
Grenada	6556	151.3	856.7	
Guyana	2015	46.5	263.3	1 July 2013
Haiti	1075	24.8	140.5	1 August 2017
Jamaica	2730	63.0	356.7	1 August 2018
St Lucia	1274	29.4	166.5	2013
St Kitts and Nevis	7954	183.5	1039.3	1 November 2014
St Vincent and the Grenadines	4440.3	102.4	580.2	January 2020
Suriname	3998	92.2	522.4	1 January 2013
Trinidad and Tobago	4619	106.6	603.6	1 January 2015
China[1]	2393			February 2024
India	765.30			2024

Source: minimum-wage.org

this helps to put the numbers into perspective. Figure 6.1 shows that the rural population of China is declining relative to India's.

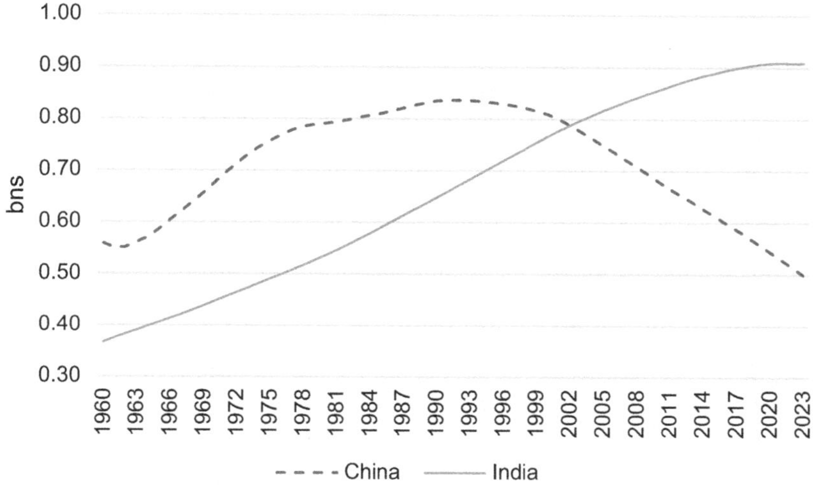

Fig. 6.1 Rural Population of China and India (bn) (Source: WDI)

6.3.2 *Considering Price and Quality of Chinese Imported Goods*

1. Are Chinese Goods Cheaper?

One explanation that can help to account for the flood of Chinese products into the markets of the CARICOM is their relatively lower price. Relatively low prices from China for their import goods have put pressure on the domestic price level of goods in most countries, including CARICOM via several avenues. First, lower-priced goods from China would replace more expensive imports from other countries. There is also evidence in other developing countries that competition through imported goods from China has reduced the price of clothing and related products (see Morris & Rankins, 2012).

Table 6.8 shows TT's comparative import prices from 10 countries, including China, for ten randomly selected commodities using HS 6-digit data. The prices per unit are shown. The indication is that the import price from China is cheaper than from other countries (Table 6.8).

Table 6.8 Prices for Selected Imports from various Source Markets 2015 and 2019 price per unit (US$)

Code	*Product*	*China*		*Germany*		*Japan*		*USA*	
		2015	*2019*	*2015*	*2019*	*2015*	*2019*	*2015*	*2019*
210,390	Sauces & preparations therefor, n.e	1.31	1.23	1.85	1.85	6.01	1.75	3.39	3.64
210,690	Food preparations, n.e.s	2.2	1.52	9.63	9.63	17.97	9.38	6.03	5.56
300,490	Medicaments (excluding goods of hea	9.92	4.49	157.3	157.3	517.14	186.32	12.16	12.65
300,510	Adhesive dressings & other articles	5.27	3.64	20.42	20.42	26.39	14.96	11.04	12.38
320,890	Paints & varnishes (incl. enamels &	2.19	3.15	45.09	45.09	51.8	64.5	7.09	6.61
321,290	Pigments (incl. metallic powders &	2.22	3.1	5.68	5.68	7.18	5.41	5.02	3.71
321,490	Non-refractory surfacing preparation	3.11	2.59	37.55	37.55	8	4.53	2.5	3.18
321,519	Printing ink (excl. black)	6.61	3.32	5.14	5.14	102.11	30.47	5.97	11.35
330,300	Perfumes & toilet waters	3.04	3.45	56.58	56.58	11	14	9.21	11.35
330,499	Beauty/make-up preparations & prepa	2.29	3.85	16.95	16.95	4.41	3.71	8.27	8.78

Source: WITS

6.3.3 But Quality Matters...

1. Export Sophistication

Existing evidence on the quality of Chinese products is scarce, as quality is difficult to measure. Some authors argue that Chinese products may be oversophisticated (Pula & Santabárbara, 2011). Alternatively, it is said that China's export structure is more sophisticated than its per capita GDP would reflect. Other researchers, such as Schott (2008) and Fontaine et al. (2008), have argued that China exports the same products as the advanced countries but a lower quality version. As shown in Table 6.9, though, there has been some increase in the sophistication of exports. This has occurred alongside increases in China's GDP per capita. This relationship is indeed intuitive and expected in that as income increases, the level of technological usage, adoption, and even innovation improves within productive sectors, which, over time, is reflected in the profile of exports (Jarreau & Poncet, 2014). In this case, Chinese goods are a limited threat compared to the goods produced by the developed world. (Specifically, Fig. 6.2 shows that China produced goods at a level of export sophistication similar to that of the USA, although its per capita GDP (in constant 2005 (international dollars) was about one quarter that of the USA).

From another angle and according to the data in Table 6.9, China produced more high-tech products as a percentage of its total exports in 2022 than other developed economies such as Germany, the UK, Japan,, and the USA. This is also consistent with the narrative presented in Chapter 4, which shows that the sophistication of Chinese exports improved over time. In 2000, 24% of China's exports consisted of high-tech goods, 42% of low-tech goods, and 18% of medium-tech goods. China's exports of primary goods decreased from 7% in 2000 to 9% in 2023.

2. Is Quality an Issue?

Ambivalent attitudes to cheap Chinese products are common in conversations in the Caribbean and other parts of the developing world. Indeed,

Table 6.9 Technological Classification of Exports from Selected Global Economies, 2000, 2019, 2021, and 2023

	Technological Classification	*% Total Exports China*	*% Total Exports Germany*	*% Total Exports UK*	*% Total Exports Japan*	*% Total Exports USA*
2000	HighTech	0.24	0.2	0.27	0.34	0.36
	LowTech	0.42	0.15	0.14	0.09	0.12
	MediumTech	0.18	0.47	0.31	0.5	0.32
	PrimaryProds	0.07	0.05	0.1	0.02	0.07
	ResourceBased	0.09	0.12	0.17	0.06	0.13
2019	HighTech	0.35	0.2	0.17	0.21	0.21
	LowTech	0.31	0.15	0.16	0.1	0.11
	MediumTech	0.23	0.47	0.35	0.56	0.33
	PrimaryProds	0.03	0.05	0.11	0.03	0.14
	ResourceBased	0.09	0.13	0.21	0.11	0.22
2021	HighTech	0.33	0.17	0.13	0.19	0.13
	LowTech	0.28	0.13	0.11	0.09	0.07
	MediumTech	0.22	0.38	0.27	0.47	0.25
	PrimaryProds	0.03	0.05	0.11	0.03	0.15
	ResourceBased	0.08	0.11	0.23	0.09	0.19
2023	HighTech	0.32	0.20	0.15	0.21	0.20
	LowTech	0.29	0.14	0.11	0.10	0.10
	MediumTech	0.27	0.47	0.35	0.55	0.31
	PrimaryProds	0.03	0.06	0.10	0.04	0.17
	ResourceBased	0.09	0.13	0.29	0.11	0.22

Source: WITS

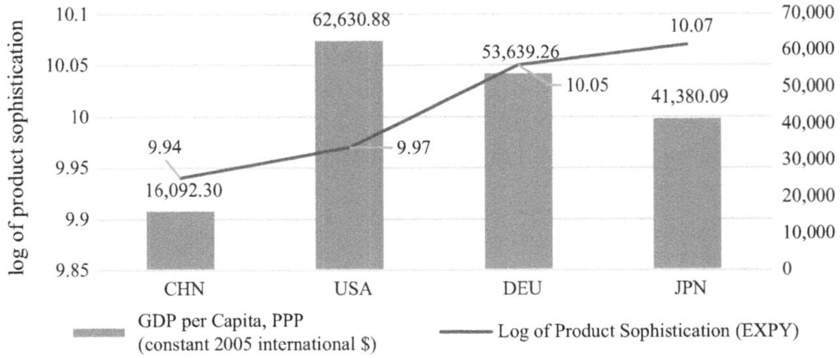

Fig. 6.2 China's production of sophisticated products, 2019 (Source: WITS)

within China, there have been incidents of milk powder and infant formula containing melamine (BBC, 2010).[3] There have also been incidents of illegal cooking oil being recycled (illegal cooking oil is also known as gutter oil and includes oil reprocessed from waste oil and extracted from drains behind restaurants), (BBC, 2011).[4] The international media is often highly critical of the quality of goods that come out of China. Some countries in Europe, as well as the USA, have raised entry barriers on goods from China entering their countries.

Many developing countries can now afford cheaper manufactured goods because of the lower price of Chinese goods. Still, at the same time, in some places, the term "Chinese goods" has become a pejorative term associated with lower quality. For example, in Mali, people buy Chinese manufactured goods but refer to them as cheap and short-lasting imitations of Western products (Chappatte, 2014, 14).

One researcher, Uyer (2018), has noted that China produces both the highest quality brands and the worst quality products on the market. Anderson (2015) reported that people negatively approach most products made in China. Indeed, although low prices can increase demand, a quality fall adversely affects demand. One has to be careful in distinguishing between goods assembled in China (like some of the top brands in the world) and goods made in China.[5]

Schniederjans (2011) has argued that consumers perceive goods of Chinese origin to be of lower quality than others. Ulgado et al. (2011, p. 3) noted that only 17% of US consumers are interested in products imported from China. Shen (2013, p. 10) notes that 12% of US consumers have never bought any Chinese goods.

Dobler (2009, pp. 717–18), notes that Chinese shop owners in Namibia sell considerable amounts of Chinese products but emphasizes that "Chinese goods are increasingly seen as cheap trinkets imported to cheat Namibians out of scarce and hard-earned cash." In Cameroon, Chinese goods are referred to as cheap junk (Ndjio, 2009, p. 617). Matthews (2011) characterizes the activities of traders who buy inexpensive merchandise from China as "low-end globalization."

In Mali, many migrant workers, rather than make a living as housemaids or houseboys for wealthy families, instead peddle Chinese goods in the town in shops called "par-terre" (meaning on the ground) in various strategic locations (Chappatte, 2014). He adds, *"cheap Chinese products have, moreover, allowed ordinary Malians to a wide range of formerly as well as prestigious manufactured products."* Chappatte goes on to note, *"the short life expectancy of Chinese products reminds Malians that they are they are bad imitations of western products, they are of poor quality."*

In the Guyanese market, the Starbroek News noted that cheap consumer products from China are well appreciated, as wages are low. However, the article also notes, *"frequently, enthusiasm for their goods only last as long as the goods themselves, which in many cases, is by no means a long time."*

In an article entitled Dangerously Contaminated Chinese Toys, the European Environmental Bureau noted that in 2019, national officials blocked 248 models of toys after they were tested for chemicals above a certain legal level. Of these 248 models of toys, 228 are categorized as "serious risk," and 219 of these serious risk toys originate in China.[6]

Indeed, Beijing was recently flooded by a growing list of foreign complaints about medical gear and testing kits that were imported from China. For example, Georgia had to cancel a contract with a Chinese company that sent flawed testing kits to Spain (Arostegui, 2020).[7] Malaysia had to switch an order from a Chinese company to South Korea as the Chinese test kits reported low levels of accuracy (Su, 2020).[8] At one point, the Netherlands, in 2020, returned 600,000 masks to China as they had faulty filters. Finland tested a shipment of personal protective equipment from China and found that they were unsuitable for hospital use.

Pula and Santabárbara (2011), however, have, challenged the view that China exports low quality products to the European market. The study estimated quality using a discrete chance model. The study found that China exports similar products to developed countries and the quality of these products are also similar to the most technologically advanced economies. The paper found that China is climbing up the quality ladder.

Wang and Wei (2015) have noted that China's exports have become increasingly more sophisticated. Using product-level data, these researchers investigate the factors leading to rising export sophistication in China. This study found that the factors that led to rising export sophistication in China include improved human capital and government policies favouring high-tech zones. Several factors were found to be important in improving the unit value of Chinese exports: processing trade, foreign-invested firms, and government-sponsored high-technology zones.

Flemming (2014) noted that almost 200,000 distributors daily purchase up to 2000 tonnes of goods from the wholesale black market. Flemming notes that more than 20% of all consumer products in the

Chinese markets are counterfeit. The Chinese often joke that in China, "everything is always fake, but your mother, and we can copy everything except your mother."

The World Trademark Review (2024)[9] estimated that China produces 80% of the world's counterfeit goods.

The increase in imports of lower-priced goods from China would have helped in a small way to contain the inflationary pressures and helped to widen the access of consumer goods available to lower-end disadvantaged consumers. At the same time, the imports of intermediate capital goods from China would have helped to diversify import sources for the Caribbean, making the region less vulnerable to supply-side shocks.

6.4 Welfare Impact of China in a Simulated Partial Scope Trade Agreement Setting

Given the sharp ascent of China in the global economy as a powerhouse, this section explores the possible impact of an FTA by CARICOM with China. The underlying assumption on which this section is premised is that it is better for a small country, (like those in the CARICOM region) to form a partnership with a large country rather than with small countries.[10] Indeed, there are several benefits on offer from this type of integration, including access to larger export markets and learnings, which help build productive capacities in smaller economies to enable them to compete under conditions of freer global trade.

Secondly, it is important to determine if the trade structures of the trading partners mirror each other, i.e., the export pattern of a home country matches that of the import structure of a partner country. Schiff (1997) refers to this as complementarity and clearly shows that countries with a high level of trade complementarity are more natural trading partners. In this regard and to determine whether China would be a suitable trade partner for CARICOM, we examine the trade complementarity between China and TT, as a CARICOM member state.[11]

As Table 6.10 shows, TT has a relatively high degree of trade complementarity with China compared to some of its other trade partners.

Given these foundational assumptions, the following section provides some trade and welfare simulations associated with forming an FTA between CARICOM and China, focusing on Trinidad and Tobago.

Table 6.10 T&T Trade complementarity indices with selected partners, 2000–2022

Year	*China*	*USA*	*CAN*	*EU-UK*	*UK*	*Chile*	*Panama*	*Guyana*
2000	26.35	24.18	19.02	25.90	18.79	33.27	32.42	38.28
2005	23.97	28.73	21.58	26.96	20.87	33.51	29.59	42.12
2010	28.46	28.63	21.22	27.91	20.76	33.99	15.15	40.62
2019	32.35	24.63	25.64	30.78	25.14	34.72	30.70	33.18
2022	29.58	21.37	21.19	31.51	28.36	35.09	34.72	39.89

Source: WITS

6.4.1 Welfare Analysis

To undertake the welfare analysis simulations, the Single Market Partial Equilibrium Simulation Tool (SMART) from the World Bank's World Integrated Trade Solution (WITS) platform was used. This tool uses partial equilibrium analysis to evaluate the trade and fiscal implications associated with trade policy. Table 6.11 shows the change in regional partner country imports (M1), imports from non-China rest of the world (nCnCrow) (M2), and the change in imports from China (M3) on account of a partial scope agreement between TT and China. The formation of this partial scope agreement is based on the list of assumptions below.

(a) import elasticities, used default in SMART (built into the system and empirically estimated for each country and every HS 6-digit product).
(b) trade source substitution indices is 1.5, the default value for SMART.
(c) all tariffs between China and T&T are set to 0 for those commodities included under the partial scope agreement.

Table 6.11 indicates that there would be trade diversion in the amount of US$587,000 from CARICOM, US$30.8 mn from the nCnCrow, and US$39.7 mn in trade created with China. There would be a loss in tariff revenues of US$47.8 mn but, overall, an increase in welfare of US$4.4 mn.

Table 6.11 Trade and welfare impacts of an FTA with China 2021

Change in CARICOM imports by TT (US$000) (M1)	*Change in imports from nCnCrow (M2) (US$000)*	*Change in imports from China (US$000) (M3)*	*Change in Revenue (US$000)*	*change in Welfare in (US$000)*
– 587.687	– 30,880.5	39,731.46	– 47,849.1	4369.887

The last column of Table 6.12 shows where the welfare benefits would be the greatest and where the greatest amount of trade would be created with this hypothetical partial scope agreement. Not surprisingly, using two-digit data, the greatest amount of trade would be created in sections that fall within the domain of manufacturing goods. This should not surprise anyone as China's comparative advantage lies in the manufacturing sector.

Table 6.12 Trade and Welfare Impacts of an FTA with China on a Product Basis, 2021

Product codes	*Change in CARICOM imports by TT (US$000) (M1)*	*Change in imports from nCnCrow (M2) (US$000)*	*Change in imports from China (US$000) (M3)*	*Change in Revenue (US$000)*	*change in Welfare in (US$000)*
72	– 1.081	– 5020.99	6088.383	– 7328.44	704.216
89	– 45.754	– 3503.07	4079.099	– 5436.49	571.817
84	– 10.116	– 1339.41	3793.292	– 4055.89	452.262
66	– 5.916	– 1644.43	3209.09	– 2252.36	304.085
82	– 80.208	– 2244.85	2092.702	– 3464.87	298.1
85	– 14.878	– 915.948	2204.965	– 2975.35	254.421
71	– 1.316	– 3972.51	3760.394	– 4419.54	253.899
65	– 0.97	– 934.522	2211.68	– 2134.15	222.881
62	– 0.054	– 1635.49	1100.563	– 2821.56	216.236
69	– 7.978	– 1967.52	2229.058	– 2374.41	211.153
67	– 0.21	– 2017.96	3236.189	– 2921.95	159.693
73	– 0.235	– 721.538	812.503	– 885.593	113.86
81	– 8.513	– 732.415	747.48	– 988.545	105.129

(continued)

Table 6.12 (continued)

Product codes	*Change in CARICOM imports by TT (US$000) (M1)*	*Change in imports from nCnCrow (M2) (US$000)*	*Change in imports from China (US$000) (M3)*	*Change in Revenue (US$000)*	*change in Welfare in (US$000)*
64	− 6.449	− 470.926	461.51	− 571.818	56.857
55	− 85.934	− 504.712	326.728	− 597.02	55.461

Source: author calculations

6.5 Conclusion

The preceding discussion does provide some evidence that China's trade impact on the region has not only been direct, as evidenced by the increase in the amount of trade observed over time, but also competitive, especially as regards manufactured goods. Indeed, this is the result of the sheer scale of the industrial sectors in China and the low cost of manufacturing compared to other jurisdictions.

Even so, trade and welfare simulations do lend justifications to the arguments that integration with China does have multiple benefits for the average regional consumer, and policymakers must remain wary as to the potential deindustrialization effects on regional industry and loss in tariff revenue. Further, the risks of deepening ties with China and its impact on the specialization pattern of regional production must be considered within context of trade with other emerging and traditional markets which are natural trading partners.

Notes

1. The lowest minimum wage applies in the province of Heilongjiang, followed by Jilin and Xinjiang where the minimum annual wage is higher at $2543. Beijing and Shanghai, have the highest the minimum wage of $4440. The remaining 21 provinces have a minimum wage of $3300 https://www.china-briefing.com/doing-business-guide/china/human-resources-and-payroll/minimum-wage#:~:text=What%20is%20the%20minimum%20wage%20in%20China%3F&text=Minimum%20wages%20in%20China%20continue%20to%20rise.&text=As%20of%20February%2019%2C%202024,%2FUS%243.7%20per%20hour).

2. Gong, Yue, et al. "Urbanisation of the Chinese Rural Population: A Literature Review of China's New-type Urbanisation." China: An International Journal, vol. 20 no. 3, 2022, pp. 181–204. Project MUSE, https://doi.org/10.1353/chn.2022.0029.
   https://clb.org.hk/en/content/migrant-workers-and-their-children
3. https://www.bbc.com/news/10565838.
4. https://www.bbc.com/news/world-asia-pacific-14894070.
5. Country of origin is very important. After Germany was defeated in World War I, to ensure that German products would not be sold, the Allied Powers insisted that the expression "Made in Germany" be imprinted on German products. Bahar (2011, 41) noted that if consumers have a positive opinion about a country, then they would positively approach the products made by that country.
6. https://eeb.org/flood-of-toxic-chinese-toys-threatens-childrens health/#:~:text=National%20officials%20blocked%20248%20models,with%20phthalates%2C%20a%20plastic%20additive.
7. https://www.voanews.com/a/science-health_coronavirus-outbreak_chinese-firm-offers-replace-faulty-test-kits-sold-spain/6186543.html.
8. https://www.latimes.com/world-nation/story/2020-04-10/china-beijing-supply-world-coronavirus-fight-quality-control.
9. https://www.worldtrademarkreview.com/guide/anti-counterfeiting-and-online-brand-enforcement/2024/article/china-multi-pronged-approach-proves-best-fit-tackle-rise-in-counterfeits.
10. See Schiff's 1997 for a discussion on the benefits of integration with a large rather than a small economy.
11. The trade complementarity index is derived using the following formula: Cii = 100(1 − sum(|mi − xij|/2)), where xij is the share of good I in global exports of country j and mik is the share of good I in all imports of country k. The index of zero when no goods are exported by one country or imported by the other and 100 when the export and import shares exactly match.

CHAPTER 7

Indirect Impact of Trade: Complementary Effects

7.1 Introduction

This chapter examines the impact of China's growth on the export sectors of various CARICOM export goods and evaluates how China's growth patterns impact CARICOM business cycles via a VAR framework analysis.

It is well known that export prices, especially for commodity-based or resourced-based economies, directly impact the economy's fiscal performance and long-term economic sustainability. As such, it is reasonable to conclude that regional exporters of energy and energy-related commodities will benefit as global prices for primary commodities increase, especially energy prices. Indeed, in the last two decades, there has been a high degree of industrial deepening in China (and India), as reflected in Table 7.1.

Consequently, there has, in turn, been an increase in the derived demand for industry-related materials, such as metals, wood, bauxite, and energy, to name a few. Only a small fraction of China's huge demand for raw material inputs can be met by domestic production, so China must rely on imports. Table 7.2 shows China's demand for various commodities.

At one point, UNCTAD pronounced that the "recent upward movement in commodity prices has been driven by very strong demand and, emerging supply constraints. Rising imports by China and for some commodities also by India, have been the main sources of additional

R. Hosein et al., *China in the Caribbean*,
https://doi.org/10.1007/978-3-031-71985-1_7

Table 7.1 Industry value added China 1960–2023

	Industry (including construction), value added (% of GDP)	*Industry value (Current US$bn)*
1960	44.39	26.51
1965	35.09	24.72
1970	40.27	37.29
1975	45.36	74.13
1980	48.06	91.87
1985	42.71	132.18
1990	41.03	148.06
1995	46.75	343.40
2000	45.54	551.65
2005	47.02	1074.86
2010	46.5	2830.53
2015	40.84	4517.54
2016	39.58	4446.13
2017	39.85	4905.70
2018	39.69	5514.85
2019	38.59	5510.63
2020	37.82	5568.14
2021	39.29	7001.79
2022	39.33	7032.49
2023	38.28	6812.38

Source: WDI

Table 7.2 China's Share of Global Commodity Consumption, 2019, 2020

	2019 (%)	*2020 (%)*
Nickel	56	32
Steel	50	59.2
Copper	50	39.5
Aluminium	47	
Tin	46	
Zinc	46	32.8
Lead	40	42.1
Rice	31	28.2
Soya	29	5.5
Gold	27	
Maize	23	
Wheat	17	17.6

Source: Bing, Roth and Santabarbara (2019), Rodrigue (2020)[1]

demand" (UNCTAD, 2005, p. 73). "Similarly, in 2015[2] the World Bank published its Commodity Markets Outlook and detailed the way in which the rapid growth rates of India and China contributed to rising commodity prices as demand from these markets increased. Specifically, the report noted that "demand from China and, to a lesser extent India, significantly raised global demand for metals and energy, especially coal, and less so for food commodities. China's consumption of metals and coal surged to roughly 50 percent of world consumption in this period, and India's consumption to a more modest 3 percent (metals) and 9 percent (coal)...if the two countries catch up to OECD levels of per capita commodity consumption, or if India's growth shifts towards industry, demand for metals, oil, and coal could remain strong."

Fathom Consulting (2024),[3] reflecting on the impact of China's demand on specific commodity markets, noted that Chinese demand has been particularly disruptive for metals and energy markets as the country's import of these commodities has increased over the period 2001–2022. The report showed that a one per cent increase in Chinese demand resulted in 0.62% in nickel prices, 0.19% in aluminium prices, and 1.2% price increase in iron.

To explain how China's growth can benefit CARICOM exporters, we collated the top 25 export commodities from CARICOM in 2023 in Table 7.3.

Based on the data in Table 7.3, the impact of China's growth on the energy sector, the wood and timber sector, and the bauxite sector of CARICOM is examined.

7.2 Energy Demand

China's energy demand is growing and in 2022, it was the world's largest energy consumer, consuming 111 exajoules as compared to 76 exajoules for the USA, which is the second-largest consumer, and 32 exajoules for India, the world's third-largest consumer (Statistical Review of World Energy, 2023). By 2025, under a Business-As-Usual scenario, the world is expected to consume 515 exajoules of energy, of which the USA's consumption would increase marginally to 78 exajoules and India's demand would continue to increase to 36. However, China's primary

Table 7.3 CARICOM's Top 25 Exports to China 2023

Product description	*CARICOM (US$000)*
Petrol./bitum. oil,crude	610,251.3
Alcohols/phenols/derivs	209,950.8
Wood in rough/squared	24,060.6
Natural gas	7915.4
Wood simply worked	7098.7
Veneer/plywood/etc	6767.5
Base metal ore/conc nes	5890.4
Fish,live/frsh/chld/froz	4877.0
Aluminium ores/concs/etc	4052.4
Coffee/coffee substitute	2520.3
Ferrous waste/scrap	2354.0
Plastic waste/scrap	1603.7
Nf base metal waste nes	1025.8
Crustaceans molluscs etc	700.6
Alcoholic beverages	238.8
Electric current	132.3
Heavy petrol/bitum oils	108.5
Crude animal mterial nes	105.2
Misc manuf articles nes	102.4
Metal store/transpt cont	52.0
Edible products n.e.s	41.6
Passenger cars etc	40.0
Fruit presvd/fruit preps	37.2
Fish,dried/salted/smoked	32.4
Fixed veg oils not soft	29.5

Source: WITS

energy consumption is expected to be 120 exajoules and remain the largest of the three (Table 7.4).

In no trivial way, then, energy demand in the global economy moving forward is heavily influenced by the economic growth and development of China, India, and other fast-growing economies.

7.2.1 *China and Global Oil Production*

Within the context of energy demand, this section will consider China's impact on the demand for crude oil and natural gas from CARICOM. As the data in Table 7.5 shows, by 2023, China's oil consumption as a

Table 7.4 Primary energy: consumption by fuel (exajoules)* 2022–2025

	2022	*2025*	*% Change 2022–2025*
China	111	120	8.1
USA	76	78	2.6
India	32	36	12.5
World	488	515	5.5

Source: Statistical Review of World Energy 2024

percentage of the world escalated to 16.54%, compared to 0.70% in 1965 (BP Statistical Review of World Energy, 2024).

As Fig. 7.1 shows, there is a clear direct relationship between crude oil imports and the price of crude oil.

Table 7.5 China's Oil Consumption, 1965–2023

	China's oil consumption as a % of World oil consumption	*World oil prices US$*	*China's import of crude oil US$bn -sitc 33*	*World import of crude oil US$bn—sitc 33*
1965	0.7	1.93		
1970	1.22	1.9		
1975	2.46	1.8		
1980	2.78	1.8		
1985	3.04	11.53		
1990	3.46	24.53		
1995	4.75	18.43		
2000	6.14	30.38	18.93	544.22
2005	8.22	56.64	59.37	1155.25
2010	10.85	79.48	162.46	1840.38
2015	13	48.66	157.29	1376.75
2016	13.24	43.29	132.08	1148.37
2017	13.67	50.8	184.28	1487.88
2018	13.96	65.23	266.23	1954.47
2019	14.35	56.99	264.97	1775.50
2020	16.08	39.16	198.24	1150.99
2021	15.71	70.86	296.3	1816.8
2022	15.32	94.53	401.1	2688.0
2023	16.54	77.58	377.9	2004.2

Source: Bp statistics

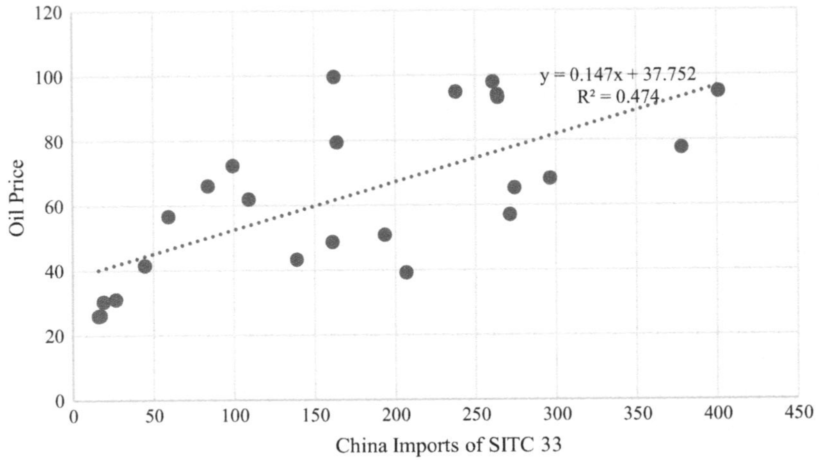

Fig. 7.1 Scatterplot showing the relationship between crude oil imports of China and crude oil prices US$, 2000–2023 (Source: author calculated)

One of China's more visible impacts, and to a lesser extent, India's, has been its influence on oil prices. As China's share of world oil consumption increased, the price of oil also tended to increase.

As seen in the scatterplot in Fig. 7.2, both variables, real GDP per capita and oil consumption, trend very closely over time, with the correlation between them standing at 91% for the period 1980–2023. The IMF (2011), to gauge the prospects for energy demand, focused on the simple relationship between per capita energy consumption and per capita real income. The estimates indicated that the relationship between per capita GDP and per capita energy consumption is non-linear.

Results also indicated that for high-income economies, an increase in per capita GDP leads to a negligible change in energy consumption, while for lower- and middle-income economies, an increase in per capita GDP of 1% leads to an increase in energy consumption of 1% (IMF, 2011).

Between 2024 and 2029, China's real per capita GDP is expected to increase by 20% (IMF World Economic Outlook, 2024). Taking a very simplistic approach, one can expect this increase in real GDP per capita to result in an increase in the daily oil consumption per capita in China to approximately 17 million barrels per day by 2030. One research group, known as the China National Petroleum Corporation Economics

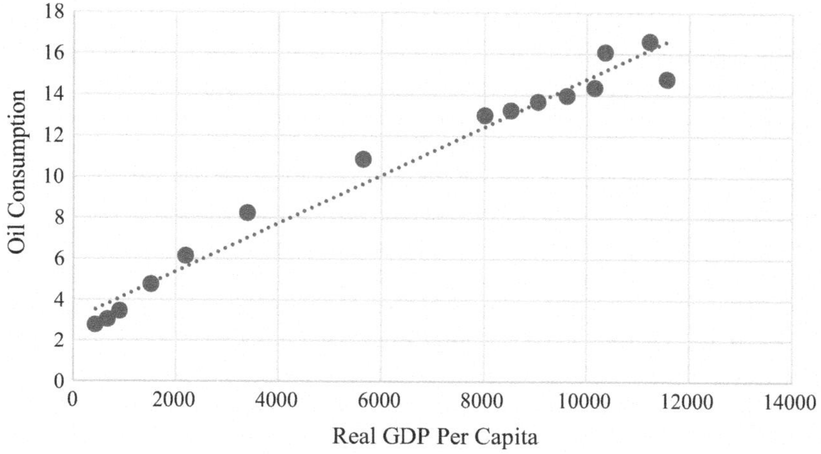

Fig. 7.2 Relationship between China's Average Daily Oil Consumption (mn barrels per day) and China's Real GDP Per Capita 1980–2023 (Source: author calculated)

and Teaching Research Institute (ETRI), however, noted that overall oil demand in China will decline after 2030, as the decline of crude oil for transportation will decrease, given the widespread electrification of vehicles (Reuters 2023[4]). In 2021 and 2022, the government of China continued its drive to increase the use of electric vehicles (EVs) in China by providing more subsidies and tax benefits to people who use EVs. China also uses a credit policy that requires manufacturers to produce more electric vehicles annually. The Global EV Outlook for 2023[5] has indicated that China is indeed the largest market for EVs, noting that "regions and cities have also recently announced targets for manufacturing, such as Chongqing's goal to produce and sell more than 10% of China's new energy vehicles (NEVs), and Jilin's aim to reach an annual production capacity of around 1 million NEVs, both by 2025, supported by policies focusing on EV manufacturing." To this end, the government has also invested in charging infrastructure and provided users with parking and licence plate privileges (Global EV Outlook, 2023). Indeed, China has forecasted new energy vehicles to reach 20% of new vehicles sold annum by end of 2025.

In 2023, CARICOM exported US$486 mn in petroleum oils to several countries (Table 7.6); the premise here is the Chinese market does provide an opportunity for increasing regional exports. One would expect that as China grows, CARICOM would sell even more petroleum oils in this market. Hayley (2023)[6] notes that "*the state oil company's Economic & Technology Research Institute (ETRI) in March forecast oil demand reaching 743 million metric tons this year for the world's top crude importer. This is equivalent to around 14.86 million barrels per day (bpd).*"

The clear indication is that as China grows, its import of crude oil increases per capita, which will put upward pressure on the price of crude oil. Even so, Horner (2023)[7] indicates that China's demand for oil is insatiable. Because China is expected to grow in the medium term, one can reasonably expect that crude oil prices would continue to be buoyant. In this regard, energy-producing Caribbean countries such as Guyana, Suriname, and TT stand to benefit in the medium term from the increase in the size of the Chinese economy. Indeed, as the Chinese economy is transformed into a more modern powerhouse, even natural resources will be required, and the region can become an import source for such resources.

Table 7.6 CARICOM Exports of Petroleum oils, oils from bitumin. materials, crude (SITC 333) US$mn, 2000–2023

	2000	*2010*	*2019*	*2020*	*2021*	*2023*
All countries All–All	1259.6	2663.4	635.9	380.1	582.9	486.5
Brazil	27.5	184.0	130.8	246.5	419.3	233.9
Colombia	246.7	559.3	289.2	100.6	129.3	215.0
Barbados	22.6	22.1	8.5	7.1	9.9	37.6
USA	0.0	13.2	80.5	25.9	0.0	0.0
Trinidad and Tobago			16.937			0.001
Jamaica				0.001	1.974	0.001
Ecuador	20.44		109.91		22.39	
France	0.21					
Gabon	123.91	836.02				
UK	0.00		0.00			
India		35.66				

Source: WITS

7.2.2 Natural Gas

China has set targets for reducing emissions of sulphur dioxide and nitrogen oxides and has also set a target for improving the number of days with good air quality to 80% annually (Lu et al., 2020,[8] World Bank, 2020[9]). The Chinese government is pushing the generation sector to switch from coal to natural gas, especially for domestic heating. The government targeted natural gas for 15% of energy consumption by 2030 (International Trade Administration 2023).[10] The BP Statistical Review 2021 indicated that China's natural gas consumption was 8.2% of its overall energy consumption profile. The consequence of these government policy directives is that China's demand for natural gas has significantly increased. Net emissions of carbon dioxide from China expanded from 3361MT in 2000 to 9464MT in 2018 (World Bank, 2020). The business-as-usual scenario, as forecasted by BP, puts China's natural gas consumption in 2035 at 19 EJ, compared to 13.6 EJ in 2021.

Table 7.7 shows that China is a small importer of natural gas from TT. Note, though, that China is set to become the largest consumer of LNG in the world, according to Wood McKensie (Thompson (2021), [11]Ang (2021).[12] Power demand has increased in China's industrial heartland (Guandong) as export-led growth has risen (Stanway, 2021).[13] China has heavily imported LNG from various countries, including the USA, Australia, and T&T, to meet its rising demand.

The Institute of Energy Economics and Financial Institute (2024),[14] however, the report notes that although the demand for LNG in China remains healthy compared to other economies, LNG will play an increasingly smaller role in the country's transition to cleaner energy sources (Table 7.8). The report noted that over the last decade, natural gas-fired electricity accounted for only 3% of China's power mix, compared to 16% generated via wind and solar sources.

China's greater push towards natural gas can only nudge natural gas prices upwards, (other things constant) and this will benefit CARICOM natural gas (T&T) exporters.

Unlike the USA, China has a relatively modest stock of oil and gas resources which it is not at the level that could meet domestic Chinese demand. Recently, (17 October 2022, in China Halts LNG Sales to foreign Buyers to ensure own supply) China advised its state-owned gas importers not to resell LNG to stabilize its own supply. Chow (2023) explained that "high prices would continue to suppress demand from

Table 7.7 T&T Exports of Natural Gas (343) to China and the World 2000–2023 000 USD

Year	*China*	*World*
2000		364,747.5
2005		2,045,738
2009	19,283.98	3,710,628
2010	8557.935	1,193,641
2015	39,189.84	2,799,923
2016	7338.612	1,447,049
2017		1,307,307
2018		1,652,853
2019	11,912.97	1,230,326
2020	1230.537	486,793.8
2021		492,202.7
2022	7915.388	1,116,833

Source: WITS

Table 7.8 Natural Gas Consumption and Imports China 1965–2023

	Natural Gas Consumption as a % of World China	*Natural Gas Prices US$ / mmbtu (Henry Hub)*	*LNG Imports bn cubic meters China*
1965	0.18		
1970	0.30		
1975	0.76		
1980	1.01		
1985	0.80	-	
1990	0.79	1.64	
1995	0.85	1.69	
2000	1.03	4.23	-
2005	1.71	8.79	-
2010	3.44	4.39	13.02
2015	5.60	2.60	27.00
2016	5.89	2.46	36.76
2017	6.60	2.96	52.93
2018	7.40	3.12	73.45
2019	7.90	2.51	84.75
2020	8.65	1.99	94.02
2021	9.40	3.84	109.5
2022	9.8	6.45	
2023	-	2.53	

Source: BP Statistical Review (2024)

the Chinese industrial and power sectors, both highly sensitive to energy cost…State energy officials have estimated that in 2022, China's annual demand for natural gas may have fallen for the first time in two decades because of weak demand from industries disrupted by pandemic controls. China was the world's top LNG importer in 2021, but Japan held the position last year. Gas prices spiked last year after Russia, following its invasion of Ukraine, cut supplies to Europe. This led Europe to import record amounts of LNG, pushing Asian spot LNG prices to historical highs."

China has, therefore, ramped up its gas production but is producing its shale gas at 1/5 of the level of the USA as there is a difference in geology, a deficit in technical skills, and the pipeline network is simply not in place (Chen, 2018). China's producing fields are generally considered to be high-cost and, as such, the country will continue to supplement local demand with imports. In 2021, China was the largest importer of natural gas in the world, superseding even Japan. The increase in demand for natural gas from China would continue to favourably affect prices, and in this regard, CARICOM exporters of gas will benefit.

7.3 Wood and Timber

China has 220 mn hectares of total forested area comprising both natural and planted forests. Regarding size, China ranks 5th in the world after Russia, Brazil, Canada, and the USA. Its planted forest is the largest in the world (Xinhua 2022[16]). However, there is a ban on commercial logging of natural forests in China, which obviously limits the supply of high-quality lumber into the Chinese market coming from China itself. Therefore, China has to import large amounts of wood (Geng, 2021).[17]

Table 7.9 shows that as China's imports of log increased, the price of logs in US$ per cubic metre (Cameroon) also increased. The correlation between the variables, China's imports of wood and the price of logs is 0.74. China's imports of logs increased from US$699.4 mn in 1984 to US$8 bn in 2021. In the same period, there was a rapid increase in log prices from US$175.6 per cubic metre in 1984 to US$370.55 by the end of 2023.

Table 7.9 Chinese Imports of Wood and Price of Logs, 1984–2023

	China mts wood US$mn	*Logs, Cameroon ($/cubic metre)*
1984	699.4	175.64
1985	761.3	173.88
1990	508.5	343.46
1995	543.6	339.51
2000	2656.6	275.43
2005	4801.4	334.37
2010	10,004.1	428.56
2015	7551.4	388.58
2016	8191.5	387.41
2017	10,224.3	395.22
2018	10,324.6	413.55
2019	8820.5	391.92
2020	7894.3	399.46
2021	8235.3	425.85
2022		395.61
2023		370.55

Source: WITS and WB

Regarding CARICOM's exports to China, this was not of any substantive value for sitc 241 (fuel wood and charcoal). For sitc 242, CARICOM's exports to China stood at US$23.9 mn in 2022 as compared to a paltry US$0.649 mn in 2000. The exports of 243 improved from 2000 to 2022 (See Table 7.10).

Table 7.10 shows trends in CARICOM exports of various wood products to China and the world. The main regional wood exporters include Guyana, Suriname, Belize, and T&T.

The Global Timber Outlook in 2020[18] noted that several factors will impact on the demand for wood in the future. These include urbanization, decarbonization, and the growing housing shortage. Global urbanization changes will impact the market for wood, especially in the context of demand for low-cost, low-carbon footprint housing. Specifically, the report noted that the urban population is forecasted to rise by 18% by 2030 and 52% by 2050 (Global Timber Outlook, 2020).

Table 7.10 CARICOM Exports of 241, 242, and 243 to China and the World (US$mn), 2000–2023

	241		*242*		*243*	
	China	*WLD*	*China*	*WLD*	*China*	*WLD*
2000	–	0.05	0.65	2.49	0.25	15.63
2005	–	0.23	1.98	10.93	1.67	25.70
2010	0.00	0.29	3.36	7.15	5.19	35.81
2011	0.03	0.24	9.36	13.46	7.03	46.96
2012	0.01	0.44	7.01	16.31	5.76	36.60
2013	0.11	0.34	9.55	16.69	4.71	33.15
2014	–	0.32	17.15	26.31	8.74	36.51
2015	–	0.34	13.48	29.02	4.39	33.48
2016	–	0.28	11.24	33.10	2.70	33.26
2017	–	0.26	18.74	60.26	1.86	30.12
2018	–	0.26	20.86	66.69	2.11	28.19
2019	–	0.29	23.06	64.48	0.74	20.69
2020	0.03	0.60	35.33	82.30	1.32	32.08
2021		0.52	23.15	64.98	4.70	34.19
2022		0.39	24.06	77.50	5.47	39.98
2023		0.26	0.09	65.30	0.54	18.51

Source: WITS

In the context of this trend, Caribbean countries can benefit from improved prices but will have to regulate the pace at which their forests are deforested.

7.4 Bauxite and Aluminium

The demand for bauxite is on the rise globally, and especially in China, the demand for aluminium is rapidly rising (Khan 2015,[20] Wood, 2020). China is the world's largest importer of bauxite. Increased demand and depletion of mines in China mean that China imports a significant amount of its bauxite (as much as 40%) even from the CARICOM (Tables 7.11, 7.12).

Table 7.11 Aluminium Trade Indicators, 1992–2023

	Imports of Aluminium ores and concentrates (incl. alumina) SITC 285 US$mn			*% of World Imports of Aluminium Ore*		*Aluminium ($/mt)*
	World	*China*	*India*	*China Imports/ World*	*India Imports / World*	
1992	4532.95	148.97	6.04	3.29	0.13	1254.28
1995	5101.05	266.14	16.08	5.22	0.32	1805.66
2000	7293.96	649.70	11.23	8.91	0.15	1549.14
2005	12,214.55	2666.44	79.99	21.83	0.65	1898.31
2010	13,558.55	2808.60	202.98	20.71	1.50	2173.12
2015	17,757.86	4527.64	460.79	25.50	2.59	1664.68
2016	14,859.29	3369.20	514.92	22.67	3.47	1604.18
2017	18,941.03	4491.27	942.04	23.71	4.97	1967.65
2018	24,042.01	4756.85	1,25.06	19.79	8.01	2108.48
2019	22,640.68	5812.11	1118.68	25.67	4.94	1794.49
2020	19,027.01	6247.65	810.97	32.84	4.26	1703.99
2021	22,311.42	6462.17	1286.55	28.96	5.77	2473
2022	24,004.47	8361.38	1464.25	34.83	6.10	2705
2023	20,791.49	9423.11	1308.55	45.32	6.29	2556

Source: WITS and author calculations

Table 7.12 Sitc 285 exports from the CARICOM, US$000 for 2019, 2021, 2023

	2019 (US$000)		*2021 (US$000)*		*2023 (US$000)*
Netherlands	215,262.4	USA	175,538.574	Russian Federation	137,967.7
USA	174,445.6	Netherlands	140,329.454	Latvia	131,071.2
Iceland	117,765.4	Canada	59,584.722	USA	107,264.9
Canada	107,585.4	Russian Federation	44,078.784	Iceland	94,902.3
Russian Federation	69,703.98	Iceland	29,452.437	Netherlands	51,967.9
Norway	64,518.29	Germany	23,666.942	Germany	26,740.4
Ukraine	52,173.33	Switzerland	22,121.273	Ghana	26,350.3
Georgia	32,535.5	Ghana	15,709.487	France	9786.6
Ghana	28,843.46	Georgia	8381.969	Georgia	8517.0
China	27,139.12	Mexico	5306.672	China	8232.5

Source: WITS

The Aluminium Global Market Report (2023)[21] explained that the global aluminium market is expected to grow at an average of 6.8% annually between 2023 and 2027. The aluminium market, in terms of demand is segmented regionally into Asia Pacific, North America, Europe, the Middle East and Africa, and South America, with the Asia Pacific market capturing the largest market share in 2022. The expectation is that Asia Pacific will remain the largest segment in terms of demand till 2030. The sectors driving this demand include packaging, transportation, building, and construction. This rising demand is likely to result in higher prices for aluminium as forecasted by the World Bank and the IMF[22] as shown in Table 7.13. Indeed, this trend augers well for exporters of bauxite (aluminium ore) in the CARICOM region, such as Guyana, Suriname,[23] and Jamaica. The respective industries in these countries are expected to expand. For example, the Jamaica Observer (2021)[24] notes that the Jamaican Bauxite Mining Limited is set to expand its operations because of technological upgrades and warehousing. Even so Linton (2024[25]) noted that production will be ramped up from mines in St Ann. According to the Jamaica Bauxite Mining Company, the park is set to include small warehouses for light and medium-sized manufacturing firms. All proposals are currently in the feasibility and pre-feasibility phases. In Guyana, the government is actively seeking to restart RUSAL operations in the Berbice region (Guyana Times, 2024).[26] The specifics of the project are currently being discussed.

As China's income continues to grow, its demand for bauxite will rise and this augers well for CARICOM bauxite exporters as MacDonald (2022) notes that the region does represent a strategic supply of natural resources.

Table 7.13 Forecasted Aluminium Prices (US$ metric Ton), 2024–2027

	WB	*IMF*
2024	2300	2723.8
2025	2400	2763.2
2026		2900
2027		2900

Sources: World Bank Commodity Prices Outlook (2024) and IMF (2024), BMI (2024)

7.5 Impact of Energy Price Changes on CARICOM

Table 7.14 captures the long-term fluctuations in the current account balances of Caribbean nations and highlights how oil prices have influenced these balances over time. Countries with strong correlations (positive or negative) are heavily impacted by oil price changes, due to their reliance either on oil exports or imports, while those with weaker correlations are less affected. The clear indication is that while a rise in oil prices benefits oil-exporting Caribbean countries, such as TT and Suriname (Guyana started to produce oil in 2019, last quarter), for the other oil-importing CARICOM countries, as oil prices rise, their current account balance tends to worsen. Thus, while China benefits CARICOM energy exporting economies by boosting international crude oil prices, there is also a boomerang effect on CARICOM non-energy exporting economies in terms of the current account balance and prices (Tables 7.15, 7.16).

Oil price increases adversely affect oil-importing economies by escalating their inflation rates via a pass-through effect. CARICOM countries have limited agricultural and manufacturing capacity; as such, the region is heavily dependent on imports to meet the demand for goods and services. This high dependence on imports leads to high pass-through inflation in the region as oil price increases drive the positive relationship between oil prices and commodity prices.

In particular, some Caribbean countries have a high dependence on imported fuel, and this has exposed these countries to associated terms of trade shocks and fiscal burdens, which have become entrenched as a structural challenge over time. The high level of oil prices has contributed to macroeconomic imbalances and adversely affected these countries' competitiveness. This is a challenge for service-based economies as services such as tourism heavily depend on imports, of which fuel is a critical subset. Consider, for example, that in the case of St Lucia, the adverse impact of rising oil prices results in declining foreign reserves; one would expect that the correlation between these two variables would be high and inverse.

Figure 7.3 shows that as the oil price rose, the trade balance of St. Lucia worsened. Indeed, the domestic economies of energy-importing CARICOM countries, such as St Lucia, suffer when energy prices increase. As energy prices rise, household discretionary income decreases, and this, in turn, reduces their expenditure on other sectors. The IMF notes that in 2012, the national electricity bill of the Caribbean was

Table 7.14 Current account balance and correlation with oil prices, 1990–2023 (% of GDP)

	ATG	*BHS*	*BLZ*	*BRB*	*DMA*	*GRD*	*GUY*	*JAM*	*KNA*	*LCA*	*SUR*	*TTO*	*VCT*
1990	– 6.74	– 1.16	3.72	– 0.35	– 21.61	– 16.63		– 6.8	– 21.62	– 9.84		9.06	– 9.8
1995	– 0.09	– 4.25	– 2.78	0.04	– 14.66	– 12.22	– 21.68	– 1.5	– 14.5	– 4.75		5.51	– 12.72
2000	– 8.08	– 7.84	– 19.42	– 3.34	– 17.94	– 16.94	– 11.53	– 4.08	– 15.7	– 10.17		6.67	– 6.03
2005	– 16.76	– 7.12	– 13.72	– 12.98	– 20.89	– 27.79	– 11.67	– 9.53	– 11.83	– 11.4	– 8.18	24.29	– 18.56
2010	– 14.55	– 8.06	– 3.32	– 6.01	– 16.24	– 26.45	– 7.18	– 7.06	– 18.23	– 13.64	14.9	18.83	– 30.58
2015	2.19	– 10.27	– 10.15	– 2.09	– 7.57	– 12.24	– 0.91	– 3.03	– 8.66	2.08	– 15.34	8.24	– 15.33
2016	– 2.43	– 5.96	– 9.14	– 9.38	– 8.84	– 10.97	– 1.12	– 0.31	– 12.73	– 4.15	– 4.84	– 3.48	– 13.05
2017	– 8.85	– 12.61	– 8.5	– 5.3	– 12.77	– 11.98	– 8.23	– 2.68	– 11.01	1.36	1.93	6.29	– 12.02
2018	– 7.05	– 8.56	– 7.87	– 4	– 40.85	– 9.95	– 24.58	– 1.55	– 7.16	4.98	– 2.97	6.81	– 12.22
2019	– 7.1	– 2.6	– 7.6	– 2.8	– 35.6	– 10.1	– 63	– 2.2	– 5.8	5.5	– 11.3	4.3	– 2.3
2020	– 16.9	– 23.6	– 6.1	– 5.9	– 35.4	– 16.4	– 16.3	– 0.4	– 10.9	– 15.3	9	– 6.4	– 15.7
2021	– 16.6	– 22.6	– 6.5	– 10.9	– 28.5	– 13.2	– 25.6	0.7	– 5.8	– 7.8	5.9	11.9	– 22.9
2022	– 16	– 13	– 8	.	– 27	– 11	– 2	– 1	– 11	– 3	2	18	– 19

(continued)

Table 7.14 (continued)

	ATG	*BHS*	*BLZ*	*BRB*	*DMA*	*GRD*	*GUY*	*JAM*	*KNA*	*LCA*	*SUR*	*TTO*	*VCT*
2023	− 13	.	− 3	.	− 34	− 14	.	.	− 13	− 2	4	.	− 13
Correl 1990–2019	− 0.54	− 0.61	0.22	− 0.6	− 0.32	− 0.54	0.21	− 0.64	0.19	− 0.17	0.43	0.73	− 0.67
Correl 2010–2019	− 0.56	− 0.56	0.79	− 0.34	0.04	− 0.7	− 0.01	− 0.9	0.12	− 0.61	0.43	0.89	− 0.88
Correl 1990–2023	0.11	0.45	0.43	0.10	0.10	0.23	0.09	0.14	0.62	0.41	0.06	0.09	0.37
Correl 2010–2023	0.33	(0.10)	0.57	0.29	0.16	0.53	0.17	0.71	0.09	0.25	0.23	0.91	0.72

Source: WDI and author calculations

Table 7.15 Inflation, consumer prices (annual %), 1990–2023

	ATG	*BHS*	*BRB*	*DMA*	*GRD*	*GUY*	*JAM*	*KNA*	*LCA*	*SUR*	*TTO*	*VCT*
1990		4.67	3.07	3.19	2.72		21.96	4.01	4.27	21.74	11.06	7.61
1995		2.07	1.88	1.32	1.87	12.21	19.91	2.96	5.63	235.56	5.18	1.74
2000	0.77	1.61	2.44	0.86	2.18	6.15	8.17	2.15	3.71	59.4	3.56	0.17
2005	2.1	1.59	6.08	1.68	3.48	6.93	15.05	3.38	3.9	9.9	6.87	3.73
2010	3.37	1.34	5.82	3	3.44	3.73	12.61	0.85	3.25	6.94	10.55	0.75
2015	0.97	1.88	– 1.11	– 0.84	– 0.52	– 1	3.69	– 2.3	– 0.98	6.89	4.66	– 1.73
2016	– 0.49	– 0.33	1.28	0.14	1.65	0.84	2.35	– 0.69	– 3.09	55.41	3.07	– 0.15
2017	2.43	1.5	4.66	0.3	0.91	1.9	4.38	0.69	0.12	22	1.88	2.15
2018	1.21	2.27	3.67	0.99	0.8	1.28	3.74	– 1.04	1.94	6.9	1.02	2.32
2019	1.43	2.49	4.1	1.5	0.6	2.09	3.91	– 0.33	0.54	4.3	1	0.91
2020	2 0.80	1.2	1.3	– 0.7	– 0.8	1.3	5.23	– 0.8	– 0.4	34.9	0.6	– 1
2021	1.6	2.9	3.1	1.6	1.2	3.3	5.9	1.2	2.4	59.2	2.1	1.6
2022	7.53	5.61	6.28	.	7.78	2.58	6.12	10.35	2.67	6.38	52.45	5.83
2023	5.07	3.05	4.39	9.79	3.48	2.70	2.82	6.47	3.56	4.07	.	4.63

Source: WDI

Table 7.16 CARICOM imports, 2000, 2010, 2019 US$

CARICOM MTS	*2000 (US$000)*	*2010 (US$000)*	*2019 (US$000)*	*2023 (US$000)*	*% change 2000 - 2023*
All countries All—All	12,663,641.0	21,657,431.0	21,848,631.0	19,324,620.0	52.6
USA	6,105,669.0	8,738,162.0	7,284,082.0	7,154,794.0	17.2
China	158,248.3	1,032,622.0	1,775,494.0	1,777,381.0	1023.2
Trinidad and Tobago	896,686.7	1,917,940.0	1,433,113.0	1,630,185.0	81.8
Japan	519,526.2	514,471.7	527,404.2	669,195.3	28.8
Brazil	190,908.2	795,287.4	956,214.9	649,633.7	240.3
Netherlands	233,998.2	372,544.4	493,876.9	555,933.4	137.6
UK	491,490.0	486,431.0	472,179.4	520,594.9	5.9
Mexico	268,202.9	322,158.7	725,558.5	429,885.3	60.3
Colombia	299,944.1	728,121.5	296,379.8	371,046.6	23.7
Turkey	36,899.4	64,135.7	381,429.9	276,155.9	648.4
Canada	341,783.9	461,500.9	495,706.6	273,666.7	− 19.9
India	28,375.2	212,595.3	288,440.7	257,449.1	807.3
Panama	65,952.0	148,020.7	209,361.9	251,536.3	281.4
Germany	159,414.1	295,220.9	319,464.9	249,733.6	56.7
Bahamas, The	5187.4	28,099.9	25,432.5	237,115.4	4471.0
Dominican Republic	18,295.6	133,070.3	232,925.8	228,144.8	1147.0
Spain	40,090.8	80,334.7	129,933.9	220,234.6	449.3
Guatemala	44,245.7	117,134.9	224,158.4	218,871.6	394.7
Suriname	52,574.2	151,007.4	204,837.8	186,208.9	254.2
Thailand	43,434.9	177,347.7	207,570.0	185,698.3	327.5
Jamaica	53,193.3	66,575.1	90,276.3	161,207.9	203.1
Nigeria	182.7	19,292.0	159,805.9	160,958.0	87,979.4
Costa Rica	32,587.6	130,924.7	156,522.6	146,158.9	348.5
Italy	110,555.1	140,184.1	166,358.3	142,484.5	28.9
Barbados	106,528.3	127,610.2	128,547.3	136,855.9	28.5

Source: WITS

approximately 9% of GDP as compared to 2% in the USA—surely, this would adversely affect the competitiveness of these oil-importing economies. Associated with rising oil prices is increasing inflation. As the inflation rate increases (on account of the high pass-through associated with electricity bills and domestic transportation) in the region, the real effective exchange rate appreciates, and this leads to a loss of external competitiveness. This reiterates a cycle of dependence on single sectors.

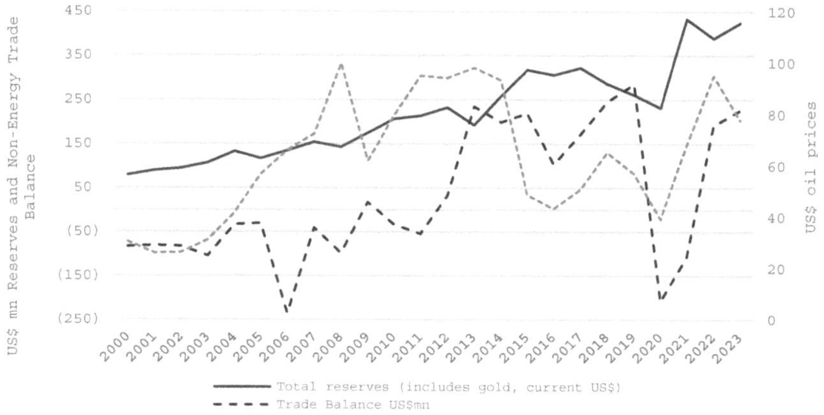

Fig. 7.3 St Lucia: the interaction of oil prices (US$), trade deficit, and total reserves (US$mn), 2000–2023 (Source: WDI and author calculations)

Indeed, it is clear, as is illustrated for Guyana in Fig. 7.4 (i.e., before it started to export oil), that both lagged oil prices and the real effective exchange rate tend to move in the same direction.

7.6 An Econometric Assessment of Growth Spillovers Impacting on the CARICOM

The extent of spillovers from developed countries to less developed countries has always been an area of interest and more so, now as the growth of many advanced economies have slowed. The growth spillover literature is premised on the notion that the domestic growth in an economy is based on three main sources: domestic shocks, global shocks, and shocks to a significant regional partner or foreign country, transmitted through a variety of channels (Furceri, Jalles & Zdzienicka, 2016, Doyle & Faust, 2005). The size of each of these various shocks varies, but in general, growth moves across countries over the long term especially when there are large bilateral trade flows or if the countries have coordinated fiscal policies (Sly and Weber 2013, Norris, Espinoza & Johan, 2015), although this may be particularly so for developed economies (Frankel and Rose 1998, Doyle and Faust 2005 and Arora & Vamvakidis, 2005). In the short term, some growth spillovers have been identified between and

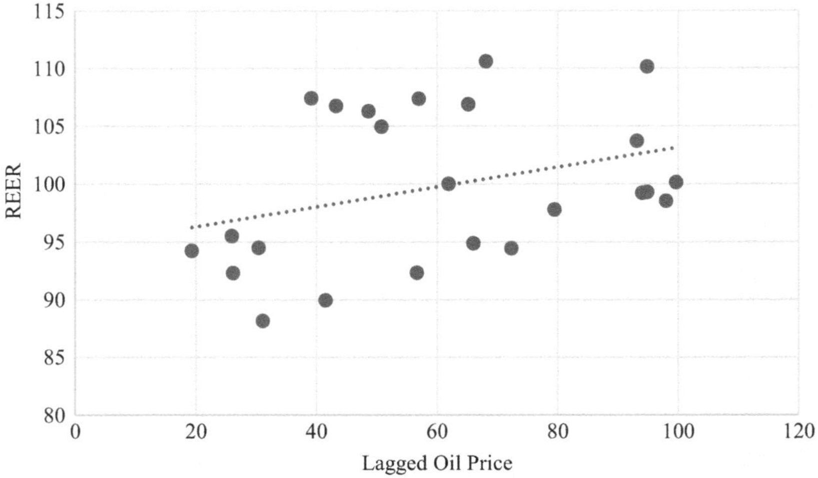

Fig. 7.4 Scatterplot of lagged oil prices and the real effective exchange rate of Guyana, 2000–2023 (Source: author calculated)

within low income and developing countries (Samake & Yang 2011, Barrot, Calderon & Serven, 2018). Blongigen, Piger, and Sly (2014) demonstrated that shocks that take place on long-term growth have larger cross-country effects than shocks to short-term growth.

Economic growth in China can spill over to the CARICOM region through a variety of channels, but it is well established in the literature that the most obvious of these channels is the direct trade channel (Hosein et al., 2017, Hosein et al., 2021). Indeed, the literature notes that countries that engage in a higher level of trade and a greater degree of financial linkages tend to have business cycles that are more synchronized. A higher level of growth in China, other things constant, is likely to lead to a higher demand for the goods and services exported by CARICOM economies. Indeed, this spillover channel could have been partially observed during the Global Financial Crisis of 2008 with economic growth in many developing countries reflecting the growth in China and other emerging market economies.

As a start, note that the trade linkages between emerging economies such as China and the economies of the CARICOM have increased sharply over time, although the developed countries continue to remain the destination economies for the export goods of the Caribbean. Using imports as a reference point, CARICOM's import from China expanded 1023% between 2000 and 2023.

Other important linkages between CARICOM and the rest of the world are remittances, FDI, and cross-border banking flows. (China is an important source of remittances for many developing countries in the Asian region). Note that India is also a major source of remittances to other less-developed countries in the Asian region (see Imbs, 2004). Russia and Saudi Arabia are other significant emerging market economies and account for about 50% of the remittance flows to the lower-income countries in their regions.

Cross-border banking flows are another important source of influence from emerging economies like China. Additionally, over time, many outbound tourists flock to CARICOM from emerging market economies. FDI flows are another critical source of linkages.

To help understand the ascent of China from a trade perspective, consider Table 7.17, which shows the top 25 exporters in the world based on the number of markets to which the indicated country exports its commodities, using 2019 data as the anchor. For example, in 2019, Portugal exported 3068 different products to 129 countries. This increased to 3091 products by the end of 2023. To understand how exports by these countries have evolved, a comparative column using 1990 data for the number of products exported and the number of destination export markets is also included.

In the final two columns, Table 7.18 shows the percentage (%) change between 1990 and 2023, and the average annual growth rate of each listed country as forecasted by the IMF for the period 2024–29. Specifically, consider China's growth rate of per capita GDP between 1990 and 2023. It is, thus, critical to determine how the economic growth performance of such a large and rapidly expanding country spills over to the CARICOM region.

From another dimension, Table 7.18 shows the top 25 export destinations of CARICOM countries for 2023. In 2023, for example, CARICOM exported to the USA a total of US$2.3 bn and to Spain TT$514.6 million. For these 25 top export destinations for CARICOM products in 2023, the table also shows data on the per capita GDP for each of these export destination economies for both 1990 and 2023.

Table 7.17 Export products and markets for selected economies, 1990, 2019 and 2023

	Number of Products 1990	*Number of Markets 1990*	*Number of Products 2019*	*Number of Markets 2019*	*Number of Products 2023*	*Number of Markets 2023*	*% Change in Products 1990 - 2023*	*% Change in Markets 1990–2023*
Portugal	1513	28	3068	129	3091	103	104.3	267.9
Ireland	1020	29	2447	131	2474	106	142.5	265.5
Poland	1413	28	3716	131	3731	106	164.0	278.6
Hong Kong, China	2062	30	2987	132	2530	107	22.7	256.7
Mexico	886	25	3072	132	3061	105	245.5	320.0
United Arab Emirates	536	26	2552	133	2383	106	344.6	307.7
Argentina	1231	28	1705	133	1532	105	24.5	275.0
Australia	2162	28	2701	133	2592	106	19.9	278.6
Sweden	2588	30	3324	133	3239	105	25.2	250.0
Denmark	2175	28	3169	134	3132	107	44.0	282.1
Singapore	2122	29	2937	134	2654	103	25.1	255.2
Canada	1678	29	3298	136	3310	108	97.3	272.4
Germany	4414	28	4475	136	4392	107	(0.5)	282.1
Italy	3988	30	4287	136	4248	106	6.5	253.3
Switzerland	2989	29	3350	137	3276	107	9.6	269.0
France	4331	30	4281	137	4205	107	(2.9)	256.7
Netherlands	3895	30	4164	137	4100	109	5.3	263.3
Turkey	967	26	3490	137	3515	109	263.5	319.2
Vietnam	147	18	2995	137	2816	109	1815.6	505.6
South Africa	993	27	3098	137	2930	108	195.1	300.0
Spain	2933	29	4191	138	4140	108	41.2	272.4
UK	3900	30	4189	138	4044	111	3.7	270.0
Indonesia	993	23	2855	138	2611	109	162.9	373.9
India	1312	27	3936	138	3780	109	188.1	303.7
USA	4688	30	4394	138	4289	109	(8.5)	263.3
Brazil	1642	29	2892	139	2907	110	77.0	279.3
China	2970	28	4461	139	4387	110	47.7	292.9
Japan	3657	29	3949	139	3668	109	0.3	275.9

(continued)

Table 7.17 (continued)

	Number of Products 1990	*Number of Markets 1990*	*Number of Products 2019*	*Number of Markets 2019*	*Number of Products 2023*	*Number of Markets 2023*	*% Change in Products 1990 - 2023*	*% Change in Markets 1990–2023*
Korea, Rep	2662	29	3615	139	3333	110	25.2	279.3
Malaysia	1906	29	3100	139	2827	108	48.3	272.4
Thailand	1597	27	3346	139	3067	109	92.0	303.7

Source: WITS

The second to last column of Table 7.18 shows the percentage change in per capita GDP of each of these export partners. The clear indication is that China experienced the fastest increase in income among CARICOM's top export market destinations. Further and, apart from Guyana (because of its massive increase in oil production), UAE and, India, China are projected (average annual real GDP growth rate for the period 2024–2029) to grow the fastest among all the listed countries. In this regard, it makes good economic sense to include the growth of China in a structural VAR modelling exercise to assess the impact of growth shocks in China on CARICOM's economic activity.

7.6.1 Empirical Results and Discussions

Various tests are deployed below to ensure the stationarity of the variables used in the model: the Augmented Dickey Fuller test, the Phillips Perron test, and the Kwiatkowski, Phillips, Schmidt, and Shin (KPSS) test. Further, a series of diagnostic tests, including the a) lag order criteria b) residual serial correlation LM test c) VAR residual normality test, were conducted. The variables were deemed to be stationary and hence, were deployed to construct the VAR.

The ordering of the variables in the VAR is critical, as the basis assumption is that economic growth in a large trade partner can impact the growth of a small economy rather than the reverse. A lag length of 1 was chosen for modelling, consistent with the other diagnostic tests applied to the period 1995–2023 (Table 7.19).

Table 7.18 CARICOM export markets, 1990, 2019, 2022 and 2023

	2023 (US$000)	*1990*	*2019*	*2022*	*2023*	*% increase in per capita GDP*	*average annual GDP growth rate 2024–2029*
		GDP per capita US$				*1990–2023*	
USA	*2,349,270*	*23,848.0*	*65,504.8*	*77,191.9*	*81,632.3*	*242.30*	*2.2*
Singapore	1,639,121	12,763.3	66,081.7	88,428.7	84,734.3	563.89	2.4
Netherlands	1,058,550	21,581.6	52,672.5	57,427.8	62,718.7	190.61	1.5
UK	935,124.3	20,913.0	42,712.6	45,730.1	49,099.0	134.78	1.4
Panama	524,939.5	2397.2	16,526.4	17,409.6	18,725.7	681.14	3.6
Spain	514,605.2	13,693.6	29,603.3	29,799.7	33,071.3	141.51	1.8
United Arab Emirates	491,017.2	27,484.6	43,981.6	52,625.1	51,908.7	88.86	4.2
Italy	333,034.4	20,500.7	33,628.2	35,043.1	38,325.8	86.95	0.6
India	314,538.9	368.8	2050.2	2366.3	2500.4	578.06	6.5
Greece	300,963.8	9679.3	19,140.6	20,818.1	22,805.2	135.61	1.6
Canada	156,327.9	21,572.1	46,431.0	55,612.9	53,547.7	148.23	1.7
Russian Federation	138,079.9	n/a	11,554.0	15,487.7	13,647.8		1.7
Latvia	131,087.8	n/a	17,828.1	21,566.9	23,153.5		2.3
Barbados	130,378.4	7772.2	18,689.7	20,184.7	22,020.3	183.32	2.5
Trinidad and Tobago	123,400.1	4221.8	17,043.9	21,252.7	19,801.0	369.02	2.2
Germany	111,712.6	20,249.1	46,810.3	48,756.3	52,727.0	160.39	0.9
St. Lucia	107,082.6	4069.8	11,773.4	12,704.0	13,545.9	232.84	1.8
Bahamas, The	95,708.78	20,460.3	33,888.8	32,298.9	34,224.1	67.27	1.7

	2023 (US$000)	*1990*	*2019*	*2022*	*2023*	*% increase in per capita GDP*	*average annual GDP growth rate 2024–2029*
		GDP per capita US$				*1990–2023*	
USA	*2,349,270*	*23,848.0*	*65,504.8*	*77,191.9*	*81,632.3*	*242.30*	*2.2*
Iceland	95,166.36	25,629.4	69,137.2	76,284.3	79,998.4	212.14	2.2
Denmark	88,462.05	26,920.6	59,678.6	68,131.9	68,299.8	153.71	1.5
Jamaica	82,886.67	1971.7	5781.8	6197.8	6875.7	248.72	1.7
France	64,142.44	22,490.3	41,924.8	42,306.1	46,000.8	104.54	1.3
Venezuela	53,875.02	2492.9	2624.4	3421.8	3659.2	46.78	3.5
China	52,458.72	346.9	10,170.1	12,642.8	12,513.9	3507.62	3.8
Guyana	47,221.93	951.0	6594.4	18,353.1	21,472.3	2157.94	20.0

Source: WITS

Table 7.19 VAR lag order selection criteria

Lag	*LogL*	*LR*	*FPE*	*AIC*	*SC*	*HQ*
0	− 319.0379	NA	765.9678	23.65778	24.78934	24.01217
1	− 253.5254	85.84387*	118.1538	21.62244	24.45133	22.50842
2	− 206.0573	42.55765	102.911	20.83154	25.35776	22.24909
3	− 122.3144	40.42759	27.76313*	17.53893*	23.76248*	19.48807*

Source: author calculations. Endogenous variables: US EU27 CHINA INDIA UK CCOM
LR: sequential modified LR test statistic (each test at 5% level)
FPE: Final prediction error
AIC: Akaike information criterion
SC: Schwarz information criterion
HQ: Hannan–Quinn information criterion
*Indicates lag order selected by the criterion

Given the AR polynomial associated with 1 lag, the estimated VAR is stable. Further, as shown in Tables 7.20 and 7.21, no root lies outside of the unit circle and the residuals are multivariate normal, at any reasonable level of significance.

Based on the VAR residual serial correlation test, it can be observed that there is no serial correlation (Table 7.22).

The VAR specified has satisfied the various model diagnostics and can thus, be deployed for variance decomposition analysis.

Table 7.20 Roots of characteristic polynomial

Root	*Modulus*
0.730872	0.730872
0.631983	0.631983
− 0.001575 − 0.533116i	0.533118
− 0.001575 + 0.533116i	0.533118
− 0.050413 − 0.086563i	0.100173
− 0.050413 + 0.086563i	0.100173

Endogenous variables: US EU27 CHINA INDIA UK CCOM
No root lies outside the unit circle
VAR satisfies the stability condition
Source: author calculations

Table 7.21 VAR Residual normality tests

Component	*JB*	*df*	*Prob*
Joint	15.33326	12	0.2237

Orthogonalization: Cholesky (Lutkepohl)
Null Hypothesis: residuals are multivariate normal
Source: author calculations

Table 7.22 VAR Residual Serial Correlation LM Tests

Lag	*LRE* stat*	*Prob*
1	50.10565	0.0593
2	46.95295	0.1046

Null hypothesis: no serial correlation at lag h
Source: author calculations

7.6.1.1 Variance Decomposition

The results in Table 7.23 show that "variance" in growth of CARICOM countries are explained by idiosyncratic shocks and that indicates that there are some benefits which can be realized by a deepening of the regional integration process, i.e., unpausing CSME. The findings also indicate the USA and EU27 also contribute 68% and 14% to the growth variance of CARICOM economies. Variance decomposition as an innovation accounting method provides an indication of how the change in the value of a variable is influenced by the changes to this variable as well as shocks from other variables over time (Enders, 2003). The USA is (the biggest trade partner to the CARICOM) significantly influences the variation of the growth of CARICOM's GDP. Of note though, is the growing importance of innovations in China and India, by extension, and how they affect CARICOM's growth variation. Specifically, observe that China and India, on average, for the first three periods contributed 3% (as compared to 6% for the UK to the growth variance of CARICOM countries).

These results are critical as the Chinese economy is projected by the IMF to grow 4.9% on average per annum between 2023 and 2028. Note in the same period, the average annual growth of the USA was 1.58%, the UK 1.75%, Germany 1.34%, and Japan 1.08%.

Table 7.23 Variance decomposition

Period	*S.E*	*US*	*EU27*	*CHINA*	*INDIA*	*UK*	*CCOM*
1	1.62	71.75	12.40	3.14	2.27	3.03	7.40
2	2.10	68.02	13.84	2.82	2.16	6.70	6.47
3	2.12	65.24	15.41	2.69	3.17	7.21	6.28
4	2.15	65.03	15.43	2.76	3.22	7.25	6.30
5	2.15	64.91	15.38	2.93	3.21	7.28	6.28
6	2.16	64.78	15.40	3.06	3.21	7.27	6.29
7	2.16	64.68	15.41	3.14	3.22	7.26	6.29
8	2.16	64.62	15.40	3.20	3.21	7.28	6.30
9	2.16	64.57	15.39	3.24	3.21	7.29	6.30
10	2.16	64.55	15.38	3.27	3.21	7.29	6.31
Average P1–P3	1.95	68.34	13.88	2.89	2.53	5.65	6.72

Cholesky One S.D. (d.f. adjusted)
Cholesky ordering: US EU27 CHINA INDIA UK CCOM
Source: author calculations

7.6.2 Impulse Responses

The IRF traces how a single shock to one of the innovations influences the current value and future values of the endogenous variables. The results are broadly consistent with the variance decomposition results discussed above. The IRF in Fig. 7.5 shows that an impulse from the USA favourably affects CARICOM for 3 periods. An impulse from China favourably affects CARICOM's GDP growth in the 2nd period. In many ways, these results show the merit of CARICOM economies engaging both their traditional and non-traditional trading partners to benefit from growth spillovers.

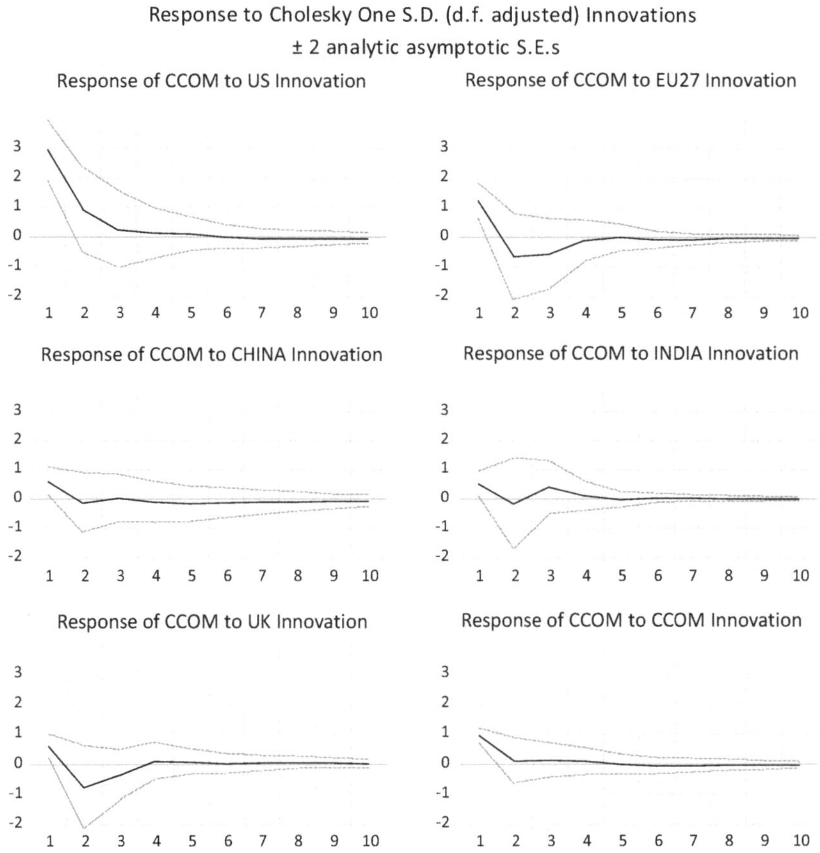

Fig. 7.5 Impulse Response of CARICOM Economies (Source: author calculations)

7.7 Conclusion

China is now the world's second-largest economy, and not surprisingly, its growth spillover influences the growth of the Caribbean. The synchronization of the Caribbean business cycle with the USA, however, remains very intact. China, as a trade partner to the region, has been increasing in importance, with various conduits through which spillovers can occur to the region, being established. These include financial assistance in the form of aid and grants, as well as agreements that result in a more pronounced political presence of China in the region.

However, structural barriers to regional spillovers may exist within CARICOM, and this hinges on the region's limited infrastructural development, its limited participation in global value chains, its dependence on the external market for consumption goods, and the need to initiate a course for deeper regional integration with a focus on CSME. Indeed, as a region, the institutions associated with CARICOM must be strengthened to improve the implementation of integration arrangements and, thereby, the region's identity.

What is clear from the discussion above is that the region's trade with China has sparked some positive spillovers via the primary conduit of trade, and indeed, this augurs well, especially for Caribbean economies with natural resource sectors. Further, the buoyancy in demand from China is likely to continue well into the medium-term period. What is needed, though, on the part of Caribbean policymakers is a series of deliberate institutional policies that deepen the basket of exports not just to China but also to other traditional and non-traditional partners.

Notes

1. https://transportgeography.org/contents/chapter7/freight-transportation-value-chains/usa-china-commodity-consumption/.
2. http://pubdocs.worldbank.org/en/716291444853736301/CMO-July-2015-Feature-China-India.pdf.
3. https://lipperalpha.refinitiv.com/2024/05/news-in-charts-assessing-chinas-dominance-in-global-commodity-markets/#:~:text=However%2C%20the%20impact%20of%20Chinese,%25%20to%2020.6%25%20in%202022.
4. https://www.reuters.com/world/china/china-oil-demand-seen-peaking-by-2030-cnpc-research-2023-12-07/.
5. https://www.iea.org/reports/global-ev-outlook-2023/policy-developments.
6. https://www.reuters.com/markets/commodities/china-2023-oil-demand-growth-seen-slower-35-year-cnpc-research-2023-06-20/.
7. https://www.wsj.com/articles/chinas-demand-for-oil-hits-record-as-iea-raises-global-forecasts-67daad8e.
8. https://www.sciencedirect.com/science/article/pii/S2095809920301430.

9. https://www.worldbank.org/en/results/2020/06/21/china-fighting-air-pollution-and-climate-change-through-clean-energy-financing.
10. https://www.bp.com/content/dam/bp/business-sites/en/global/corporate/pdfs/energy-economics/statistical-review/bp-stats-review-2021-china-insights.pdf.
11. https://www.woodmac.com/news/opinion/china-becomes-the-worlds-largest-lng-market/.
12. https://www.spglobal.com/platts/en/market-insights/latest-news/lng/090221-analysis-high-lng-prices-trigger-gas-demand-destruction-in-chinas-downstream-sectors.
13. https://www.reuters.com/world/china/china-energy-crunch-triggers-alarm-pleas-more-coal-2021-09-28/.
14. https://ieefa.org/sites/default/files/2024-06/IEEFA%20Report%20-%20LNG%20is%20not%20displacing%20coal%20in%20China's%20power%20mix.pdf.
15. https://www.reuters.com/business/energy/china-2023-gas-demand-likely-grow-lng-outlook-cloudy-petrochina-intl-exec-2023-03-03/.
16. https://english.www.gov.cn/news/topnews/202210/05/content_WS633cdb88c6d0a757729e0ddc.html.
17. China has halted logging as a strategy to maintain its natural environment and safeguard its long-term development.
    https://www.researchgate.net/publication/347854934_Impact_of_Forest_Logging_Ban_on_the_Welfare_of_Local_Communities_in_Northeast_China.
18. https://greshamhouse.com/wp-content/uploads/2020/07/GHGTO2020FINAL.pdf.
19. https://jamestown.org/program/the-caribbean-and-u-s-china-strategic-competition-next-phase-of-the-new-cold-war/.
20. https://publications.iadb.org/publications/english/document/caribbean-Economic-Alchemy-Has-Magic-Returned-to-Bauxite.pdf.
21. https://www.thebusinessresearchcompany.com/report/aluminum-global-market-report.
22. https://knoema.com/infographics/ffzioof/aluminum-price-forecast-2021-2022-and-long-term-to-2035.
23. Bauxite exports account for 70 per cent of total exports of Suriname. Other exports include gold, oil, hardwood and bananas with

the primary export partners being the USA (23 per cent of total exports), Canada (20 per cent), Belgium, United Arab Emirates, Norway, Guyana, and the Netherlands. https://tradingeconomics.com/suriname/exports.

24. https://www.jamaicaobserver.com/business-report/jamaica-bauxite-mining-diversifies-_236663.
25. https://jis.gov.jm/jbm-to-facilitate-increase-in-bauxite-production/.
26. https://guyanatimesgy.com/govt-actively-working-to-reopen-rusal-operations-in-berbice-river-bharrat/.

CHAPTER 8

China's Competitive and Indirect Trade Impact

8.1 Introduction

The rapid growth of China has, in many regards, promoted that economy to the point that it is today very much a major global economic player. China is now the 2nd largest economy in the world. The empirical literature provides varying results on the impact of China on Latin America and the Caribbean (LAC). Blazquez Lidoy et al. (2007), Scott (2004), and Meller and Contreras (2003) have indicated that the export structure of Latin America and the Caribbean (LAC) is different from that of China. These researchers indicated that China, a giant economy, offers both opportunities and threats to other economies linked to it by trade or other types of spillover-associated flows. Indeed, according to Blazquez Lidoy et al. (2007), Latin America clearly benefits from China's global integration. Using a data set of 620 different goods and two indices of trade competition, the researchers found no significant trade competition between China and LAC. This study found that those LAC countries that mainly exported raw materials faced less competition in the USA's market.

Other researchers, such as Lall and Weis (2004), found similar results.[1] Although Lederman et al. (2006) found some evidence of substitutability, they noted that this is small. This chapter specifically focuses on the following research questions: Are CARICOM and China competing in

R. Hosein et al., *China in the Caribbean*,
https://doi.org/10.1007/978-3-031-71985-1_8

the USA‘s market? This is critical, as CARICOM can ill afford to lose market shares in its main export markets. How extensive is the degree of competition between China and CARICOM in the USA's market, and how has this competition evolved? What is the actual proportion of CARICOM exports under threat from China? This chapter reflects on this issue of competitive threat.

8.2 Understanding the Trading Size of China

Table 8.1 shows the top 25 merchandise exports in the world. As can be seen, China posted a merchandise export level of US$3380 bn in 2023, which is 7.8 times that of India. Note that in 2023 China was the largest world exporter, having surpassed the USA.

China, has a significantly more diversified export base that other economies in the region as shown in Table 8.2 below. As such, deepened trade with China, can offer benefits to regional exporters. There was considerable growth in the number of exported products and partner countries for some CARICOM countries, which must be encouraged (Table 8.2).

8.3 CARICOM and China's Share of Major Export Markets

Table 8.3 shows the main export destinations of CARICOM countries. The evidence shows that the main export destination of CARICOM was the USA in 2023, followed by Singapore, the Netherlands, and the UK (See Table 8.3). Table 8.3 also shows that China's top export destination is the USA. As such, the competitive threat from China to CARICOM is assessed for the US market.

Table 8.4 shows the USA's imports from CARICOM and its member states and imports from China and the world. The clear and not surprising indication is that CARICOM is a small import source for the USA. In 2000, China's exports to the USA accounted for 8.2% of the USA's imports; by 2021, this had escalated to 18.5%. The USA imported less than 0.7% of its total imports from CARICOM in 2000 and 2019.

The USA is a significant export destination for CARICOM member states. In 2023, Jamaica had the highest importance, at 47%, followed by

Table 8.1 Top 25 highest exporters of merchandise in 2023 and fastest growing exporters 2000–2023

	Merchandise exports US$bn 2023	*Fastest growing economies in terms of exports to the World 2000–2023%**	
China	3380.02	Djibouti	155.3
USA	2019.54	Sierra Leone	96.7
Germany	1688.42	Rwanda	46.7
Netherlands	934.57	Armenia	27.6
Japan	717.32	Mongolia	27.3
Italy	676.96	Guyana	25.2
France	648.48	Lao PDR	24.4
Korea, Rep	632.23	Viet Nam	23.4
Mexico	593.01	Mozambique	21.7
Hong Kong SAR, China	573.87	Burkina Faso	19.6
Canada	569.26	Congo, Dem. Rep	19.3
Belgium	562.44	Chad	19.2
UK	520.69	Azerbaijan	18.4
United Arab Emirates	487.78	Georgia	17.9
Singapore	476.25	Panama	17.3
India	432.00	Cambodia	15.9
Russian Federation	423.92	Albania	15.6
Spain	423.22	Uganda	14.3
Switzerland	420.17	Guinea	13.5
Poland	381.52	China	12.6
Australia	370.87	Eritrea	12.4
Viet Nam	353.78	Poland	11.0
Brazil	339.70	Latvia	11.0
Saudi Arabia	322.26	Mauritania	10.3
Malaysia	312.85	Lithuania	10.2

Source: WDI

*Exports to the world were obtained from the World Bank's WDI from 2015–2019. The export growth rate over this period was calculated and ranked by country

Belize, at 20%. However, in 2023, Suriname and Antigua and Barbuda were not significantly dependent on the USA as an export market (Table 8.5).

Table 8.2 Number of export partners and products sold for selected export markets, 2000, 2023

	Number of Products 2000	*Number of Markets 2000*	*Number of Products 2023*	*Number of Markets 2023*	*% change Products 2000–2023*	*% change in Markets 2000–2023*
Antigua and Barbuda	41	26	44	26	7.32	–
Bahamas, The	112	52	86	39	(23.21)	(25.00)
Belize	103	40	110	40	6.80	–
Barbados	182	44	107	46	(41.21)	4.55
China	4461	139	4387	110	(1.66)	(20.86)
Dominica	75	36	41	23	(45.33)	(36.11)
Grenada	36	24	41	25	13.89	4.17
Guyana	98	47	109	43	11.22	(8.51)
Haiti	115	17	103	35	(10.43)	105.88
India	3227	142	3780	109	17.14	(23.24)
Jamaica	198	60	191	51	(3.54)	(15.00)
St. Kitts and Nevis	32	11				
St. Lucia	41	17	54	16	31.71	(5.88)
Russian Federation	3100	118	2957	96	(4.61)	(18.64)
Suriname	63	33	132	35	109.52	6.06
Trinidad and Tobago	360	62	422	58	17.22	(6.45)
USA	4778	160	4289	109	(10.23)	(31.88)
St. Vincent and the Grenadines	65	30	34	14	(47.69)	(53.33)

Source: WITS

8.4 Empirical Analysis of the Competitive Threat from China to CARICOM in the USA's Market

8.4.1 Export Similarity Index (ESI)

CARICOM, as compared to other labour-intensive Southeast Asia and South Asian countries, is far removed and, thus, not likely to be threatened by China. Others may argue that exports from CARICOM are

Table 8.3 CARICOM's and China's top 10 export markets in 2023

CARICOM's Partners	*Export value (US$000)*	*China's partners*	*Export value (US$000)*
United States	5108	United States	501,221
Singapore	1639	Hong Kong, China	274,519
Netherlands	1362	Japan	157,500
United Kingdom	1049	Korea, Rep	148,982
Spain	731	Vietnam	137,607
Panama	626	India	117,679
United Arab Emirates	498	Russian Federation	110,935
China	434	Germany	100,565
Belgium	364	Netherlands	100,195
Italy	352	Malaysia	87,370

Source: WITS

mainly commodity-oriented or tourism-based and, therefore, seemingly unlikely to be threatened by China's exports in third markets. (which tend to be manufacturing goods). As China has grown over the last 40 years, academics have made several attempts to evaluate the threat of competition to other countries (see Jenkins 2008, Moschella & Atkinson, 2020).[2] These studies measured the threat of competition by looking at the export structure of the affected country. They used a rationale that if these export structures are similar, then the exporter is more likely to be affected by China's exports. One commonly used index is the Export Similarity Index (ESI) developed by Finger and Kreinin (1979) to measure the export similarity of two countries. The index is calculated as follows:

$$ESI = 100 * \sum \min\left(X_{i1,} X_{i2}\right)$$

The ESI, as outlined by Kreinin and Finger (1979), assumes there are three different countries or region, say i, j, and k. The index provides an understanding of the export similarity of i and j in the third region k. $x^1{}_{jk}$ represents the export share of commodity 1 by region j in country k. $x^1{}_{ik}$ is the export share of commodity 1 from region i to country. The larger the ESI ($0 \leq ESI \leq 100$) the greater is the similarity of the export share of both i and j in k for commodity i. If the export share of i and j to k of all the commodities are the same, then the index will take on a value of 100. The closer to zero the greater the dissimilarity of the export shares.

Table 8.4 Imports by the USA from the listed economies, 2000, 2010, and 2023, Total Imports from World (US$000s)

USA's Import Partner	*2000 (US$000)*	*2010 (US$000)*	*2023 (US$000)*	*Total World Imports 2023 (US$000)*	*% of Total Imports (2023)*
Antigua and Barbuda	2291.6	5269.6	13,433.8	173,384.8	7.7
Bahamas, The	275,009.3	835,692.1	1,874,690.2	3,172,483.3	59.1
Belize	93,555.4	129,635.4	57,845.8	275,644.2	21.0
Barbados	38,638.2	44,274.1	49,867.7	284,898.8	17.5
CARICOM–CARICOM	3,959,649.1	9,320,358.3	10,093,001.7	31,306,753.3	32.2
China–China	100,012,803.5	382,962,830.4	448,017,376.4	2,483,247,023.8	18.0
Dominica	6926.4	1626.0	2271.6	20,397.0	11.1
Grenada	27,072.4	8288.5	17,278.4	42,018.8	41.1
Guyana	139,144.5	108,085.4	3,369,046.2	11,844,550.9	28.4
Haiti	296,922.2	564,956.8	849,367.8	1,013,414.7	83.8
Jamaica	648,172.4	329,839.8	406,806.5	1,014,119.6	40.1
St. Kitts and Nevis	36,805.9	52,966.9	22,512.4	80,439.3	28.0
St. Lucia	22,260.8	17,909.4	10,777.6	61,799.9	17.4
Suriname	135,210.1	208,399.5	81,829.1	1,690,050.6	4.8
Trinidad and Tobago	2,228,813.2	7,012,054.3	3,330,104.7	11,586,910.6	28.7
St. Vincent and the Grenadines	8826.7	1360.7	5565.8	40,547.2	13.7
World	1,215,276,101.3	1,955,206,660.0	3,168,471,121	19,931,737,171	15.9

Source: WITS

Table 8.5 CARICOM exports to USA relative to the World, 2023

	USA xts (US$000)	*World xts (US$000)*	*USA xts / World xts*
Antigua and Barbuda	131.31	4821.61	2.72
Belize	41,860.82	203,880.63	20.53
Barbados	38,767.86	240,714.16	16.11
Grenada	3552.72	38,228.55	9.29
Guyana	1,482,804.05	8,325,348.68	17.81
Jamaica	718,120.77	1,521,867.75	47.19
Suriname	64,032.07	2,223,179.36	2.88
Total CARICOM	2,349,269.60	12,563,529.48	18.70
China–China	501,220,723	3,379,747,835	14.83

Source: WITS

The ESI between CARICOM and China is shown in Fig. 8.1. Since 2000, CARICOM's export structure has become less similar to China's; its ESI is tending towards zero. CARICOM's ESI with China declined from 9.9 in 2000 to 3.3 in 2021, increasing to 4.9 by 2023. This should surprise no one as CARICOM and China export different categories of goods. Figure 8.2 shows that the number of zeros of CARICOM supersedes that of China, implying that China has a much more diverse basket of exports to the USA than CARICOM.

The ESI applied by Jenkins (2008) compares the similarity of the export composition of two countries and is not an accurate measure of export threat. These measures do not accurately estimate export competition, as they do not capture the scale of exports by any country and do not allow for the analysis of export competition between a large and diversified exporter such as China and a small exporter whose exports are specialized in a particular sector, such as commodity exporters and energy-rich countries. ESI-type measures only measure the similarity of the export structure of two countries and, therefore, cannot accurately estimate China's export threat to CARICOM over a period, i.e., if the export structures of both China and CARICOM remain the same, the ESI-type measures will remain static. As such, ESI-type measures will not account for the rapid growth of China's exports and export share over the review period.

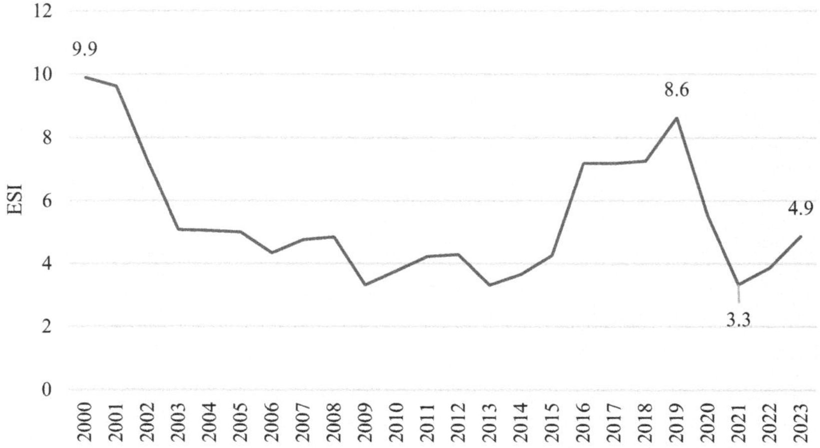

Fig. 8.1 Export similarity index of China and CARICOM in the USA's market, 2000–2023 (Source: author calculated)

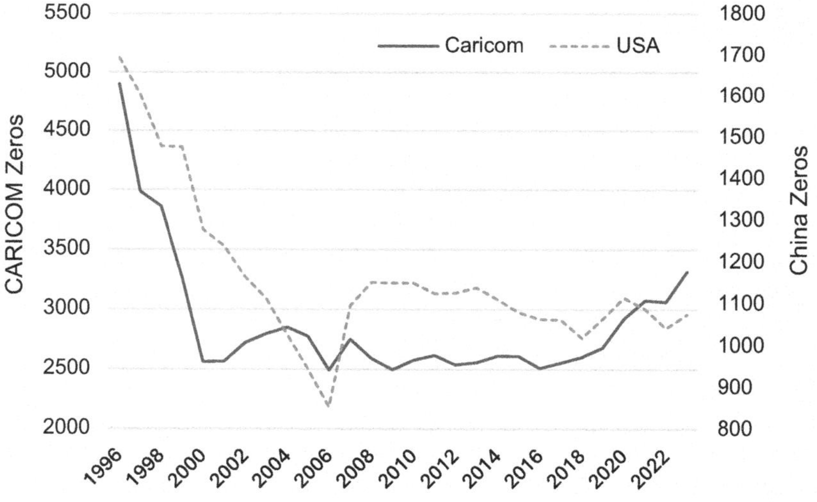

Fig. 8.2 Number of Zeros for traded sectors between the USA and Selected Trade Partners (1996–2023) (Source: WITS)

The ESI-type measures also do not distinguish between the major and minor export products of the countries examined, as the methodologies favour the similarity of export structures. This bias towards similarity can be illustrated by considering that the export of electronics, a major export product for China, is a minor export product for CARICOM and, as such, cannot be analysed using the ESI-type measures. Another shortcoming of these traditional measures is that their results provide one estimate of export similarity between two countries and not the direction of the export threat. Due to the nature of the formulas applied, the estimate of traditional measures implies that country A's export threat to country B in a third market is the same as country B's export threat to country A.

8.4.2 RCA

The RCA, is calculated using the Balassa index ranges and from 0 to $infinity$. Scores below 1 indicate that the commodity is at a comparative disadvantage whilst scores above 1 indicate a situation of comparative advantage. Hinloopen and Van Marrewijk (2001) divided the theoretical range into four classes.

Class A $0 < BalassaIndex \leq 0$ industries with comparative disadvantage (a).

Class B $1 < BalassaIndex \leq 2$ industries with weak comparative advantage (b).

Class C $2 < BalassaIndex \leq 4$ industries with medium comparative advantage (c).

Class D $4 < BalassaIndex$ industries with strong comparative advantage (d).

This section follows Proudman and Redding (2000) and Brasilia et al. (2000) and calculates the transition probability matrix using the abovementioned classes. Table 8.6 shows the transition probability matrices (TPM) for China, USA, Trinidad and Tobago, Jamaica, Guyana, and Suriname for 2000–2022 and 2021, where 2022 data is unavailable. The TPM deployed shows the probability of moving among the different classes of a to d between 2000 and 2022. Regarding China, the first transition probability matrix (TPM) shows the probability of a firm or sector starting in a state of comparative disadvantage in 2000 and remaining in that state in 2022 was 0.77. For the USA, the corresponding number was 0.86, but for TT it was 0.96. For China, the probability that a sector between 2000 and 2022 moved from a state of weak comparative disadvantage to a state of comparative advantage was 0.21. The corresponding probability for the USA was 0.12, but for TT, it was a paltry 0.02. For China, the probability of a sector starting in a state of comparative disadvantage in 2000 and moving to a state of moderate comparative advantage by 2022 was 0.02, with the corresponding number for the USA being 0.01 and for TT, 0.

A careful look at the transition probability matrices above shows that the sum of the leading diagonal for Trinidad and Tobago in the transition probability matrix by far supersedes that of the USA and China, indicating that the TT export structure between 2000 and 2021 was much more persistent than the export structure of China and the USA.

Also, the structure of RCA between China and T&T in the US market should be considered (Fig. 8.3). The correlation score is – 0.09, implying no similarity in the export structure between China and T&T in the US market. For Jamaica, Guyana, and Suriname, note that there is a tendency over time for exports to lose comparative advantage. This indicates that policymakers in these economies must invest in building sustainable export capacity.

8.4.3 *Correlation*

For two countries A and B, both of which export to C, one commonly used method for assessing the competitive threat of A–B is to estimate the correlation between the export structures in C's market of country A and country B. A similar approach was adopted by Shafaeddin (2004), Lederman et al. (2007) and IDB (2006). Shafaeddin (2004) concluded that there is some competition for manufactured goods between China and South Asian countries, as well as Latin American and African economies.

Table 8.7 shows the correlation between China's revealed comparative advantage with the world using two-digit SITC data and that of Trinidad and Tobago, Jamaica, Guyana, and Suriname with the world in 2023. The correlations are very low. This indicates that CARICOM economies generally have different export structures from China with the global economy, which was also partly reflected in the export similarity index calculated above.

Table 8.6 Transition probability matrices for selected economies' trade with the World 2000–2022

From	To a	b	c	d
China to World 2000–2022				
a	0.77	0.21	0.02	–
b	0.35	0.49	0.16	–
c	0.32	0.32	0.37	–
d	0.10	0.25	0.65	–
USA to World 2000–2022				
a	0.86	0.12	0.01	0.01
b	0.38	0.54	0.08	–
c	0.21	0.47	0.26	0.05
d	0.33	–	0.67	–
T&T to World 2000–2021				
a	0.96	0.02	0.00	0.00
b	0.50	0.38	0.13	–
c	0.17	0.50	0.33	–
d	0.25	0.17	0.08	0.50
Jamaica to World 2000–2021				
a	0.88	0.02	0.02	0.03
b	0.50	0.25	0.13	0.13
c	0.40	–	0.20	0.40
d	0.29	–	0.07	0.57
Guyana to World 2000–2022				
a	0.88	–	–	0.01
b	0.83	0.17	–	–
c	0.50	–	–	0.50
d	0.31	0.15	0.38	0.15
Suriname to World 2000–2022				
a	0.81	0.03	0.01	0.01
b	0.83	–	0.17	–
c	0.50	–	–	0.50
d	0.50	–	–	0.50

Source: author calculated

8.4.4 *SICT (Static Index Competitive Threat) and DICT (Dynamic Index of Competitive Threat)*

One problem associated with the correlation between the RCA of a very diversified economy such as China and a small Caribbean exporter is that many of these small Caribbean countries (using, say, 5-digit SITC data)

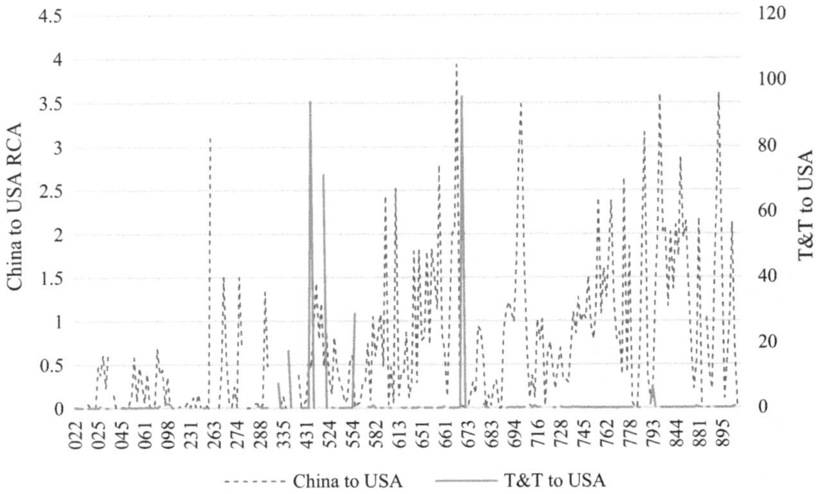

Fig. 8.3 RCA Scores for China and T&T Exports to the USA, 2021 (Source: author calculated)

Table 8.7 Correlation between China's RCA with the world and the RCA of the listed economy with the world, 2023

TT (2022)	*Jamaica*	*Guyana*	*Suriname*
− 0.044	− 0.122	0.020	− 0.212

Source: author calculations

would have a higher number of zeros than China, so the correlation between RCA_{China} and a CARICOM member state is likely to be low.

Additionally, the correlation approach also does not help to identify where the threat comes from, but rather, is just a generalized number that gives an idea of the similarity in export strength, by sector. To assess the level of competitive threat, this is insufficient. In this section, we follow Jenkins (2008) and identify that the extent of the threat faced by a country, i, from China depends on the proportion of the country's exports that is accounted for by goods in which China is internationally competitive. If country A has a high proportion of its exports in products for which China has a comparative advantage, then the exports of these products are threatened by Chinese exports of the same, even if the products under consideration account for a small share of China's total exports. The greater the share of a country's exports which are made up of such products, then the greater the threat from China.

In this regard, following Jenkins (2008) the index of competitive threat SICT can be defined as:

$$SICT = 100 \sum_{i=1}^{n} ix_i$$

where i = 1 ... n and refers to the n products which country A exports to market k and in which China has a comparative advantage.

The steps involved in calculating this SICT:

1. Calculate the RCA of China for year t for each of the goods exported by China to the USA.
2. For country A, we then take the sum of shares of all of its export goods to the USA, in which China has an RCA>1. This number represents the proportion of country A's exports under possible competitive threat from China.

A careful observation of the SICT would show that it can increase in value because the number of products under competition from China increases (extensive margin) and because China further penetrates existing product markets (intensive margin). An assessment of the formula would show that SICT → 0 as both countries develop more dissimilar export structures and towards unity if China's exports to the USA, the same commodities as CARICOM. SICT is also unity if China fully exports all US market requirements. In such a scenario, there will not be any exports by CARICOM (or any other country) to the USA.

Table 8.8 shows the top 25 sectors of CARICOM under threat, given China's increasing presence in the USA's market. This analysis can help regional policymakers better target interventions to specific sectors to maintain export share relative to competitors.

8.4.5 DICT Index

Jenkins (2008) also proposed a dynamic index of competitive threat (DICT). The DICT is calculated by summing the share of CARICOM's

Table 8.8 Top 25 CARICOM export commodities under competitive threat from China in the US market, 2000, 2019, 2021

Total		*0.182115*			*0.014125*			*0.309957254*
Product code	*rcachn2000*	*sictcar2000*	*Product code*	*rcachn2019*	*sictcar2019*	*Product code*	*rcachn2021*	*sictcar2021*
034	1.579	0.006	581	1.040	0.000	001	3.930	0.000
058	1.819	0.001	635	2.040	0.001	012	3.610	0.000
278	5.277	0.004	642	2.052	0.001	017	3.600	0.000
291	9.454	0.000	658	3.047	0.000	022	3.480	0.001
522	1.193	0.107	692	1.200	0.000	024	3.160	0.004
541	2.366	0.000	695	1.759	0.001	025	3.100	0.000
635	2.037	0.000	699	1.476	0.000	034	2.910	0.004
642	1.193	0.002	743	1.085	0.000441	035	2.860	0.001
658	3.421	0.000	745	1.117	0.000	036	2.790	0.003
692	1.026	0.000	759	1.646	0.000	037	2.640	0.002
695	1.993	0.002	764	2.797	0.002	042	2.520	0.001
697	4.392	0.000	786	2.478	0.001	043	2.440	0.000
699	1.898	0.000	813	3.623	0.001	045	2.420	0.000
751	3.048	0.000	821	2.331	0.000	046	2.410	0.000
764	1.039	0.000	831	2.294	0.000	047	2.380	0.000
778	1.194	0.001	841	1.397	0.000	048	2.180	0.002
813	7.623	0.001	842	2.210	0.001	054	2.140	0.003
841	1.338	0.005	845	1.937	0.001	056	2.120	0.000
842	1.942	0.001	851	2.571	0.000	057	2.100	0.000
845	2.097	0.017	881	2.027	0.000	058	2.080	0.003
846	1.705	0.029	892	1.778	0.000	059	2.060	0.004
881	1.781	0.000	893	2.520	0.000	061	2.060	0.007
885	3.552	0.001	894	3.771	0.000	062	2.030	0.000

Total		*0.182115*			*0.014125*			*0.309957254*
Product code	*rcachn2000*	*sictcar2000*	*Product code*	*rcachn2019*	*sictcar2019*	*Product code*	*rcachn2021*	*sictcar2021*
893	4.382	0.000	898	1.110	0.000	071	2.030	0.001
899	5.946	0.000	899	1.860	0.001	072	2.020	0.001

Source: WITS and author calculations
rcachn—RCA China exports to USA
sictcar—Static Index of Competitive Threat CARICOM exports to USA

exports, which China's exports grew faster than world exports to the partner country market over the review period. Regarding the empirical results, in 2000, 1.44% of T&T's exports were under a static competitive threat in the US market, relative to China, although this declined to 0.3%. For Barbados, the associated trend is that the SICT declined from 28.9% in 2000 to 10.7% in 2020. Similar trends are observed for Guyana, Jamaica, St Lucia, and Suriname. Regarding the DICT, this also declined from 2000 to 2020 for all the listed CARICOM economies. The DICT estimates are higher than those of the SICT for some economies, indicating that China's dynamic threat is more significant than the competitive threat of the exports in which it specializes in the USA market (Table 8.9).

8.4.6 *TradeCAN*

The Trade Competitiveness Analysis of Nations (TradeCAN) tool was developed by UNECLAC and assesses whether sectors/commodities are missed opportunities, retreats, rising star, or declining star sectors. This tool maps a country's existing export sectors to specific markets to show the relationship between changes in the trade partner's demand level for certain sectors/commodities and the home country's responses. The four categories of competitiveness can be represented using the matrix in Fig. 8.4.

A declining star is a sector in which a country's export share is falling but international demand is rising. A retreat is a sector in which both international demand and export share are falling.

A missed opportunity is one in which international demand is rising but export share is falling, and a rising star is a sector in which export share is rising and international demand is rising.

Considering the market share ratio, we can observe that over the period 2000–2022, at the triple digit Standard International Trade Classification (SITC) level, 33 sectors were considered as rising stars, and 10 missed opportunities; these 43 sectors are considered as dynamic as these are sectors for which demand by the importing countries, in this case, China, is rising. Stagnating sectors refer to those for which Chinese demand is declining and include the categories of declining star sectors and retreats, totalling 66 sectors. Over the period 2000–2022, for CARICOM, there are more stagnating sectors in the Chinese market than dynamic ones (Table 8.10).

Table 8.9 SITC and DICT of CARICOM with China in the US market, 2000–2022

	Barbados	*Guyana*	*Jamaica*	*St Lucia*	*Suriname*	*T&T*
SICT for Selected CARICOM members and China in the US market						
2000	28.92	10.63	44.65	86.95	54.53	1.44
2005	14.95	5.03	4.65	17.91	2.28	0.23
2010	7.21	3.20	2.21	71.39	4.30	0.11
2015	29.61	2.65	3.44	46.66	16.09	0.23
2016	3.19	2.51	3.87	38.56	37.43	0.32
2017	7.25	2.46	2.99	68.36	37.29	0.28
2018	7.86	3.71	2.98	55.58	30.38	0.22
2019	9.48	6.30	2.97	35.31	29.52	0.26
2020	10.65	2.37	3.02	47.84	14.19	0.26
2021	0.20	5.32	23.33	–	0.18	0.91
2022				–		
DICT for Selected CARICOM members and China in the US market						
2000	0.42	12.89	54.61	0.11	0.06	34.62
2005	0.31	3.85	28.53	0.06	0.07	58.90
2010	0.44	6.98	34.79	0.29	0.62	43.18
2015	0.57	5.87	26.34	0.36	0.14	87.74
2016	–	5.91	34.05	–	–	45.57
2017	0.43	8.90	27.07	0.33	0.14	37.84
2018	0.28	5.91	20.61	0.38	0.02	33.09
2019	0.59	4.64	25.54	0.24	0.21	24.01
2020	0.29	6.40	31.76	0.14	0.24	21.49
2021	0.59	5.11	22.96	–	0.25	28.01
2022	0.29	7.62	–	–	0.77	–

Source: author calculated

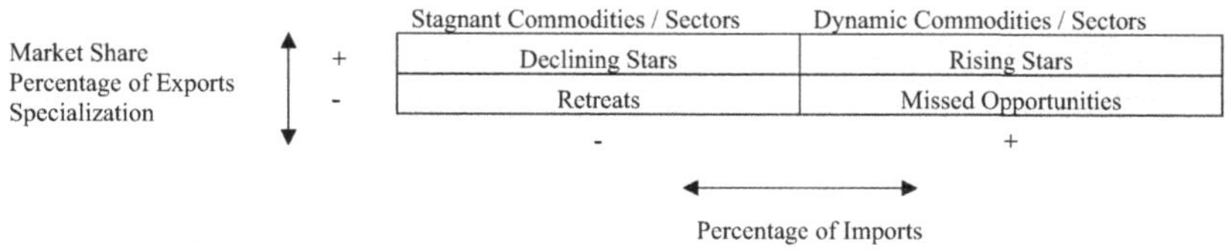

Fig. 8.4 Competitiveness Matrix

Table 8.10 TradeCAN Categories for CARICOM exports to China 2000–2022

Rising star	*Declining star*	*Missed opportunity*	*Retreat*
33	43	10	23

Source: author calculations

Consider Table 8.11 which shows the missed opportunity sectors for CARICOM in the Chinese market for the period 2000–2022; these sectors include live animals, crustaceans, alcoholic beverages as well as aluminium ores.

Even so, the International Trade Centre,[3] which provides a range of analytical resources for businesses to support the development of trade relations globally, shows that there is extensive unrealized export potential in the Caribbean and the Chinese market. Consider Table 8.12, which shows the main sectors that comprise the commodities identified in Table 8.11.

A second way to calculate a DICT-type index is deployed in the business literature using market shares, and this measure is also drawn on in this study (Lall & Albaladejo, 2004). There are five permutations based on world market shares:

(a) partial threat
(b) no threat

Table 8.11 Missed opportunity sectors for CARICOM in the Chinese market 2000–2022

Live animals except fish
Crustaceans molluscs etc
Alcoholic beverages
Aluminium ores/concs/etc
Pearls/precious stones
Women/girl clothing wven
Headgear/non-text clothg
Footwear
Medical/etc instruments

Source: author calculations

Table 8.12 Caribbean export potential in the Chinese Market

	Export potential US$mn	*Actual exports US$mn*	*Unrealized potential US$mn*
Animals and animals products	4.9	0.145	4.755
Fish and shellfish	127	41	86
Beverages	17	3	14
Mineral primary products	911	162	749
Textiles	11	4.5	6.5
Machinery and electronic equipment	24	4.6	19.4

Source: ITC, Export Potential Map

(c) direct threat
(d) China under threat and
(e) mutual withdrawal.

A partial threat in the context of the discussion herein occurs when both China and the CARICOM country experience increased market shares, but China's market share grows faster than that of the indicated CARICOM member state. In this type of setting, there is the possibility that the growth of China is stifling the growth of CARICOM economies. However, this threat is classified as partial, as China's export growth can also be complementing the growth of CARICOM export products. China's export growth in commodity X may facilitate the USA, for example, building scale in a particular sector and purchasing even more of commodity X, from say, the CARICOM.

No threat: Both China's market share and that of the listed CARICOM member state grow, but the growth of the CARICOM member state increases even faster, so that the growth of China is not a threat. Indeed, it is possible that the growth of China can spur the growth of CARICOM economies. A direct threat is where China increases market share and CARICOM economies lose market share. China under threat: It is possible that China can be under threat as it loses market share and the CARICOM member state gain market share. Mutual Withdrawal: The

Table 8.13 Share of exports under threat from China Exports in the US Market (%)

Country	*Partial threat*	*No threat*	*Direct threat*	*China under threat*	*Mutual with-drawal*
TTO	15.5	0.3	36.0	1.5	0.2
BAR	0.9	22.3	5.5	13.6	0.8
GUY	0.0	0.3	12.7	1.9	5.1
JAM	0.7	3.4	9.6	0.2	2.8
STL	44.7	37.2	3.1	7.8	0.5
SUR	0.0	17.6	1.1	31.5	5.0

Source: author calculated

final permutation is that both China and CARICOM lose market share at the same time.

Table 8.13 shows the different levels of "threat" calculated for various CARICOM countries for the year 2020. Of concern to policymakers are the categories of partial threat and direct threat. 15.5% of T&T's exports to the USA are under partial threat by China, while a further 36.0% are under direct threat. This is not trivial and shows that T&T has to pay particular attention to the growing presence of the Chinese in its main export market. For Guyana, there is the direct threat of China in the USA's market for 12.7% of its exports. The corresponding direct threat number for Jamaica was 9.6%. 44.7% of St. Lucia's exports are under partial threat from China. Surprisingly, 31.5% of the exports from Suriname to the USA are such that China is under threat as the threat for all other listed CARICOM economies is much less (Table 8.13).

8.4.7 *Understanding the Displacement of CARICOM's Exports*

China's displacement of CARICOM's exports in its top three destinations is ascribable to decreasing competition at the product level through the application of an extension of the Constant Market Share (CMS) analysis. The CMS analysis here is an extension as applied by (Batista, 2008) and (Jenkins & Edwards), attributes the increase/decrease of an exporter's market share over time to its competitors in a zero-sum game.

The analysis applied by Batista (2008) and Jenkins and Edwards (2015) allows for the estimation of CARICOM's market share loss to

China is derived as follows:

$$k^t_{CARICOM} \equiv X^t_{CARICOM}/X^t_K$$

$k^t_{CARICOM}$ represents CARICOM's export share in partner market K, with $X^t_{CARICOM}$ representing CARICOM's exports at base year t and X^t is the world exports to the partner market K at base year t.

The CMS methodology attributes a country's export share gain or loss to various competitors in a zero-sum game. Here, the relative growth rates of exports of the home country and its competitor in the partner market are at the core of the methodology in estimating the market share gain/loss from/to a competitor in the partner market K. CARICOM's change in market share $\Delta k_{CARICOM}$, between the base year t and final year t + 1 of CARICOM.

The loss of market share by CARICOM to China with respect to product i can be determined by the formulation below:

$$\Delta k_{CARICOMi,CHINAi} = \Delta k_{CARICOMi} * k^t_{CHINAi} - \Delta k_{CHINAi} * k^t_{CARICOMi}$$

The aggregate loss of CARICOM's market share to China is illustrated by summing over all products:

$$\Delta k_{CARICOM,CHINA} = \sum x^t_K * \Delta k_{\mathrm{CARICOMi,CHINAi}}$$

where x^t_K is the share of product i in world exports to partner market k.

Following this approach and using data for the periods 2000 and 2019, we find that CARICOM did not lose a significant amount of market share in the USA. This should surprise no one, given the low degree of correlation between China's export structure and CARICOM's and the low level of export similarity. The region's major exports centered around unsophisticated products and energy commodities whilst China's major exports diversified into sophisticated manufactured exports. The commodities in which CARICOM lost the largest market share in the USA are listed in Table 8.14.

Table 8.14 CARICOM commodities losing market share to the USA 2000–2019

Sorted	*– 0.0173* *Change Kcar* ktch*	*0.058792* *Change Kch* ktcar*	*– 0.0753* *Change KHCI*
846	– 0.0041	0.0266	– 0.0307
285	– 0.0001	0.0101	– 0.0102
512	– 0.0018	0.0072	– 0.0090
522	– 0.0034	0.0055	– 0.0089
059	– 0.0019	0.0008	– 0.0027
278	– 0.0046	– 0.0021	– 0.0025
844	– 0.0001	0.0015	– 0.0015
845	– 0.0004	0.0010	– 0.0015
075	– 0.0004	0.0009	– 0.0014
036	– 0.0008	0.0005	– 0.0013
676	– 0.0005	0.0006	– 0.0011
291	– 0.0015	– 0.0005	– 0.0010
034	– 0.0002	0.0003	– 0.0005
642	0.0000	0.0004	– 0.0005
695	– 0.0001	0.0003	– 0.0004
554	0.0000	0.0004	– 0.0004
334	– 0.0001	0.0003	– 0.0004
841	– 0.0001	0.0003	– 0.0004
813	– 0.0002	0.0002	– 0.0004
098	– 0.0001	0.0003	– 0.0004
692	– 0.0001	0.0003	– 0.0004
122	– 0.0005	– 0.0001	– 0.0004
634	0.0000	0.0003	– 0.0004
772	– 0.0001	0.0003	– 0.0003
843	0.0000	0.0003	– 0.0003

Source: author calculated

8.5 Conclusion

This chapter reflected on the impact of China's rapid growth and its emergence as an engine of growth in the global sphere. Indeed, China is now the second-largest economy in the world and is projected to continue to grow. This growth will undoubtedly have a competitive impact on developed and developing economies alike, such as those in the CARICOM region.

Indeed, China's comparative advantage poses a competitive threat to CARICOM exports, especially in the US market, where CARICOM's share remains minimal compared to China's growing presence. As the region navigates global integration, policymakers must appreciate China's existing and potential competitive threat to CARICOM merchandise exports. CARICOM countries must identify and harness their export strengths to maintain market relevance. Enhanced collaboration among CARICOM states could lead to strategic responses to China's competitive pressure. Policymakers are encouraged to focus on sectors with untapped export potential to better position themselves against external competition. Adapting to these evolving trade dynamics will be crucial for CARICOM's economic sustainability and growth in the global marketplace.

Notes

1. Lall and Weis (2005) concluded that "The direct threat to exports to third country markets appear small; Latin America and the Caribbean's (LAC's) trade structure is highly complementary to that of China (p. 163).
2. https://itif.org/publications/2020/08/31/competing-china-strategic-framework.
3. https://www.intracen.org/.

CHAPTER 9

Considering the Chinese Yuan (Renmimbi) as a Global Reserve Currency: Implications for the CARICOM Region

9.1 Introduction: Setting the Context

China (as with the USA in 1945) has emerged, since 2008, as a more entrenched giant player in the global economy and indeed, is the world's second-largest economy, and its economic significance continues to grow and is expected to remain this way in the medium to long term (Cerdeiro & Jain-Chandra, 2023[1]; Pettis, 2023[2]; Lau, 2023[3]). With a large and rapidly expanding GDP, strong trade relationships, and significant foreign exchange reserves, China's economic size and growth make the yuan an attractive currency for international use. As China's economic influence expands, the yuan's prominence as a reserve currency could increase (Haque, 2023[4]; Llu, 2022[5]).

Indeed, there is evidence that shows that the Chinese government has been actively working to internationalize the yuan and enhance its role in global finance (Chen & Westbrook, 2023[6]; Zhang & Tao, 2014[7]; Huang & Lynch, 2013[8]). This includes initiatives such as promoting the use of the yuan in international trade settlements and increasing its convertibility. These efforts demonstrate China's commitment to opening its financial markets and making the yuan more accessible for international transactions, which can boost its attractiveness as a reserve currency.

Kun and Hao (2023)[9] reflected that the yuan has been increasingly used as a settlement for trade since 2015 due to the institutionalization

R. Hosein et al., *China in the Caribbean*,
https://doi.org/10.1007/978-3-031-71985-1_9

of new trade models to accelerate and promote the yuan's internationalization. In the first instance, China has signed agreements with several countries to settle payments in the yuan. Consider, for example, that in March 2023, China and Brazil agreed to use their currency instead of the US dollar for trade. Similar agreements were signed with Russia, Venezuela, UAE, Oman, Bahrain, Qatar, Kuwait, and Saudi Arabia from 2016 to 2022. By 2024, in addition, to the more than 40 currency swap agreements, the People's Bank of China has authorized 31 yuan clearing banks in 29 countries and regions to support trade settlement.

This process of cross-border trade settlement in yuan is institutionally guaranteed with the requisite infrastructure and technology support provided by the Chinese government. In 2015, China launched the Cross-Border Interbank Payments System (CIPS) as a strategy to build a stable financial infrastructure and service platform for settlement in yuan. This can encourage the increased usage of the yuan as a medium of exchange for trade. As of the end of February 2023, CIPS had 1366 participants: 79 direct and 1287 indirect participants, from 109 countries and regions (Friesen, 2023[10]; IMF, 2023[11]).

There is considerable work to be done, but the point is that the current global geopolitical situation creates the right environment for the yuan to make further progress as a reserve currency.

The current global reserve system is heavily reliant on the USA, which can create risks for countries in times of economic or geopolitical volatility. As the global economy becomes more multipolar, there is a growing desire among some countries (Russia, China, Iran, Afghanistan, Brazil, South Africa,, and others) to diversify their reserve holdings and reduce dependence on a single dominant currency (Papa, 2023[12]; Zakaria, 2023[13]; Sullivan, 2023[14]; Patrick, 2024[15]). The yuan, as an alternative reserve currency, can offer diversification benefits and help mitigate risks associated with concentrated exposure to one currency. This potential for risk mitigation and portfolio diversification could contribute to the yuan's adoption as a reserve currency.

The authors acknowledged that the process of becoming a widely accessed currency is complex and can take time and some of this was witnessed with the switchover from the pound to the US dollar, as well. The yuan's path to becoming an important reserve currency will depend on factors such as China's continued economic growth and acceptance by other countries. Of course, while the yuan has the potential to play a more significant role in the future, the US dollar's position as the dominant reserve currency is likely to remain for the foreseeable future, but the proportions will likely change.

9.2 Evolution of Global Reserve Currencies

The first known dominant currency was the Assignat, issued by the National Assembly of France issued during the French Revolution. This form of paper currency held this position from 1789 to 1815, when it was succeeded by the British pound (Holt et al., 1919).[16] Daudin et al. (2021) provide some details of Britain's strength relative to other European empires; consider that in 1790, Britain's trade was estimated to be 49% of total world trade (See Table 9.1).

The British pound ascended to its stature between the mid-1800s to around WWI because Great Britain's prominence in world trade led to demand for Great Britain's goods worldwide. Great Britain became one of the largest exporters in the world, such that in 1870, the nation was responsible for 20% of world exports (Keller et al., 2020[17]) as shown in Table 9.2.

This dominance continued even as other nations started reaping the benefits of industrialization but slowly dwindled after 1890 (Steinsson, 2022).[18] Coinciding with Great Britain's dominance of commodity trade during this period was its dominance in capital exports to the rest of the world (Holt et al., 1919). This was done as Great Britain sought to develop potential suppliers of raw materials that were vital to the nation's industrial survival (Karlstroem, 1967). This resulted in a net export of nearly £4000 mn between the period 1848–1913 (Karlstroem, 1967). At the time, most transactions were undertaken using the British Pound as it was pegged to gold. When WWI broke out in 1914, countries began to suspend their dependence on the gold standard as military expenses increased (Congressional Research Service, 2022).[19] Note that most of the cotton for example which was a necessary raw material in the production of textiles, was sourced for the American South in the 1860s; with the disruptions caused by the Civil War, cotton was sourced from Egypt and India as the mills required steady cotton supplies. Straussman et al. (2016) showed that during this period, Great Britain's strength as an exporter of cotton and textiles increased significantly (See Table 9.3).

The UK maintained its gold standard during this period but soon began to borrow to fund its involvement in the war. By 1931, the UK

Table 9.1 European trade 1790 (£mn)

	Imports		*Exports*		*Re Exports*		*Total*	*Share ROW*
	From Europe	*From ROW*	*Towards Europe*	*Towards ROW*	*Towards Europe*	*Towards ROW*		
Britain (1784–86) (Including Trade with Ireland)	11.3	11.5	6.3	7.3	2.8		40	49
France (1787)	12.8	11.7	9.7	5.3	6.0		45.9	38
Netherlands (using 1770 trade composition)	9.3	3.6	8.3 (incl re-exports)	0.7 (incl re-exports)	3.8 (colonial goods) 2.4 (European goods)		21.9	20
Spain (1788–92) ROW: America	3.6	2.0	3.5	1.9	1.4	2.2	19	36
Portugal (1796–1800) ROW: Brazil	4.1	2.9	1.4	1.3	3.9	1.4	15.3	35

Source: Daudin et al. (2021)

Table 9.2 Openness and Trade Growth for Selected Economies 1700–1870

Region (example)	*Openness 1700*	*Openness 1760*	*Openness 1820*	*Openness 1870*	*Trade Growth 1700–60 (%)*	*Trade Growth 1760–1820 (%)*	*Trade Growth 1820–1870 (%)*	*Share of world exports in 1870 (%)*
UK	8	15	8	19	1.5	1.8	4.9	19.5
Continental Europe (France)			5	12	2.3 (1717–1780)	− 2.1 (1787–1821)	4.6	44.4 (France 11.2%)
Japan				3			14.3 (1860–70)	0.3
India				7	(0.2) (EIC) (− 2.2) (Surat)	(2) (EIC)	3.8	5.5
China			0 (1840)	1			1.8 (1830–70)	2.1
Southeast Asia (Dutch East Indies)			(1)	(5)		(2.6)	4.8 (1822–1870)	2.1 (Dutch East Indies: 0.9%)
Ottoman Empire	< 2	< 2	2	6			4.3	1.7
Latin America (Mexico)			(8)	(12)		(0.6)	2.2	Latin America and Caribbean: 9% (Mexico 0.6%, Brazil 1.9%)

(continued)

Table 9.2 (continued)

Region (example)	*Openness 1700*	*Openness 1760*	*Openness 1820*	*Openness 1870*	*Trade Growth 1700–60 (%)*	*Trade Growth 1760–1820 (%)*	*Trade Growth 1820–1870 (%)*	*Share of world exports in 1870 (%)*
Latin America (Brazil)								
Africa (Nigeria)				Africa: 16)			3.2	3.1 (Nigeria: 0.1%)
Africa (Slave Trade)	0.3	0.7 (1790)	0.3	0	0.8		– 100	n/a
Australia			7 (1826)	21			10.7	1,6
USA	(9 Mid-Atlantic/ 24 Lower South, 17,202)	(9 Mid-Atlantic/ 22 Lower South 1770)	6	5	3.7% Mid-Atlantic/ 4.3% Lower South 1720–70)	2% (USA 1790–1820)	4.3	8.4

Notes: Openness = Exports/Gross Domestic Product in current prices (if in parenthesis, data refers to estimates in constant prices). Trade growth per year is measured in constant prices. The share of world exports is measured in current prices and refers to 1913 borders. Data for 1820

Source: Keller et al. (2020)

Table 9.3 Britain's cotton consumption and exports mn 1760–1826

	Raw cotton consumption in Great Britain	*Exports of cotton textiles from Great Britain*
1760–1769	£3.5	£227
1820–1829	£1665.5	£25,605
	British imports of cotton piece goods from India	British exports of cotton from textiles
1772–1774	£697	£221
1824–1826	£363	£17,375

Source: Straussman et al. (2016)

had no choice but to abandon the gold standard. The USA became the global lender of choice as the USA by that time had amassed significant gold reserves; the pound sterling was replaced by the dollar as a leading international reserve currency (Costigan et al., 2017).[20]

Considering Great Britain's key position during this period, many nations that imported from Britain began storing reserves of the pound that would eventually be utilized through imports from Great Britain. Brezis (1995, pp. 6, 8) noted, "There is evidence of substantial inflows of capital from foreign countries to Britain, in particular from Holland, the latter investment being used to finance both private assets and the British government debt." Some of these transactions included Dutch investment in the East India Company stood at £10 million in 1770, and by 1791, one-sixth of the stock of the Bank of England was held by the Dutch. In 1773, Britain borrowed £1 million sterling to fund sugar production plantations in the British West Indies. Dutch investment in British debt in 1737 stood at £10 million, which increased to £30 million by 1762 and £46.6 million by 1774 (See Table 9.4).

This practice continued several years after WWI in 1918, and the emergence of the Great Depression in 1929 led to a decline in the pound's dominance (Pettinger, 2017). During the decades of the 1920 s and 1930 s, as shown in Fig. 9.1, the UK was plagued by unemployment, which rose sharply (by 10%), and deflation, despite efforts to devalue the pound to pre-war levels (Pettinger, 2017).

The British pound remained a dominant global currency until the early twentieth century, and it maintained the gold standard. Dawnay (2001)[21] noted that the economic conditions in the UK during the WWI period and immediately after, resulted in some unrest, such as labour strikes,

Table 9.4 The British balance of payments 1711–1900 (decade averages £m p.a)

	Trade and services	*Transfers*	*Current account, net of debt service*	*Debt service*	*Current account*	*Increase in foreign reserves*	*Inflow of capital*	*Balance of foreign debts*
1711–20	0.18	0.11	0.29	– 0.10	0.19	0.46	0.27	4.70
1721–30	– 0.85		– 0.85	– 0.23	– 1.08	0.18	1.26	17.33
1731–40	– 0.72	0.02	– 0.70	– 0.78	– 1.48	0.08	1.56	32.91
1741–50	1.52	0.14	1.66	– 1.48	0.18	0.04	– 0.14	31.57
1751–60	2.20		2.20	– 1.42	0.78	0.10	– 0.68	24.81
1761–70	0.42	– 1.00	– 0.58	– 1.12	– 1.70	0.02	1.72	42.00
1771–80	0.24		0.24	– 1.89	– 1.65	1.70	3.35	75.45
1781–90	– 1.50	2.00	0.50	– 1.89	– 1.39	1.41	2.80	103.40
1791–1800 (a)	– 2.55	0.00	– 2.55	– 2.58	– 5.13	1.28	6.41	167.50
1791–1800 (b)	– 2.55	15	12.45	– 2.58	9.87	1.28	– 8.59	– 17.54
1801–15								– 10.00
1816–20	7.44	– 0.36	7.08	1.74	8.82	1.60	– 7.22	– 46.10
1821–30	3.52	– 0.37	3.15	4.43	7.58	1.11	– 6.47	– 110.76
1831–40	– 1.92	– 1.04	– 2.96	6.65	3.69	0.78	– 4.47	– 155.41
1841–50	– 1.70	– 2.15	– 3.85	8.49	4.64	0.66	– 5.30	– 208.36
1851–60	8.30	– 2.21	6.09	14.11	20.20	3.11	– 17.09	– 379.23
1861–70	12.15	– 1.58	10.57	26.17	36.74	5.61	– 31.13	– 690–49
1871–80	0.58	– 1.41	– 0.83	53.17	52.34	2.62	– 49.72	– 1187.67

	Trade and services	*Transfers*	*Current account, net of debt service*	*Debt service*	*Current account*	*Increase in foreign reserves*	*Inflow of capital*	*Balance of foreign debts*
1881–90	2.50	– 1.73	0.77	74.47	75.24	0.66	– 74.58	– 1933.44
1891–1900	– 44.11	– 0.74	– 44.85	96.48	51.63	5.15	– 46.48	– 2398.22

Source: Karlstroem (1967)

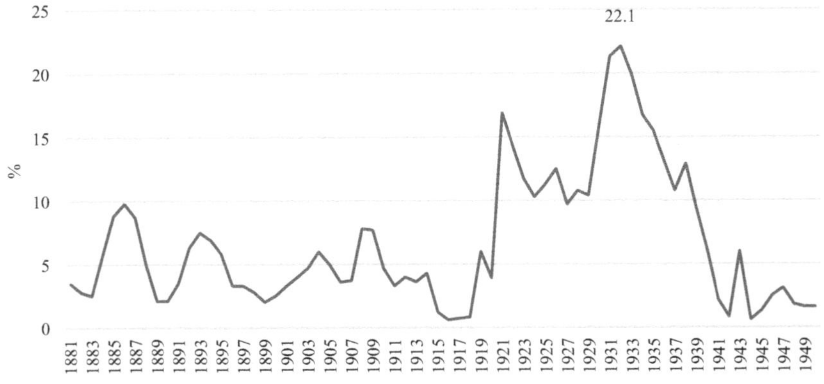

Fig. 9.1 Annual Average Unemployment in the UK (Source: Pettinger (2017))

which culminated in a run on sterling in 1931, which effectively ended the Gold Standard. The next few years saw a breakdown of the standard globally (1930–1933) as countries began to focus on rebuilding their economies in the post-war era. Protectionism increased and trade declined. The strength of the pound sterling subsequently declined and was replaced by the US dollar (Karlstroem, 1967), which was increasingly demanded as a global currency, as shown in Table 9.5.[22]

Regarding gold holdings, the USA has held more of the world's gold supply than the UK since 1913, 27% of the total world supply compared to 4% held by the UK. Gold holdings continued to grow; by 1945, the USA had 63% of the world total, while the UK held a mere 5%.[23] This switch from the British pound to the US dollar as the world's dominant currency after WWII was mainly due to the economic and political conditions prevailing at the time which allowed the US economy to signfiicantly build up its gold reserves relative to Great Britain.

During WWII, the USA supplied weapons and other amenities to the Allies, who paid for such goods in gold. This resulted in the USA amassing extensive reserves. This made returning to the gold standard after the war difficult, as the reserves of many countries were depleted. In 1944, after WWII, delegates from 44 countries met at Bretton Wood, New Hampshire, to develop a system to manage foreign exchange so that no country could be disadvantaged (Ghizoni, 2013[24]). The delegation agreed that the world currencies would no longer be linked to gold but pegged to the US dollar. This is known as the Bretton Woods

Table 9.5 US and UK International Asset Position (end of year) 1913–1965

	1913	*1920*	*1930*	*1940*	*1945*	*1950*	*1960*	*1965*
US Gold holdings	1.3	2.5	4.3	22	20.1	22.8	17.8	14.1
As a % of world total	27	34	39	73	63	68	47	34
Foreign-owned liquid dollar assets	0.4	0.8	2.3	3.9	6.8	7.1	17.3	24.1
US International investment position, net long term	− 3.2	4.0	9.5	3.3	7.8	23.6	50.1	58.0
UK gold holdings	0.2	0.8	0.7	2.8	1.6	2.9	2.8	2.3
As a % of world total	4	11	8	9	5	9	7	7
Foreign-owned liquid sterling assets				8.0	14.0	9.8	10.9	11.8

Source: Karlstroem (1967)

Agreement, which established the authority of central banks globally to maintain the exchange rates between domestic currencies and the US dollar. The Bretton Woods Agreement, therefore, established the US dollar as the official global reserve currency in 1944, replacing the British pound. One of the main reasons for this was the economic dominance of the USA at the time. After WWII, the USA emerged as the world's largest creditor nation, with its industrial and military power relatively unscathed by the war and in the process amassing over two-thirds of the world's gold reserves. In addition, the Bretton Woods Agreement created the International Monetary Fund (IMF) and the World Bank, both of which were headquartered in the USA. This gave the USA a significant role in global economic decision-making, as well as a mechanism to enforce the dominance of the US dollar (Chen, 2024[25]). In 1971 the US ended the convertability of the US$ to gold thereby establishing the US$ as fiat currency and ending the Bretton Woods system.

9.3 Why Did the US Dollar Become the Dominant Currency?

Best (2023)[26] defines an international or global currency as any currency that can be freely used and/or exchanged for another within or outside of the geographical boundaries of the country that issues it. The US dollar is one of the world's strongest currencies and was first printed in 1914, a year after the establishment of the Federal Reserve. The Federal Reserve was created to respond to the unreliability and instability of the existing currency system, where individual banks issued banknotes.[27] The establishment of the Federal Research Bank coincided with the period when the US economy bypassed that of the UK as the largest global economy (See Table 9.6).

The rise of the US dollar is no surprise as the USA at the point in time was one of the world's leading economic and military power (WTO, 2013[28]). Globally, there are over 180 currencies in circulation, but only a few of these currencies play a role in foreign exchange reserves and the finance of international trade.[29] The US dollar has become the main currency in international transactions for various reasons.

The US historically has been one of the largest economies in the world, and the dollar is used in all transactions with the USA (Bertaut, von Beschwitz & Curcuru, 2021).[30] The US dollar is also a stable currency, so investors tend to stock up on US dollars during periods of economic

Table 9.6 GDP per capita in selected wealthy countries, 1870–1930 US$

	Belgium	*Denmark*	*Netherlands*	*New Zealand*	*Switzerland*	*UK*	*USA*
1870	4291	3193	4422	4941	2954	5829	4803
1875	4560	3366	4584	5879	3599	5950	5105
1880	4886	3476	4666	5973	3869	5997	6256
1885	5002	3625	5137	5718	4773	6132	6424
1890	5464	4022	5078	5985	5309	6845	6665
1895	5598	4415	5212	5805	5632	6996	7160
1900	5947	4809	5306	6851	6612	7594	8038
1905	6188	5333	5735	7731	7185	7603	9121
1910	6478	5906	6030	8474	8048	7718	9637
1915	6150	6022	6258	8247	7459	8639	9164
1920	6315	6363	6727	8992	7364	7017	10,153
1925	7438	6978	8019	8435	8385	8199	11,150
1930	7936	8513	8931	7906	9969	8673	10,695

Source: https://world101.cfr.org/historical-context/world-war/how-did-united-states-become-global-power

uncertainty (Lioudis, 2024[31]). In addition, the main US players, such as the US government, the US Central Bank, and the Federal Reserve Bank of the USA, have played a strong role and have a good track record in maintaining the dollar's stability over time.

The US economy also has a political system that is considered stable (Beartaut, Beschwitz, & Curcuru, 2021) and there is a respect for property rights and contracts, which makes the US dollar a stable basis on which to do business. Indeed, this characteristic makes the US dollar attractive to investors from all around the world (Lioudis, 2024).

The USA has a sophisticated and large financial system consisting of a vast network of banks, investment firms, and other financial institutions, each of which can handle complex international transactions (Federal Reserve System Publication, 2021).[32] The sophisticated financial system of the USA makes it relatively easy for people to buy and sell dollars and use these dollars to make payments and investments in and out of the USA.

The USA has a long history of international trade and, for decades, and significantly, since WWII, the dollar has been the premier currency in these transactions (Siripurapu & Berman, 2023).[33] Over this extensive period, the dollar has become widely accepted, and many of the world's

Table 9.7 World currency composition of official Foreign exchange reserves US Dollars, Billions (1999, 2024)

	1999Q1	*2024Q1*
Total Foreign Exchange Reserves	1605.92	12,349.92
Allocated Reserves	1239.41	11,497.44
Claims in U.S. dollars	882.33	6766.77
Claims in euro	–	2262.45
Claims in Chinese renminbi	–	246.94
Claims in Japanese yen	74.77	654.14
Claims in pounds sterling	34.01	562.23
Claims in Australian dollars	–	248.37
Claims in Canadian dollars	–	295.22
Claims in Swiss francs	3.57	22.27
Claims in other currencies	20.12	438.05
Unallocated Reserves	366.50	852.48

Source: Currency Composition of Official Foreign Exchange Reserves (COFER), International Financial Statistics (IFS)

governments and businesspeople rely on the dollar to do their financial transactions. This momentum will be hard to change (Siripurapu & Berman, 2023; Best, 2023[34]).

The USA also has a powerful military and exerts a lot of power in international affairs, and this has helped to reinforce the strength of its currency (Ministry of Foreign Affairs, the People's Republic of China, 2023[35]; Strange, 1971[36]).

According to the available data, the US dollar is by far the most frequently used currency in global trade (Table 9.7).

9.4 Will the Chinese Yuan Challenge the US Dollar as the Dominant Currency in the World?

Some 14 years after the global financial crash of 2008 and the utterances of the then-Chinese Central Bank Governor on how to create a new global currency, the Chinese yuan is still far from that destination.[37] In 2016, the Chinese were able to get their currency included in the IMF special drawing rights. The inclusion of the yuan as a reserve currency reflects China's growing economic importance in the world and its increasing use in international trade and finance. It also represents a significant milestone in China's efforts to increase its currency's global use and acceptance.

Chuluun (2023)[38] reflected on the fact that China has maintained one of the highest levels of growth in the world for more than 25 years and has successfully transitioned over 800 million persons out of poverty over the last few decades. China, is the second-largest economy behind the US economy, and has become the largest exporter in the world and one of the most important trading partners for Japan, Germany, Brazil,, and even Argentina, as well as other countries. Despite this, the yuan lags behind other major international currencies. Still, the shock of the Ukraine-Russia war may have resulted in a change in the tides for the yuan as the dominance of the US dollar began to wane (Thibault 2024).

China has been preparing for the ascent of the yuan since the financial crisis of 2008, with the implementation of the Cross-Border Interbank Payments System (CIPS) in 2015 to support more intense cross-border trade, using the yuan as a medium of exchange (Chen, 2024). In 2018, China launched the world's first yuan dominated crude oil futures, which allowed exporters to sell oil in yuan. For the last decade, China has also become the world's largest creditor, with state-owned enterprises extending loans to several developing economies (Yue & Wang, 2022)[39] As Table 4.13 in Chapter 4 shows, by the end of 2023, Pakistan and Angola were China's largest debtors, with a total debt of US$48 bn (Table 9.8).

China has also been developing one of the world's first central bank digital currencies and has extended the trading hours[40] for the yuan to facilitate greater international involvement. Tran (2022),[41] though, raises the concerns that increasing availability of the digital version of the fiat currency of China, e-CNY, will not necessarily have the impact as intended, given that China's capital market is not as open as other economies, its underdeveloped financial markets and the lack of full convertibility of the yuan; further, foreigners using the e-CNY will have to be monitored by the Chinese which users may be reluctant to accept. Subrahmanyam (2023)[42] notes, "While digital payments are popular in China, the rollout of a national digital currency puts the government in a space designed to thwart central control. e-CNY also is a key part of China's efforts to digitize its domestic economy to, in part, expand state control while also strategically positioning China to influence the global financial system."

China has signed several bilateral currency swap[43] deals with central banks, but these signings were mainly about status and typically had little,

Table 9.8 Debts to China for countries which are a part of the Belt and Road Initiative, 2019, 2020

	Outstanding public external debt to China in 2020 US$mn	*The net change in 2020 compared with 2019 (US$mn)*	*% change in 2020 as compared to 2019*
Guinea	1291	628	94.8
Lesotho	115	43	60.3
Burkina Faso	89	32	55.2
Sierra Leone	63	19	42.9
Rwanda	258	63	32.5
Chad	311	76	32.2
Bangladesh	4572	972	27
Cote d'Ivoire	2944	547	22.8
Uganda	2606	457	21.3
Comoros	93	15	19.7
Nepal	248	33	15.2
Madagascar	155	20	14.7
Malawi	234	29	14.4
Djibouti	1341	146	12.2
Papua New Guinea	944	100	11.9
Mali	637	63	11.1
Zambia	3218	316	10.9
Mongolia	1232	99	8.7
Cambodia	3902	293	8.1
Senegal	1316	90	7.4
Niger	302	− 25	− 7.6
Ghana	1456	− 125	− 9.1
Tanzania	1963	− 208	− 9.6
Congo, Rep	2086	− 279	− 11.8
Central African Republic	26	− 17	− 40.0

Source: Yue and Wang (2022)

even questionable, practical value (IMF, 2023).[44] The IMF (2023) indicated that as of 2022, China had 38 bilateral swap lines outstanding, totaling 4 trillion RMB.

Chuluun (2023)[45] notes that as of June 2023, the yuan was the 5th most traded currency in the world, compared to its 35th place in 2001. This represents an extraordinary progression in global ranking, and it should be noted that the yuan is also the 5th most actively used currency globally for payments as of April 2023, compared to 30th place in 2011. Perez-Saiz and Zhang (2023)[46] acknowledge, "the increasing use of RMB in a country's transaction with China is likely to reduce the sensitivity of its trade volume to the U.S. dollar exchange rate. A wide adoption of RMB may also imply a stronger spillover effect of China's monetary policy." Note, though, that the volume of the yuan's trading remains less than a tenth of that of the US dollar; the actual share of the yuan in global payments is 2.3% compared to 42.7% and 31.7% for the US dollar and the Euro, respectively. The yuan also accounts for less than 3% of the world foreign exchange reserves as of the end of 2022, compared to 58% for the US dollar and 20% for the euro (See Table 9.9).

Although the Chinese economy has been open since 1979, the domestic financial market of the Chinese economy has remained restricted. So the lack of investment opportunities in the financial markets of China has impacted the relative global strength of the yuan. Since 2017, though, there has been an increased pace of financial liberalization. China achieved this by deregulating aspects of the domestic capital markets and encouraged investments in RMB bonds which impacted on global indices (Perez-Saiz & Zhang, 2023). The authors noted that, while China significantly lags behind other major global currencies, "if these trends continue, they will help deepen China's financial integration with the rest of the world and reduce barriers to the global use of RMB" (p. 4).

Brazil and Russia have recently shown great interest in China (See Table 9.10).

One of the primary factors determining a currency's role in the global financial system is its liquidity and depth in global financial markets. While the yuan has made significant progress in recent years in terms of internationalization, it still lags behind the US dollar in terms of liquidity and

Table 9.9 Global use of currencies, 2022 (per cent)

Currency	*Share of Forex trading (%)* *	*Share of Official reserves (%)*	*Share of global payments (%)* **
US Dollar	88.5	58.4	41.9
Euro	30.5	20.5	36.3
Japanese Yen	16.7	5.5	2.9
British Pound	12.9	4.9	6.1
Chinese Renminbi	7	2.7	2.2

Source: Otero-Iglesias and Gonzalez-Agote[47]

Table 9.10 Brazil and Russia Imports from China in US$bn, 2000–2023

	Import Partner	*2000*	*2010*	*2020*	*2023*
Brazil	China	1.3	27.8	36.7	56.0
	World	59.9	192.4	166.1	252.4
	China/World	2.2	14.5	22.1	22.2
Russian Federation	China	0.9	39.0	54.9	
	World	33.9	228.9	231.7	
	China/World	2.8	17.0	23.7	

Source: WITS, author calculated

depth of its financial markets. Yongding (2023)[48] explains that, in 2021 and 2022, the cross-border receipts and payments totaled 36.6 trillion and 42 trillion yuan, respectively. The author noted that "the RMB's share in China's cross-border payments and receipts has risen from close to zero in 2010 to a record 48% at the end of March 2023." However, the US dollar is still the most widely used currency for trade and investment transactions, and it is also the primary reserve currency held by central banks around the world (Yongding (2023)).

Another factor that determines a currency's role in the global financial system is the stability and predictability of the issuing economy. While the Chinese economy has grown rapidly over the past few decades, it still faces challenges related to debt, financial regulation, and political risks, which could impact the stability and predictability of the yuan over the long term. Consider the Table 9.11 below which shows that China continues to lag behind the US on key pillars of governance.

The yuan has made significant progress in recent years in terms of internationalization, and it is likely to continue to play a more prominent role in the global financial system in the coming years (Fulcher, 2023[49]). The Chinese government has taken several steps to promote the international use of the yuan, including establishing offshore yuan trading centres and signing currency swap agreements with other countries (Chen, 2024). The IMF (2023) reflected that China, in 2009, began permitting cross-border settlements with some restrictions, then launched the initiative nationwide in 2011. In addition, the inclusion of the yuan in the International Monetary Fund's Special Drawing Rights (SDR) basket in 2015 was a significant milestone in the yuan's internationalization. In 2017, financial liberation was accelerated by opening of domestic capital

Table 9.11 World Governance Indicators China and the US

	China (Percentile rank)					*USA (Percentile rank)*				
	Control of corruption	*Government effectiveness*	*Regulatory quality*	*Voice and accountability*	*Rule of law*	*Control of corruption*	*Government effectiveness*	*Regulatory quality*	*Voice and accountability*	*Rule of law*
1996	48.4	43.2	45.1	12.0	33.7	91.4	89.1	95.7	91.0	92.5
2000	49.5	50.8	37.0	10.0	35.3	92.0	91.8	95.1	89.1	93.0
2005	32.2	51.0	49.5	7.7	32.1	91.7	90.2	95.6	89.9	91.4
2010	33.8	57.9	40.7	5.2	38.9	84.8	91.9	91.9	85.8	92.4
2015	48.6	67.8	43.3	4.9	41.3	89.9	89.4	85.6	84.2	90.4
2016	48.6	67.3	41.3	7.4	41.8	90.4	91.3	91.8	84.2	91.3
2017	47.6	68.3	46.2	7.9	46.2	88.9	92.8	92.8	81.3	91.8
2018	46.6	69.2	44.7	9.2	49.5	88.5	92.8	92.8	79.7	89.9
2019	44.7	71.6	42.8	6.8	46.2	85.1	91.3	88.9	76.3	89.9
2020	54.3	72.1	44.2	4.8	52.4	82.7	87.0	87.5	72.9	88.9
2021	58.2	76.4	41.3	5.3	53.8	83.7	88.5	90.4	74.9	88.9
2022	55.19	68.0	36.8	7.3	52.83	82.6	86.8	91.0	72.9	88.7

Source: World Governance Indicators

markets and the financial sector to foreign investors. Additionally, Chinese bonds have been included in major global indices (Schipke et al., 2019).

The rapid growth of China is a factor that the USA must consider in the context of changing global geopolitics. China, an emerging developing economy, is now the largest merchandise trader in the world, with a positive and growing trade balance as shown in Fig. 9.2.

Amadeo (2022[50]) reflected on whether the Chinese yuan can replace the US dollar as the next global currency. The author noted that while BRICS and China in particular, have been pushing for a new global reserve currency, the process of dethroning the US dollar is much more complicated than anticipated. The Economist (2023) attempted to explain why any attempt to de-dollarize the global financial system would be challenging. This is because the Bank of International Settlements noted that some 90% of foreign exchange transactions and 85% of spot transactions, forward and swap markets are undertaken in US dollars and that about 50% of global trade estimates are denominated in US currency. The Economist (2023), however, indicates that what is more likely to emerge in the next few decades is a multipolar global system, where the US dollar is used in the Americas, the Euro in Europe, and the yuan in Asia. The report noted, though, that the global reserve currency is likely to remain the US dollar.

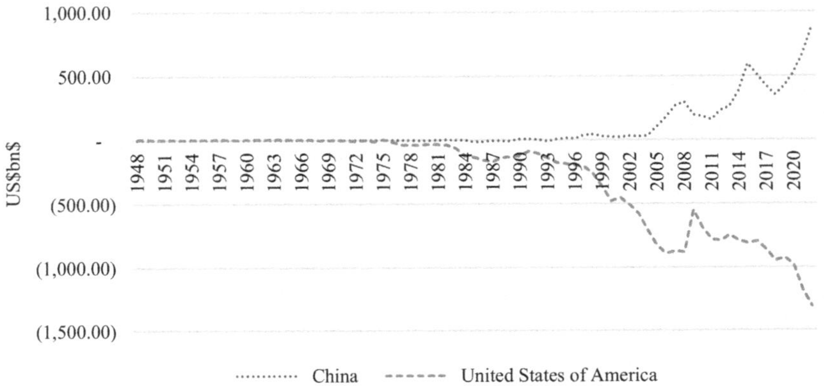

Fig. 9.2 China and US trade balance with the world (US$bn) (Source: WDI)

Hypothetically, though, for the dollar to be dethroned as a global reserve currency in favour of the yuan, the following would have to occur as proposed by Amadeo (2022):

1. Central banks globally would have to maintain at minimum, $700 billion yuan in reserves; Amadeo (2022), building on the work of Oakly (2013[51]), proposed that the reserve allocation should approximate China's share of international trade and GDP.
2. China would have to institute a policy to allow free trade of the yuan and relax its exchange against the US dollar. The liberalization of the Chinese capital market is a requirement by the IMF for a currency to be held as a reserve currency.
3. China would have to institute a policy of openness regarding its future intentions with the currency. This is because a reserve currency is considered a safe asset provision as discussed by Perez-Saiz and Zhang (2023).
4. China's financial markets must become transparent. Since the 2008 financial crisis, China has been making strides to improve the yuan trade on foreign exchange markets. This requires a more open financial and political system, and some progress has been made to date. For example, in 2015, China backed the Renminbi Trading Hub for the Americas.
5. Chinese monetary policy must be globally perceived as "stable."
6. The yuan as a currency option must match the reputation of stability similar to the US dollar given that an enormous number of US Treasuries backs it.

9.5 Impact of RMB as a Reserve Currency on US Dollar?

Using the Chinese currency as a reserve currency would have several benefits to China in terms of increasing global trade and economic integration and inclusion to the global financial system (Lim, 2023). This move can, over time, reduce the influence of the USA on global geopolitics as the strength of the US dollar as a reserve currency weakens. This move can also help to mitigate risks associated with volatility due to unilateral measures and the reduction in the use of the dollar as a dominant currency reserve (Pistilli, 2023).[52]

While the potential impact of the Chinese currency as a reserve currency is unknown, given that the dollar is still more widely used, some experts argue that as the yuan stabilizes against the dollar and is increasingly used as a substitute for the dollar in trade, it may result in weakened power of US-based sanctions, which may in turn contribute to further weakening of the dollar, accelerating the trend towards de-dollarization (Zhang, 2023[53]). This can ultimately negatively impact the US economy and reduce the standard of living of Americans.

Countries like Russia and India have also begun to trade in their own currencies as a strategy to de-dollarize, with Kenya and Malaysia even signing agreements with other nations to engage in trade in their local currencies or via other forms of exchange (Zeidan, 2024[54]).

As countries continue to diversify their reserve holdings in currencies other than the dollar, the US can face competition from emerging currencies such as the Yuan, which alters the balance of power in global markets (Zeidan, 2024). The ultimate impact, though, will be dependent on adoption, perceived stability, and the extent to which it can offer an alternative to the hegemony of the dollar. Lim (2023, p. 324) notes, that "attempts to stimulate greater RMB usage in offshore centres like London and Singapore are fundamentally predicated on confidence in the RMB's dollar peg. Insofar as the Chinese central government continues to accumulate large dollar-denominated reserves while permitting offshore RMB holders to transact through the current rather than the capital account, RMB internationalization would not engender a moment of rupture in global monetary history. What it demonstrates, rather, is the CPC's path dependence on the dollar-centric global monetary system that, in turn, sustains its absolute domestic financial control. All signs are suggesting, indeed, that this national-level continuity is the overarching goal of RMB internationalization."

A potential shift towards greater use of the yuan as a reserve currency could have significant and negative implications for the US economy and its investors, with the main sectors likely to be impacted being oil and gas, banking and finance, commodities, international trade, technology, tourism and travel and the foreign exchange market. The increased use of the yuan as a reserve currency can alter currency correlations, impact market volatility, and stimulate new trading arrangements ((Zeidan, 2024; Zhang, 2023).

In unpacking the nuances of this debate further, what is important to consider is the impact on trade of a world that is less tied to the dollar

(Zhang, 2023). Two issues intersect here: global capital flows, which may be considered the obverse of trade, and current account flows.

Notwithstanding the issue of trade and capital flows, Pettis (2023) noted that it would be difficult for China or Russia to upend the dominance of the US dollar. This would require a US policy-directed limit on the ability of foreigners to leverage US financial markets as an absorber of last resort for global savings (Lim, 2023; Zeidan, 2024). The author noted that the general line of reasoning was that the USA will never likely abdicate its hegemonic status through deliberate steps to reduce or end the dominance of the US dollar, despite the cost of maintaining this position in the US economy. Any moves to dethrone the use of the dollar globally will be opposed by Wall Street, the State Department, and the US military.

An additional consideration is that trade and savings imbalances would be difficult to monitor and report in a global economy that does not use the US dollar as its primary mode of exchange. Economies in the global space are highly interconnected and have structural domestic deficiencies, and any type of shift that results in a reduction of global trade imbalances would have economically and politically disruptive impacts, especially for countries that have persistent trade surpluses (Lim, 2023). Consider, for example, if the USA and other major economies undertook to eliminate the role of their domestic financial markets as foreign exchange absorbers and, consequently, no longer run current account and trade deficits. Developed economies account for 70–75% of the world's current account deficits, which would imply that these economies would have to convert their trade surpluses into deficits (Pettis, 2023, Economist, 2023) To explain this further, assume that a large, developed country which runs a perpetual trade surplus is forced to reduce the value of this surplus, which can impact on an economy's growth capacity, as the economic adjustment results in;

1. An increase in unemployment.
2. An increase in consumer lending to raise domestic demand.
3. An increase in government deficit.
4. A decline in domestic savings.
5. An increase in investment.

These adjustments in the context of global spillovers can be disruptive given industry linkages and are the reason why US trade deficits with various countries, result in the persistence of the dominance of the US$ as a global currency (Lim, 2023[55]).

To this end, Fulcher (2023, p. 10) notes that "Navigating the geopolitical landscape and fostering cooperation with other countries will be essential for the RMB's internationalization. By engaging in constructive dialogue and promoting economic collaboration, China can work to alleviate concerns about its political and economic influence and create a favorable environment for the RMB's acceptance as a global currency. Ultimately, the successful internationalization of the RMB will depend on China's ability to address these challenges and demonstrate its stability, reliability, and attractiveness as an international reserve asset. Achieving this objective could enhance China's role in the global financial system and contribute to a more diversified and resilient international monetary order."

9.6 Considerations for CARICOM

The internationalization of the Chinese yuan does present a host of economic implications for CARICOM, which, against the backdrop of the preceding chapters, warrants examination. As China's economic influence expands, internationally and regionally, CARICOM nations must remain alert to reduce the likelihood of global marginalization. Deepening financial integration with China can help to mitigate some risks. First, using the RMB rather than the US dollar to facilitate trade with China can result in deepened trade relations and improve access to Chinese markets. This also provides opportunities for trade with other economies which use the yuan as a reserve currency. This integration may, therefore, open pathways for greater investment and trade partnerships, ultimately stimulating local economies. The prospect of elevated trade levels could provide the impetus to drive regional growth and create a more robust economic environment for CARICOM nations.

The concern though is associated with increased economic dependency on a single trade partner. To navigate this challenge, CARICOM must establish robust regulatory frameworks and modern financial infrastructures to monitor and manage their economic interactions with China (and other trade partners) effectively. Miller (2023) emphasizes the importance of these mechanisms to ensure that deepened integration does not lead to the entrenchment of vulnerabilities.

Furthermore, while the advantages of engaging with the internationalized RMB are considerable, CARICOM member states must adopt a strategic approach when interacting with China (and other trading partners). This strategy should focus on diversifying economic ties to reduce dependence on any one nation and enhance their economies' long-term stability and resilience. By fostering a more diversified trade environment, CARICOM countries can leverage their relationship with China while safeguarding their economic interests in an increasingly interconnected world.

The yuan's internationalization presents both opportunities and challenges for CARICOM nations. A cautious and strategic engagement with China and a commitment to strengthening local regulatory frameworks will be essential for navigating the complexities of this evolving economic landscape in the coming years.

9.7 Conclusion

The international financial environment over the last decade has changed, with the presence of China, becoming more pronounced. The evolution of the Chinese yuan's role in the global economy represents a pivotal shift that could reshape international trade dynamics and financial systems. As China solidifies its position as a leading economic power, the yuan's potential to challenge the US dollar's dominance as the primary reserve currency is becoming increasingly tangible. The strategic efforts by China, such as establishing currency swap agreements, promoting the yuan in international trade, alongside interventions such as the increase in the number of offshore RMB centres, and creating the CIPS, and its connectivity to SWIFT, lay the groundwork for the yuan's greater international acceptance.

However, the path to becoming a widely adopted reserve currency is fraught with challenges. Despite significant strides since its inclusion in the IMF's Special Drawing Rights (SDR) basket, the yuan still lacks the liquidity, transparency, and political stability that underpins the dollar's longstanding dominance. Furthermore, the geopolitical landscape, marked by rising tensions and economic nationalism, complicates the yuan's trajectory. As countries explore alternatives to the dollar, the shift could potentially lead to a multipolar currency system, but the dollar will likely maintain its lead for the foreseeable future.

For CARICOM nations, the internationalization of the yuan presents opportunities and challenges. By engaging strategically with China and leveraging the yuan for trade, CARICOM can enhance economic ties and access to Chinese markets, fostering regional growth. It is imperative, though, for regional economies to diversify their economic partnerships to avoid over-reliance on a single trading partner.

While the yuan's ascent could signify a shift in the global financial order, its journey is contingent on several factors, including China's economic policies, the geopolitical environment, and the responsiveness of international economies to adapt to these evolving dynamics. As the global landscape continues to change, proactive engagement and strategic diversification will be critical for CARICOM to navigate the complexities and opportunities this change presents (especially in the context of a global environment where the USA seems increasingly intolerant to a greater participation of China).

Notes

1. https://www.imf.org/en/News/Articles/2023/02/02/cf-chinas-economy-is-rebounding-but-reforms-are-still-needed.
2. https://carnegieendowment.org/chinafinancialmarkets/89466.
3. https://www.chinausfocus.com/finance-economy/the-prospects-for-the-chinese-economy-in-2023-and-beyond.
4. https://www.linkedin.com/pulse/yuan-become-worlds-reserve-currency-ariful-haque/.
5. https://foreignpolicy.com/2022/09/21/china-yuan-us-dollar-sco-currency/.
6. https://www.reuters.com/markets/currencies/chinese-banks-seize-russia-oil-trade-internationalise-yuan-2023-04-28/.
7. https://www.adb.org/sites/default/files/publication/156336/adbi-wp481.pdf.
8. https://carnegieendowment.org/2013/09/01/does-internationalizing-rmb-make-sense-for-china-pub-53119.
9. http://global.chinadaily.com.cn/a/202305/17/WS646430b9a310b6054fad35d9.html.
10. https://www.hks.harvard.edu/sites/default/files/centers/mrcbg/files/200_AWP_final.pdf.

11. http://www.imi.ruc.edu.cn/docs//2023-07/420b178614dc4eb6916fff2605fe948b.pdf.
12. https://fortune.com/2023/06/25/dollar-reserve-currency-brics-brazil-russia-india-china-south-africa/.
13. https://www.washingtonpost.com/opinions/2023/03/24/us-dollar-strength-russia-china/.
14. https://foreignpolicy.com/2023/04/24/brics-currency-end-dollar-dominance-united-states-russia-china/.
15. https://carnegieendowment.org/research/2024/10/brics-summit-emerging-middle-powers-g7-g20?lang=en.
16. A Brief History of Europe From 1789 To 1815; https://tile.loc.gov/storage-services/public/gdcmassbookdig/briefhistoryofeu00holt/briefhistoryofeu00holt.pdf.
17. International Transactions: Real Trade and Factor Flows Between 1700 and 1870.
18. https://eml.berkeley.edu/~jsteinsson/teaching/originsofgrowth.pdf.
19. https://crsreports.congress.gov/product/pdf/IF/IF11707.
20. Thomas Costigan, Drew Cottle, and Angela Keys. "The US Dollar as the Global Reserve Currency: Implications for US Hegemony." World Review of Political Economy 8, no. 1 (2017): 104–22. https://doi.org/10.13169/worlrevipoliecon.8.1.0104.
21. https://www.telegraph.co.uk/news/1399693/A-history-of-sterling.html.
22. https://www.elibrary.imf.org/view/journals/022/0004/003/article-A007-en.xml.
23. "By 1947, the United States had accumulated 70% of the world's gold reserves. The United Kingdom had gone from being the world's greatest creditor to the world's greatest debtor. Countries had sold off most of their gold and dollar reserves, as well as their foreign investments, to pay for the war. What few reserves remained were now quickly running out. Trade deficits meant there was little hope of replenishing them." https://www.imf.org/external/np/exr/center/mm/eng/mm_dr_01.htm.
24. https://www.federalreservehistory.org/essays/bretton-woods-created.
25. https://www.investopedia.com/terms/b/brettonwoodsagreement.asp.

26. https://www.investopedia.com/articles/forex-currencies/092316/how-us-dollar-became-worlds-reserve-currency.asp.
27. The Federal Reserve represents the culmination of the efforts to manage and mitigate the risk observed during several periods of economic tumult in the USA. In its earliest form, centralized banks were established but this created some challenges for rural areas. These centralized banks were controlled by eastern banking powers and were deemed to be untrustworthy. This resulted in the creation of state-chartered free banks which issued their own currency which was backed by gold reserves. In 1863, with the passing of the National Banking Act, these free banks were allowed to provide a standardized currency which was backed by US securities. The unstable financial markets which resulted in market crashes and depressions over the period 1893 and 1907, were alleviated only through the private sector infusions from JP Morgan. In 1912, the House Committee on Banking and Finance took the decision to decentralize banking which led to the establishing of the 1913 Federal Reserve Act.
28. https://wtocenter.vn/tin-tuc/21265-how-the-united-states-dollar-dominated-the-global-trade-space.
29. These include the UK pound, the Euro, and the Japanese Yen.
30. https://www.federalreserve.gov/econres/notes/feds-notes/the-international-role-of-the-u-s-dollar-20211006.html.
31. https://www.investopedia.com/articles/forex/09/factors-drive-american-dollar.asp.
32. https://www.federalreserve.gov/aboutthefed/files/the-fed-explained.pdf.
33. https://www.cfr.org/backgrounder/dollar-worlds-reserve-currency.
34. https://www.investopedia.com/articles/forex-currencies/092316/how-us-dollar-became-worlds-reserve-currency.asp.
35. https://www.fmprc.gov.cn/mfa_eng/wjbxw/202302/t20230220_11027664.html.
36. The Politics of International Currencies. Strange, S., World Politics, Vol. 23, No. 2 (Jan. 1971), pp. 215–231 (17 pages).
37. Xin (2023), noted, "Efforts to internationalise the yuan received a shot in the arm in the aftermath of the 2008 global financial crisis. In 2009, China's then central bank governor, Zhou Xiaochuan, tabled ideas on how to create a new global currency to replace

the dollar, the dominance of which, China blamed for the world's recent economic woes. Yet 14 years later, Beijing's journey to make the yuan an international currency has been anything but smooth sailing. One reason is excessive reliance on a 'top-down' approach to internationalisation. In 2016, for instance, China was able to get the yuan included in the International Monetary Fund's Special Drawing Rights (SDRs), foreign exchange reserve assets based on a basket of currencies, giving the Chinese currency greater status alongside the dollar, euro, yen and pound. However, SDRs cannot be held by private parties doing little for international adoption of the yuan among businesses. China has also inked dozens of bilateral currency swap deals with other central banks, but these were mostly about status, and they are of questionable practical value. In theory, if a foreign central bank inks a currency swap deal with China, it recognises the yuan as a source of emergency liquidity support. But it would be a bad deal for China to give yuan to a foreign central bank in exchange for an obscure, depreciating currency." https://www.scmp.com/comment/opinion/article/3216563/china-still-has-lessons-learn-making-yuan-international-alternative-us-dollar?action%5Bfollow_topic_package%5D%5BcheckedIndex%5D%5B0%5D=0&action%5Bfollow_topic_package%5D%5BcheckedIndex%5D%5B1%5D=1&action%5Bfollow_topic_package%5D%5BcheckedIndex%5D%5B2%5D=2&action%5Bfollow_topic_package%5D%5BcheckedIndex%5D%5B3%5D=3.
38. https://fortune.com/2023/06/01/china-yuan-ukraine-war-us-dollar/.
39. https://greenfdc.org/brief-chinas-role-in-public-external-debt-in-dssi-countries-and-the-belt-and-road-initiative-bri-in-2020/.
40. The People's Bank of China (PBOC) said it would extend trading hours for its interbank foreign exchange market to 3 a.m. (1900 GMT) from 11:30 p.m. (1530 GMT), according to an online statement. Following the adjustment, the new daily trading hours will be from 9:30 a.m. (0130 GMT) to 1900 GMT. The PBOC said the decision was to "cover more trading sessions in Asian, European and North American markets." https://www.reuters.com/article/china-yuan-trading/update-1-china-to-extend-fx-market-trading-hours-to-further-internationalise-yuan-idINL1N33K0GJ/.

41. https://www.atlanticcouncil.org/blogs/econographics/internationalization-of-the-renmibi-via-bilateral-swap-lines/.
42. https://www.chinacenter.net/2023/china-currents/22-1/chinas-digital-currency-the-hopes-and-fears-of-the-e-cny/.
43. China has employed Bilateral Currency Swaps (BSLs) with 41 countries globally between 2009 and 2020, which results in an amount exceeding 3.5 trillion RMB ($554 billion). These BSLs were employed by China to reduce dependence on the dollar as is allows bilateral trade and investment to be facilitated in RMB (Tran, 2022).
44. https://www.imf.org/-/media/Files/Publications/WP/2023/English/wpiea2023077-print-pdf.ashx.
45. https://fortune.com/2023/06/01/china-yuan-ukraine-war-us-dollar/.
46. https://www.elibrary.imf.org/view/journals/001/2023/077/001.2023.issue-077-en.xml.
47. https://www.thedialogue.org/blogs/2023/06/chinas-rmb-isnt-set-to-outpace-the-dollar-in-latin-americayet/.
48. http://www.cf40.com/en/news_detail/13474.html.
49. https://www.middlebury.edu/institute/sites/default/files/2023-07/WP-%20The%20RMBs%20Delicate%20Dance-%20Justin%20Fulcher_0.pdf.
50. https://www.thebalancemoney.com/yuan-reserve-currency-to-global-currency-3970465.
51. https://www.cnbc.com/2013/05/10/heres-what-china-is-secretly-planning-for-the-yuan.html.
52. https://investingnews.com/brics-currency/.
53. https://www.gisreportsonline.com/r/yuan-unseating-the-dollar/.
54. https://gjia.georgetown.edu/2024/04/18/de-dollarization-the-belt-and-road-initiative-and-the-future-of-the-chinese-yuan/.
55. https://www.cambridge.org/core/journals/journal-of-global-history/article/on-the-rationale-and-implications-of-chinas-rmb-internationalization-a-global-historical-perspective/88B691ED0F1F3BC5A4FE86E331C3A67A.

CHAPTER 10

China, the Caribbean, and the Hemisphere

10.1 Introduction: Does Size Matter?

China is identified as a large, powerful, and influential country in the world. There are other large countries which are also powerful and influential. However, it is important to establish that China is a big, powerful, and influential country in dealing with its relations with smaller countries of the Caribbean and simultaneously, in the context of economic, geopolitical, and military competition with other big countries.

In terms of sheer physical size, Russia, spanning Europe and Asia, is the largest country in the world by far, 17.1 million square kilometres.[1] Canada is the second-largest and the USA is the third-largest country in the world. China in fourth place, is not far behind. Including land and water, China is 9.6 million square kilometres. The USA including Alaska, is 9.8 million but China has a larger land mass than the USA. Canada is 9.9 million square kilometres.[2]

The Caribbean consists of small countries in the Western Hemisphere. The Caribbean landscape, sea, and land is 2.7 million square kilometres.[3] CARICOM is 433,000 square kilometres.[4] The Caribbean, as well as CARICOM, notwithstanding their size, have, always traded with large countries.

As colonial production centres for the metropole, colonial Caribbean countries exported commodities to European countries, and received

R. Hosein et al., *China in the Caribbean*,
https://doi.org/10.1007/978-3-031-71985-1_10

investments from Europe, and the level of development or underdevelopment achieved, was largely dependent on, and, ultimately determined by, this relationship with Europe.[5]

Today, trade, investment, and development relationships continue to exist with the USA (CBI), Canada (CARIBCAN) with the EU (CARIFORUM- EU EPA). For the English-speaking CARICOM, a similar agreement as with the EU obtains with the UK. The Caribbean has traditionally had some preferential trading arrangements with the EU, the USA, and Canada and continues to do so today. Trade, investment, and development links with these traditional partners, remain strong.[6]

The size of China is unlikely to be daunting to the Caribbean, and CARICOM, as a trade, investment, and development partner. It would also come as no surprise to China if the Caribbean as a whole, or CARICOM, seeks a concessionary relationship with China. The really troublesome issue, already raised earlier, would be those countries which persist in their relationship with Taiwan, as they would be immediately excluded by China which would make the CARICOM negotiating position difficult as a block, especially if China views the Belt and Road Initiative as the vehicle through which and, as a platform upon which China-Caribbean relations can be built.[7]

10.2 The Belt and Road Initiative

The Belt and Road Initiative was seized upon immediately by Trinidad and Tobago. In alliance with Chinese companies, an investment park was built in Phoenix Park. Belt and Road can be concessionary from the point of view of Caribbean countries because China is willing to engage any country on any matter it wants to raise, and if it is practical and feasible, and sometimes even when it is not, they will negotiate the terms. Negotiation of terms allows a small, developing country to put its cards on the table and to say exactly what it wants and what terms and conditions it will prefer. China will have its own point of view and articulate that, but for Belt and Road to work, countries across the world would have to come on board, deals worked out and desirable terms and conditions agreed, and parties would have to make things work by operating in a mutually satisfying way. Here is a perspective on Belt and Road articulated by a Senior Lecturer of the Institute of International Relations at the St Augustine Campus, Annita Montoute made in 2023, "The initiative provides the commensurate infrastructure to support and facilitate the unimpeded movement of goods, services and capital, allowing for the trans-border flow of personnel and technology." The industrial park coincides with the vision of the Caribbean country's government, which values "consistent high quality foreign direct and domestic investment" as "key to sustained growth." The park offers opportunities for Trinidad and Tobago to expand and diversify its manufacturing base towards non-traditional manufacturing, as it will house between 60 and 80 factory shells, directly employ more than 4500 persons, and contribute about 1.6 billion U.S. dollars annually to GDP. Caribbean countries are similar in many ways, all small by international standards, with small populations and limited bases. Caribbean countries share similar challenges that BRI projects could help overcome or alleviate. Montoute (2023) described the BRI as a reflection of China's pursuit of a multidimensional, comprehensive, and holistic global engagement, in keeping with the changing landscape. In addition, the Belt and Road Initiative does not have a set of broad ideological conditions which countries must adhere to participate. Technically, that means that the model allows countries to develop projects with China that are specific to their needs.[8]

The Belt and Road Initiative can be considered as an open window through which, what a country can do, and how much it can achieve, depends on how strategically it chooses its project for support from China, and how well it negotiates to get the best value, not only for money, but also the best value out of the relationship with China. From China's point of view, the Belt and Road Initiative can be the pivot that draws Caribbean and Latin American countries into a constructive economic relationship with China. At the same time, it can open the door for small developing countries to do certain things that they may have felt they would never get the chance to do before, and now, based on open negotiations and China's appreciation of its size and weight in relation to such countries, agreements may be made that such countries will consider desirable and concessionary. A strengthening of relationships with multiple countries clustered in the Caribbean but spread throughout Latin America is bound to have hemispheric and geopolitical implications.

The other issue related to size is quantum of population and, consequently, size of market. The Caribbean has 44 million people.[9] CARICOM has 19 million.[10] China has a population and market of 1.4 billion.[11] From the Caribbean point of view, a small amount of anything sold to China could be quite substantial for a Caribbean company. One million bottles of pepper sauce sold is $^1/_{14}$th of 1% of China's market.

For example, a calypso, soca, steel band, chutney, jazz, or variety concert to 100,000 people in China, means delivery to a larger audience than any audience that perhaps ever has been delivered to in the Western Hemisphere.

By the same token, a Chinese grocery catering to a market of 50,000 or even 1,000,000 people makes little sense in the big scheme of things. However, a chain of stores across the region catering to a market of 19 million or 44 million makes sense in terms of export, business venture, and returns. Investment for China only makes sense in a region of such small markets, if the location also provides a raw material which can be processed efficiently for demand in a global market or some significant part of it. Hence, oil, natural gas, LNG, asphalt, bauxite, timber, are important resources to China. If the location/destination provides a logistical advantage to manufacture goods and design services to nearby markets or to tranship them with greater customer satisfaction to third countries, this would certainly present an opportunity. In the context of pullbacks of investment, especially by US companies and some other Western countries from China and the evolution of the concept of nearshoring, this could be an important consideration in China's outward investment strategy.[12] While Mexico is the main beneficiary now, the Caribbean offers China some opportunities as discussed in previous chapters.

10.3 Respect Among the "Big Players"

China wants respect among the big players with influence at the power centres, (the USA, G20, Europe, Russia) but it desperately wants influence in the developing world as well (trade, investment, loans, development, ports and airports, technology penetration, Belt and Road, BRICS, alternative currencies to the US dollar, multilateral agencies, organizations like WTO, UN Security Council, UN General Assembly). Indeed, while China wants respect and consideration as an equal big power, it wants to lead the developing world in the transformation of the world order to break the hegemonic control of the West and to create a stronger balance in favour of developing countries and in so doing enhance its own role in the world.[13]

Another issue is geographical positioning. Ports and airports and waterways are critical for this. Globally the COVID pandemic, revealed how vital logistics, transportation, ships, containers, and ports are, and how these impact on availability, access, shortages, and prices.[14]

Transportation routes and sea-lanes are critical in the Ukraine war, the Red Sea, and elsewhere as sea route disruptions can bring chaos to economies, trade, and livelihoods and provoke military tensions.[15]

Another issue is how does the geographical location of the Caribbean and China's trade, investment, financing, and development engagement with the Caribbean dovetail with China's larger quest to lead a developing world challenge to the existing world order, build alliances as a counterweight to the dominant West, and to pursue trade, investment, technological, and military competition with the USA, with an expansionist thrust in this hemisphere which includes the building of ports, airports, and the deployment of communications technology?

As has been noted in Chapter One, China is today, a major maritime power, building ports all over the world and carving out shipping lanes which are vital for commercial trade, but which can also be of strategic value for military purposes. In Chapter One, it was also noted that, apart from over 2000 minor ports plus 34 major ports in China, Chinese companies own or operate terminals in 96 ports in 53 countries around the world, 40 of them in Latin America. The Maritime Executive of 24 March 2024, announced that the government of Peru had awarded a contract to a subsidiary of Chinese company, Jinzao to build what will be Peru's third-largest port. Another port built in Peru by a Chinese company will come into operation within the next few years.[16]

10.4 Ports and Finance

Chapter 1 took note of the fact that some Chinese-controlled ports are being converted to military purposes. In addition, China has 11 satellite ground stations in hemispheric countries such as Venezuela, Argentina, Bolivia, and Brazil. The chapter also took into account China's pivotal influence in finance in the Western Hemisphere, and China's strategic roles in the Inter-American Development Bank and the Caribbean Development Bank. Chapter 1 also took note of the Foreign Affairs Committee's observation that China was also active in providing security assistance to countries in this hemisphere.

Such issues which raise concerns about China's geopolitical strategic positioning in this hemisphere are bound to increase suspicion about

China's intentions from the USA and consequently have repercussions for geopolitical tensions which may manifest here as elsewhere.

There can be little doubt that the emergence of COVID in China, spread throughout the world as a global pandemic, killing millions and causing inordinate suffering and fear, has increased suspicion, prompted caution, and increased tension between the USA and China.[17] The issue of what caused COVID and whether it emerged from a food source, market, or laboratory has not been clearly and finally resolved and may well be a source of continuing controversy in the future.

China's approach to stem the spread of COVID inside China did not win support nor respect, Chinese vaccines were not thought to be as effective as those produced in the West, and despite cooperation by China with World Health Organization authorities, (WHO), scepticism on the depth of cooperation by China and suspicion on the origin of the COVID virus persist (The Guardian, 2022).[18]

During the pandemic, the minimum 15% taxation issue, to circumscribe companies from moving their business location to avoid taxes, was settled,[19] but concerns also began to heighten overdependence of countries on supplies from elsewhere, the extent to which some level of self-sufficiency could be assured by an individual country, and the concept of nearshoring gained currency as American companies, in particular, moved production systems from China to Mexico and elsewhere, in the Americas.[20]The concepts of self-sufficiency and nearshoring and near sourcing for a greater sense of security by countries have also gained currency generally.[21]

10.5 Political Stability

The Taiwan question, alleged Chinese spying on the USA, China's alleged stealing of US technological research and innovations, competition for dominance in telecommunications technology and artificial intelligence, and competition in space both for telecommunications and satellite advantage and for vital resources all par for the course in contemporary competition and the quest for geopolitical, technological, and economic advantage, have been contributing to increasing competitive as well as military tensions between China and the USA.

The relocation of US companies away from China has been occurring since 2020 (Britt 2023,[22] Atkins 2023[23]). Moreover, in the post pandemic era, China has been undergoing an economic downturn and with this, the population has been becoming increasingly restless, and protests, always a factor in Chinese life, because of economic stress, arbitrary decisions, high handed officials, and ethnic assertion, have been increasing.[24] Britt (2023) noted that companies such as Intel, Microsoft, Nike, and Dell have begun to consider relocation of their production facilities out of China to countries such as Vietnam and India.

In this context, the three things that China is most worried about: escaping the middle-income country trap, avoiding war with the USA, and economic and political stability inside China, are suddenly threatened (Vinhas de Souza 2024[25]). Pulling 800 million people out of poverty could not have been an easy task; in fact, it is a formidable achievement, of which China should be duly proud. However, any rolling back of that now would be a severe reversal, affecting the size and well-being of the Chinese middle class, which would inevitably have socio-economic and political impact inside China.

The tensions over Taiwan have heightened due to a combination of factors; Nancy Pelosi's visit (Global Times 2022), the balloon incident over US land space (AP News 2023) and recent elections. Since 2022, there has been increased military activity in the maritime areas around Taiwan as well as the South China Sea. This includes confrontations involving the Philippines and China on the high seas. Not only have there been higher traffic in the waters around China, but also reports of significant increases in the production of boats and ships in Chinese ship building facilities.

The issue of political stability in China is paramount. China is a big country, densely populated, very diverse, and protests occur by the hundreds every day and as economic stresses increase, and greater political control is exerted, the number of protests daily has been increasing and the geographical spread of these protests, widening.[26]

It was hardly a surprise that the recent annual congress of the party was muted and subdued, and that the focus was on stability, rather than China's current economic challenges and geopolitical stresses. Why? Because China's ability to address economic recovery as well as manage geopolitical challenges, depend on internal stability, the effective management of protest and dissent, and the avoidance of unruly rebellions and chaos are essential to China's economic success and prosperity and geopolitical power and leverage.

10.6 Chinese Migrants to USA

On 1 April 2024, CNN reported on the challenges that Chinese illegal immigrants were facing to cross the border between Mexico and the USA. The article reports that eight dead bodies of Chinese migrants were found on the coast of southern Mexico.[27] The pertinent facts related to the purpose of this chapter and this book are quoted as "The number of Chinese migrants illegally entering the US from Mexico has skyrocketed in recent years. In 2023, more than 37,000 Chinese citizens were picked up by law enforcement crossing illegally into the US from Mexico," US government data shows—compared with an average of roughly 1500 per year over the preceding decade. Chinese people are on track to be the fastest growing group making those crossings according to a CNN analysis, earlier this year of law enforcement data. The influx of Chinese migrants spotlights the urgency many now feel to leave their homeland, even amid, what Chinese leader, Xi Jinping has claimed is a "national rejuvenation."[28]

Xiong et al. (2024)[29] note that "three years of Covid-19 lockdowns and restrictions left people in China out of work and disillusioned with the ruling Communist Party's increasingly tight grip on all aspects of life under Xi….hope that business would fully rebound once restrictions ended a year ago has vanished with China's once envious economic growth stuttering …other migrants nod to restrictions on personal life in China where Xi has overseen a sweeping crackdown on free speech, civil society and religion in the country of 1.4 billion."[30] The recent marked increase in illegal immigration from China to the USA gives some indication of the challenges that some citizens in China are currently facing and some of the difficulties that China as a country is currently going through but it also points to the challenge of an expansionist foreign policy intention, amid economic challenges and political resentment at home for China (Washington Post, 2024).[31]

10.7 China Challenges: Economy and Taiwan

COVID-19 dealt an economic whiplash to China, and following all the restrictions, illnesses, and deaths, the real estate crash came and with it a myriad of other problems. Consumer demand was subdued, jobs were lost, unemployment increased, a rollback of numbers who had entered the middle class was likely, businesses were moving out of China, a reduction of growth was certain, and with it, the need to export more, to increase production and consumer demand at home, to invest abroad, to encourage foreign investment to China, to do whatever was required to secure economic stability, to prevent loss of economic gains, and maintain economic momentum and competitiveness.[32] The middle-income country trap was a looming challenge in 2024 that had to be addressed. Events preceding the 2024 election in Taiwan and the results of that election (China's favoured candidate had not succeeded) asserted the One China policy that was more urgent in a context in which the new president of Taiwan wanted a more autonomous Taiwan and welcomed collaboration with the USA.[33] Taiwan was also the world's largest producer of quality semi-conductor chips essential to the Artificial Intelligence industry. US artificial intelligence companies were relocating from China, and China itself was restricting AI-driven companies and their ability to operate in China in relation to US restrictions on China (Britt, 2023).[34]

Showing strength and becoming more assertive with Taiwan and the One China policy would make the issue of sovereignty more urgent. This could mean more aggression in the waters surrounding China and Taiwan and stricter protection of maritime borders in the Taiwan Strait and the waters around China, principally the South China Sea.[35]

Such aggression on the high seas, accompanied by an ambitious boatbuilding strategy and a defensive, somewhat aggressive posture towards sovereign territory, makes some countries around China worry, as Chinese military capability and man-made islands are established. Such things are bound to unsettle the USA.[36]

The combined impact of aggressive and strategic economic, harbour, logistical, and technological partnerships challenges the hegemonic position of the USA in the Western Hemisphere. In a way, the territorial approach to regional domains counterbalances each other. China wants to be the dominant power and influence in Asia and have dominant maritime and military control to protect its sovereignty, borders, and the waters around China. In the Western Hemisphere, the USA might be prepared to accommodate economic competition and the reach for more significant political influence by China. However, the USA is hardly likely to be comfortable with strategic capability, which can be leveraged for military advantage and would probably actively resist military positioning and technological dominance of the Western Hemisphere by China.

10.8 Increased Geopolitical Tension

Geopolitical tensions are bound to affect relations between the USA and China and vice versa, the Caribbean and China and vice versa, and China's bilateral relationships on a one-to-one basis with other hemispheric countries and on a general basis between China and other countries and their relationships with the USA.

Not only will China and the USA have to manage their relationship with each other, but each country or cluster of countries will also have to manage their relationships with China on the one hand and the USA on the other. So, this involves not only a unique navigation challenge for both China and the USA with each other, including how they treat and engage other countries in the hemisphere, but also how they balance relations in the South China Sea and the Taiwan Strait, the tone of engagement on issues of global competition in finance, technology, investment and trade, and how each of these powers, counterbalance policy and action in the Western Hemisphere for economic gain, political influence, and geopolitical advantage.

Growing tensions between the USA and China can lead to war between two large powers, a frightening prospect that both countries want to avoid. On the other hand, countries in this hemisphere would want to keep the temperature of tensions lower and the hemisphere peaceful and free from military confrontation. It is interesting to note that the bottom line stressed by China President Xi Jinping to US President Joe Biden in his early April 2024 meeting with Xi Jinping was "no clash, no confrontation.“ This is in keeping with an often articulated position by the Chinese president to avoid war with the USA.[37]

Economic setbacks within China can make China more aggressive as a military power for at least two reasons (Beckley 2023,[38] Panella 2024[39]). The first is to mitigate against a perception of weakness or vulnerability. The second would be to boost the military industries, whether firepower, bombs, planes, drones, ships, or other technologies and devices, to increase employment and boost the economy. That can also lead to defensive and aggressive responses by others and further move the world to an escalated level of military tension, heightening the prospect of war. The most favourable assumption must be that both China and the USA would be reluctant to escalate to the point of war, because it would be bad for both countries and bad for the world. And it is a positive development, worthy of note, that "no clash, no confrontation" was addressed as the bottom line of USA-China relations going forward, at least for the rest of 2024.

10.9 FDI Flows and Political Stability

Internally, Xi Jinping is addressing the issue of foreign investment and political stability. The Chinese leader wants a vibrant Chinese economy well connected to the world, which, in turn, will help maintain political stability.[40]

The National People's Congress, in March 2024, faced concerns about how China would deal with a perceived real estate crash, a withdrawal of demand by Chinese consumers, a shift away from China by foreign investors, loss of jobs, and high youth unemployment, and a significant slowing of growth. The meeting was largely closed to the outside world, not much press coverage, and quite muted in tone; the focus was on political stability. From Xi Jinping's and China's perspectives, considered and expressed in a 3000-strong Party and Parliament meeting, political stability precedes economic recovery and growth.[41]

"The collapse of the Real Estate Sector has wiped out huge chunks of household savings over the course of two years," making Chinese citizens resistant to the government's policy thrust "to encourage personal consumption" (Caraway, 2024). The Chinese consumer is hardly persuaded, and not only have there been many protests, but the number of protests has been growing.[42]

Notwithstanding, the main goals announced were stability, development of critical sectors such as nanotechnology, biomedicine, and artificial intelligence, and stimulating the economy. The meeting set a target of 5% growth, modest compared to a decade ago but in keeping with current achievements. As Gunjan Singh of the Deccan Herald says, it is a "bumpy road ahead" for China, but Chinese leadership is united behind Xi Jinping and summoning the resolve.[43]

When Xi Jinping started his unprecedented third term as China's president, Bloomberg reported him as saying that he would focus on stability, strengthening Party Leadership, and national security. He faced a future of slower growth and increasing tensions with the USA over Taiwan.[44] China is currently experiencing an economic downturn, its population is restless, and tensions with the USA continue. Although pathways have been crafted to ease the tensions, China's military stance is still bold and aggressive.[45] According to Al Jazeera, as reported by Lyndal Rowlands, it was announced that China's defence spending would increase by 7.2% in 2024, the same as in 2023. She writes, "Beijing's defence budget has more than doubled since 2015,[46] but according to William Hartung of the Quincy Institute, the US continues to outspend China on its military by a substantial margin…according to the latest SIPRI estimate, US military spending at $877 bn was about three times higher than Chinese military spending at $292 bn in 2022."[47]

Military strength and stability are important anchors, and promoting consumer demand, if times are tougher and consumers are hesitant, is nonetheless important. But how will China get its economy to grow, even if the target is a relatively modest 5% by China's standards?

After the Two Meetings Congress, Xi Jinping proactively invited US businesspeople and investors to meet with him in Beijing. He asked them to "continue to invest in China" and pledged further reforms to open the country's market to foreign firms.[48] In a CNN report by Laura He and Wayne Chang, the authors write, "Chinese leader Xi Jinping met more than a dozen US CEOs and academics" on Wednesday after China's 3000-strong national congress of Party and Parliament "to woo back foreign investors and mend strained relations with the United States."[49] The article continues, "Xi also called for "a better future" between China and the US." He added, "Whether in traditional fields such as economy, trade, and agriculture, or emerging fields such as climate change and artificial intelligence, China and the United States should help boost each other's development."[50] The CNN article continues, "About 100 global CEOs, as well as heads of international organizations, such as the International Monetary Fund and the World Bank, were in the Chinese capital this week for the annual China Development Forum." According to Chinese state media, more than 30 of them are US Executives.[51]

China is thoughtful and strategic in its approach to internal political management of governance, stability, and economic recovery. Still, it is also quite pragmatic in ensuring that outward-reaching engagement serves its national interests well.

10.10 The Chinese Dream

Notwithstanding all the above and an agreement in principle not to descend into conflict and confrontation, in April 2024, talks between the presidents of the world's two most powerful countries, China and the

USA, may be headed on a collision course based on ideological differences. One might call this the clash between the Chinese Dream and the American Dream, one based on democracy, a modifying capitalism and citizen welfare; the other based on the Communist Party idea of socialism with Chinese characteristics, a more equitable prosperity for all and a broad-based notion of democracy anchored in stability.

The "American Dream" is an idea that keeps the USA going and the migrants coming. The American idea that everyone can pursue happiness under freedom and democracy is essential to being American and a vital attractor to immigrants. It would be difficult to say if, perhaps, some of the 37,000 illegal Chinese migrants who crossed the US border from Mexico in 2023 might have been summoned or motivated by the American dream or just trying to escape from a feeling of economic distress and possibly repression in China.[52]

The path now being pursued by the Chinese leader is "National rejuvenation," as espoused by Xi Jinping, leading to the achievement of the "Chinese Dream" or "China Dream." The objective is set for 2049 when China will celebrate 100 years of socialist achievement as a world power.[53]

The situation becomes extra complicated when China, which regards itself as a large developing country that wants to escape the middle-income country trap, finally achieves not just developed country status but very developed country status. This is in a context in which the entire Make America Great Again (MAGA) movement sees America as facing a receding future with a diminishing quality of life within the USA itself.

The vision of the China Dream or Chinese Dream, and its intended big celebration 100 years after the establishment of the People's Republic of China in 2049 and Xi Jinping's advocacy for a national rejuvenation to make the attainment of the Chinese Dream manifest, is a powerful magnet for Chinese ambition and drive. However, it is also a counterpoint for a divided and fragmented America, where the American Dream seems cracked, if not broken, and multiple visions of a better America constantly clash and compete.

10.11 Global Superpower, Multipolar World, and the Need for Limits

The USA's achievement has been so formidable that the country achieved superpower status, which it has continuously enjoyed since the end of the Second World War. A multipolar world, though, means that other countries like China will rise and space must be made for them. Space would only be made for a country based on value. Value is determined by the amount of mutual goodwill and the level of trustful cooperation. As the world turns, several countries compete for space and make no apologies, sometimes making bold assertions about it. Besides China, of course, there are Russia, India, Iran, North Korea, Turkey, Venezuela, and Cuba. Each country has perspectives and individualized, special goals, and each will cooperate and collaborate as required to achieve what it views as desirable goals.

If space is not made for them, they will claim it, and to claim space, they must be strong and aggressive. Strength, aggression, and China's space seizure mean that, in perception, the USA will recede. A multipolar world already reduces the USA's supreme superpower status, but China's superpower status creates a countervailing force capable of challenging the USA militarily while it competes aggressively on every other plane.

Terms and conditions for cooperation, collaboration, and non-aggression are absolutely critical for such countries. Also critical are terms of competition and rules of competitive advantage and established boundaries for domains of needed control, which might be so strong that concessions might have to be made.

It may well end up that the USA will have to make concessions to China on Taiwan, the South China Sea, and Asia in exchange for concessions by China in its Western Hemisphere thrust. A lot depends not only on the level of aggression and restraint but also on its tone.

The tone of the relationship dramatically changed during and after the pandemic. Still, since Nancy Pelosi's visit to Taiwan and the spy balloon over the American sovereign space incident, there have been genuine attempts at recalibration of USA-China relations, even as tensions in specific spheres escalate, whether spying, intellectual property infringements, investments and restrictions on investments, technology, and restrictions on technology, microchips, artificial intelligence, and the list can lengthen.

One thing is clear: there is a need to set limits and establish rules between competing countries and for all countries to abide by. The USA wants a world where it can maintain some control, whatever the circumstances—for example, veto power in the United Nations Security Council. China considers itself a world superpower and a developing country. It wants to rewrite the rules with the support of other developing countries, which it wants to lead because it feels that a rebalancing of power needs to take place in a multipolar world in which the scale is not tipped so heavily on the side of the USA and other Western powers. China is in the G20, but it also helped form BRICS and plays a significant role in its development. China wants to lead Africa, Asia, Latin America, the Caribbean, and the entire developing world, but competing ambitions and aspirations are not limited to the USA and China alone or Russia, China, and the USA. India, soon to be the most populous country in the world and the world's largest democracy, wants to play a role with the big powers in the world and has leadership aspirations for the developing world. In this regard, India's successful sponsorship of Africa to enter the G20 as the 21st member is a case in point.

India is also a founding member of BRICS. Therefore, we see here, between India and China, cooperation and competing ambitions for leadership of the developing world, as well as for leading the transformation of the world order, the rebalancing of power, and the rewriting of rules, but perhaps from different perspectives. The American Dream and the Chinese Dream might be very different, but so might the Indian Dream and the Chinese Dream. Thus, in the unfolding multipolar world, there may be a clash of dreams, even though there might be a common pursuit of self-interested national prosperity and peace as well as wider world prosperity, peace, and stability for collective progress.

10.12 Navigating a Recalibration

There can be little doubt that since the COVID-19 pandemic, the approach towards strengthening a relationship between China and the USA has been one of navigating a recalibration. Suddenly, the tensions escalated only to seek a more restrained, collaborative path to recalibration again.

From the West's point of view, there is mistrust and scepticism about what caused the outbreak of COVID. It is the escalation of costs and loss of control over logistical problems. It is the rethinking of offshoring, the withdrawal and relocation of investment, and a renewed and heightened interest in self-sufficiency, independence, and management of the dependence risk. From China's perspective, this is a defensive response based on mistrust and smacks of aggression, fear, and the desire to harm China.[54]

China's response is self-protection, strengthening itself to the point of invulnerability, resisting aggression, and being prepared to fight. It is making the moves required to give China power, influence, and strength in a multipolar world and alter the terms of power and the rulemaking process.

10.13 The Chinese Communist Party, Power and Ideology

The paramountcy of the Chinese Communist Party is an important principle in China's political ideology and development thrust. Xi Jinping has constantly stressed this since becoming Party General Secretary in 2012, although he is also president, head of Government, and Supreme Commander of the Military.

The CPC determines government policy, foreign policy, and military strategy. The Chinese Leader always emphasizes that the Party must be close to the people, listen to their points of view, and reflect on their wishes and aspirations while offering examples of exemplary leadership and constantly correcting the Party when it goes off course to maintain its moral authority and leadership strength.

Here is the Chinese leader's view of the importance of the Chinese Communist Party, given on 1 July 2021, at the ceremony marking the Centenary anniversary of the Communist Party of China:

"We must uphold the firm leadership of the Party. China's success hinges on the Party. The more than 180-year-long modern history of the Chinese nation, the 100-year-long history of the Party, and the more than 70-year-long history of the People's Republic of China all provide ample evidence that without the Communist Party of China, there would be no new China and no national rejuvenation. The party was chosen by history and the people. The leadership of the party is the defining feature of socialism with Chinese characteristics and constitutes the greatest strength of this system. It is the foundation and lifeblood of the party and the country, and the crux upon which the interests and wellbeing of all Chinese people depend. On the journey ahead, we must rely closely on the people to create history. Upholding the Party's fundamental purpose of wholeheartedly serving the people, we will stand firmly with the people, implement the Party's mass line, respect the people's creativity, and practice a people-centred philosophy of development. We must continue to adapt Marxism to the Chinese context.

We must uphold and develop socialism with Chinese characteristics. We must accelerate the modernization of national defence and the armed forces. A strong country must have a strong military, as only then can it guarantee the security of the nation. At the point that it was engaged in violent struggle, the party came to recognize the irrefutable truth that it must command the gun and build a people's military of its own. The people's military has made indelible achievements on behalf of the party and the people. It is a strong pillar for safeguarding our socialist country and preserving national dignity, and a powerful force for protecting peace in our region and beyond.

We will elevate our people's armed forces to world-class standards so that we are equipped with greater capacity and more reliable means for safeguarding our national sovereignty, security, and development interests. The Chinese nation does not carry aggressive or hegemonic traits in its genes... We will work to build a new type of international relations and a human community with a shared future, promote high-quality development of the Belt and Road Initiative through joint efforts, and use China's new achievements in development to provide the world with new opportunities.

The party will continue to work with all peace-loving countries and peoples to promote the shared human values of peace, development, fairness, justice, democracy, and freedom. We will continue to champion cooperation over confrontation, to open up rather than close our doors, and to focus on mutual benefits instead of zero-sum games. We will oppose hegemony and power politics and strive to keep the wheels of history rolling toward bright horizons.

We Chinese are a people who uphold justice and are not intimidated by threats of force...we will not allow any foreign force to abuse, oppress or subjugate us...we must ensure great unity and solidarity and balance commonality and diversity... We should strengthen theoretical and political guidance, build broad consensus, bring together the brightest minds, expand common ground, and seek convergence of interests, so that all Chinese people, both at home and overseas can focus their ingenuity and energy on the same goal and come together as a mighty force for national rejuvenation...We will stay true to the letter and spirit of the One Country, Two systems policy...No one should underestimate the resolve, the will, and the ability of the Chinese people to defend their national sovereignty and territorial integrity...it is certain that with the firm leadership of the Party and the great unity of the Chinese people, we will achieve the goal of building a great modern socialist country in all respects and fulfill the Chinese Dream of national rejuvenation."[55]

Xi Jinping's Governance of China IV is structured to start with Socialism with Chinese characteristics and the fundamental role of the Party in that it speaks to Party leadership matters and the necessity of putting people first and at the centre of development; it then speaks to challenges that must be confronted including resistance to "US Aggression" and help and support for North Korea; it deals with China's COVID response and the economic consequences; it deals with the strategy and stages of getting to high-quality development, and the strengthening of what Xi Jinping calls " whole process democracy" with the people of China, the strengthening of socialism and a socialist based economic rejuvenation, as essential to public well-being and social progress, and he also stresses the environmental side, speaking to the need for harmony between humanity and nature.[56]

The issue of national security is fundamental. "... we must consider development and security as of equal importance," Xi Jinping says, "We must assign the highest priority to political security.[57] This means that we must ensure the security of our State power, and political system... we must continue to promote global security for all."[58]

Food security is important to the Chinese leadership. "We must keep food security in our own hands," says Xi Jinping.[59] China-Asian relations are critical in international, economic, and foreign relations. Cooperation between China and the African continent is also highly valued. Xi Jinping outlines perspectives on China's relationship with Russia, the USA, Saudi Arabia, and the Middle East, among others. It is not by accident that the book is structured to end with a focus on the party's role in political and economic transformation and military strength. The connection between these fundamental issues is obvious—the paramountcy of the Party, the oneness of the Party with the people in maintaining Party leadership and National harmony and order. The link between these and economic strength, success and advance, and the importance of military strength and capacity to guarantee continued progress, security defence and foreign policy power. Xi Jinping emphasizes in a context where Party leadership is fundamental to economic, political, governmental, and military power, that corruption must be resisted and eradicated, and that the Party must perpetually engaged in self-reform.

10.14 The People's Republic of China and the Community of Latin American and Caribbean States (CELAC)

The first China CELAC meeting took place on 8 January 2015 in Beijing. The purpose of that meeting was to cement relations between the 33-member CELAC Block and China and create institutions and infrastructure for more effective collaboration.

This CELAC forum came just after the APEC Summit at which China had asserted its intention to engage in a more robust foreign policy and two years after he visited Trinidad and Tobago and his one-to-one meetings with CARICOM leaders, and on which journey he also met with the presidents of Costa Rica, Mexico, and the USA. By 2024, the Belt and Road Initiative, which would have been launched in 2013, has had significant buy-in in terms of sign-on by countries.

This is how the CELAC-China initiative is seen in various quarters. Jorge Hine, the Chilean Ambassador to China at the time, saw the initiative as coming at a point when growth in China and Latin America was slowing. Still, trade between the two regions was significantly increasing. He saw opportunities in Chinese investments and in deeper cooperation arrangements. He saw President Xi Jinping as having a deep interest in the region, having visited twice in two years, and he felt that the Chinese president discerned significant value from China's engagement with CELAC "in the forging of a new multipolar world order in the new century."[60]

Beatrice Rangel, a member of the Latin American Advisory Board of Dialogue and director of a Consulting firm, believes that China's thrust towards Latin America and the Caribbean is purely economic for now, but this will change with time. She observes that the Western Hemisphere has 25% of the world's energy resources and that at any rate of growth, low or high, China has energy deficits.[61] She also regards CELAC as "a good geopolitical platform for China, from which that country can operate in the Western Hemisphere. Upon the death of Venezuelan President Hugo Chavez, CELAC has become a character looking for a script. China can fill that void by using the organization to better secure its economic interests, wrapping them in the nice foil of international cooperation. We have seen this happen before as world powers seek order."[62]

Margaret Meyer, Director of the China Latin America program at the Inter-American Dialogue, sees China as an increasingly important economic partner for Latin America. She sees trade as growing significantly as well as the flow of Chinese investments, taking the form of mergers and acquisitions in extractive industries and agriculture. She notes that China has become a financial lifeline for Venezuela and Ecuador and is emerging as the major source of financing for other countries in the region. She sees China's relationship with CELAC as a diplomatic overture for economic purposes.[63]

Anton Edmunds, president and CEO of the Edmund's Group, International, LLC sees Latin America and the Caribbean as fragmented in their development and social and political agendas and is not very optimistic. "China today is a slowing economy whose leaders will be focused primarily on domestic growth and employment.[64] A mature and pragmatic approach with the larger regional economies will centre around market access for Chinese goods and services, with raw materials to be exploited continuing to be the key. Smaller economies in Central America and the Caribbean will, however, be relegated to the sidelines with sporadic initiatives, the best that they can expect. That said, a key plank of China's political agenda, which is to be active within this hemisphere, will ensure a presence. While the bulwark against Taiwan's influence may no longer be needed, Chinese interests align with those of some Latin American countries, in a common desire to try to keep the United States in check. China, as an economic power, provides cover, with well-known positions on non-interference in internal matters by external parties, notably the West, appealing to many."[65]

There can be little doubt that some see China as a countervailing force against the power of the USA and Europe in the Western Hemisphere for finance, infrastructure, investment, trade, markets humanitarian aid, and for facilitating economic growth but also as a partner for developing countries in international institutions to present an alternative view of world development.

CELAC was established in 2011, and China was involved from the beginning. At that founding meeting, Hugo Chavez read out aloud a congratulations letter from Hu Jintao, the then-leader of China, on the formation of the community block of nations.[66]

President Xi has taken a keen interest in the region, visiting Trinidad and Tobago, Costa Rica, Mexico in 2013, Brazil, Argentina, Venezuela, and Cuba in 2014, early in his Presidency. His pursuit of consolidating the BRICS group has generated interest and energy. Within the hemisphere, there is support for China as a containment force against China.

At the same time, some countries are fearful that some of the negatives of China's relationship with Africa and Asia could also befall Latin America and the Caribbean.[67]

The Congressional Research Service of the US Congress has taken an interest in China's interest in Latin America and the Caribbean. In their " In Focus" publication of 23 June 2023, Ricardo Barrios and Carla I Rios, analysts in Asian and Latin American Affairs respectively acknowledge that "Beijing's diplomatic initiatives in LAC have helped advance China's economic priorities, institutionalize its engagement in the region, and garner support in international fora.[68] Some analysts assess that the PRC's activities in LAC do not appear to be challenging the United States directly or militarily, yet reflect a global strategy to counter US influence."[69] The In Focus Newsletter takes notice of two important things 1) that a joint CELAC-China Action Plan 2022–2024 had been adopted to guide cooperation in politics, security, economy, and infrastructure and 2) that Xi Jinping in 2023 had described CELAC as China's "key partner in enhancing solidarity, among developing countries and furthering South-South cooperation."[70] The paper argues that CELAC can be a forum that succeeds in neutralizing and isolating Taiwan. The document notes that since 2017, five LAC governments have established formal diplomatic ties with China and have cut off relations with Taiwan.[71] The document presents a point of view from the Joe Biden administration, which concedes that the Western Hemisphere impacts the USA more than any other region does. Because of that, the Biden administration will seek "to further deepen partnerships in LAC to advance economic resilience, democratic stability, and citizen security." It also vows to protect LAC from "external interference or coercion, including from the PRC."[72]

The document reports that the US Southern Command is concerned about China's investments in deep-water ports and cyber and space facilities, which "can have a potential dual capacity to align commercial and military activities."[73] The authors also note a range of legislation on the books, pending or contemplated, that focus on setting parameters for strategic competition in the hemisphere on the one hand and greater economic prosperity for countries of the Western Hemisphere on the other.[74]

Alicia Barcena, Executive Secretary of ECLAC views cooperation between China and Latin America and the Caribbean as an "opportunity to reduce global asymmetries and support transformative, inclusive economic recovery that promotes sustainable development in line with the 2030 agenda." Others are more sceptical. They feel that China imposes few conditions on loans that it offers and turns a blind eye to environmental issues.[75]

Barcena senses the inevitable tensions inherent in China's hemispheric push: "Latin America and the Caribbean must seek to maintain, cultivate and deepen, constructive, harmonious and respectful relations with all the actors in the international system, while setting our compass on our own interests in regards to the urgent task of constructing our development route."[76] In other words, do things together in your best interest with China, but do not forget that you must live in this hemisphere with the USA.

10.14.1 Belt and Road

How does the Belt and Road Initiative fit in this strategy of China in relation to CELAC and the Caribbean and Latin America, and, what are the possible benefits and fallouts in this regard from the smaller countries in this partnership?

We can see a pattern emerging and a strategy at work by China. The 2008 China policy paper on Latin America and the Caribbean, by which time significant engagement of Asia and Africa had been achieved. Note that the BRICS group was created in 2006 by China, Brazil, Russia, and India. China had its sights on the Caribbean and Latin America as part of a global plan. CELAC was created in 2011, and China was very much in the picture, as noted earlier. The Belt and Road Initiative was launched in 2013 by President Xi Jinping, and in that same year, he visited Trinidad and Tobago. The Chinese president seized the opportunity to meet with and engage with all CARICOM leaders with diplomatic ties with China one-on-one. During that same trip, President Xi Jinping also paid visits to Costa Rica and Mexico, following which, in 2014, the Chinese president visited Venezuela, Cuba, Argentina, and Brazil. Then came the major summit of China and CELAC in 2015, after the APEX meeting in China's Great Hall of the People. And in 2015, Africa, with whom China has had a working relationship since the 1950s, agreed on an action plan (2016–2018). In 2014, the BRICS Summit was convened in Brazil, and in 2017, in South Africa.

10.14.2 *Worthy of Note*

It is important to summarize some developments already mentioned that are worthy of note:

(1) China has surpassed the World Bank, the Inter-American Development Bank,, and the IMF combined as Latin America's top lender for Energy and infrastructure projects. It is a larger lender in the Americas than the 22 Paris Club governments combined (Yueh 2024[77] Vehla and Santo 2024[78]).
(2) China is the largest export market for Brazil, Chile, Peru, Cuba, and Uruguay currently
(3) Imports from Latin America by the USA have fallen by 40% in the last 15 years
(4) China is a member of the IDB and the CDB, with significant shareholdings and influence in both banks. China enjoys observer status in the Organization of American States (OAS). It is difficult to conclude, other than that, that China has been positioning itself to play a bigger, more influential role not only in the Caribbean and Latin American region but in the hemisphere, focusing on both the Caribbean and Latin America. It should be noted that neither the USA nor Canada are members of CELAC. Based on asset size, China owns four of the largest banks in the world. These banks play a significant role in sustaining China's economic growth but also play an influential developmental role in the global financial landscape.

The four banks are:

(a) Bank of China
(b) China Construction Bank
(c) The Industrial Commercial Bank of China
(d) Agricultural Bank of China.

In addition, China has two main Development Finance Institutions (DFI's) that lend to governments, and intergovernmental bodies; for example, CARICOM or CELAC could technically be eligible; and they lend to majority State-owned entities, from Latin America and the Caribbean, whether wholly owned or partially owned by government, could technically be eligible. Generally, the security for such lending would be sovereign guarantees.

There can be little question that, regarding financial infrastructure and the banking and loan availability side, China has been ready for some time for government projects and continues to be. On the trade, investment, and development side, the Belt and Road Initiative puts China in a good position to play a key role in the development and partnership between the Caribbean and Latin America. China has been very strategic in getting to a point where for any project that a country wants or any kind of need that a country has, China is able to get that project or initiative to the point of execution.

10.14.3 The Promise, Opportunity, and Challenge of Belt and Road

In addition to the China Development Bank and the Export–Import Bank, China has established the China Silk Road Fund to support the Belt and Road Initiative, initially launched as "One Belt, One Road" in 2013. The fund was established at the end of 2014 to provide investment financing to support trade, economic cooperation, and connectivity under the Belt and Road Initiative. Fundamentally, it is a Chinese government guidance fund to foster increased investment in countries signed up for Belt and Road. According to the Asia Society Policy Institute and the Silk Road Fund Overview website, the ideal espoused is to promote development and prosperity in China and developing countries involved in the Belt and Road Initiative.[79] However, good intentions and mutually acceptable benefits can never be assured; they must be worked at, in order for mutually acceptable goals to be achieved.

Executive Director of ECLAC, Alicia Barcena, argued during a high-level forum of China-CELAC in 2017 that BRI, which she referred to by its original name of "One Belt, One Road," is a "civilizational proposal of interconnectedness and shared prosperity." She continued, "The One Belt, One Road initiative represents a renewal of, and a profound commitment to the values that are fundamental to our global, economic, and social wellbeing: interconnectedness, deeper trade and investment ties, transparency and openness, and the need for economic growth to be coupled with social progress ...I call on the nations of Latin America and the Caribbean to harness the potential that this initiative... has for refining capitalism through peoples' equality and dignity."

This promise not only enhances trade, investment, cooperation, and development but also transforms international economic arrangements and expectations and spreads the benefits of development across countries and internally within countries across a national population or regional population.

Throughout the chapters of this book, the growth in trade, investment, cooperation, infrastructure development, and economic, financial, and political relations between China, the Caribbean, and Latin America has been underscored. Opportunities have been seized, challenges have been weathered, and perils, some anticipated, some as yet, probably unforeseen, may surface.

Within the CELAC group and between Latin America and the Caribbean countries, there are countries of various sizes, capacities, levels of readiness, and economic and strategic potential, given the diversity of countries in the region based on physical size, population numbers, demography, and current levels of development.

Already, we see Latin American countries fast off the block and making tangible gains and progress, as well as Caribbean countries struggling with capacity deficits and structural challenges to meet the demands of twenty-first-century engagement as the world transforms economically and technologically.

In Chapter 4 of this book, it is noted that since 2019, there has been a shift to increased imports to China from low and middle-income economies of the developing world, which includes an increase from Latin America and the Caribbean. It seems that China, as a large economy, can have a pull-forward and/or pull-up effect on other economies. A simple benefit for a small developing country can be higher exports to China and the ready availability of goods and services from China at competitive prices. On the investment side, countries receiving FDI inflows from China, beyond the immediate benefits of investment, business generation, and their generally positive impact, can also benefit significantly from technology transfer if effectively managed. It is clear that as China grows, it will provide market opportunities and potential for trade and investment growth that will benefit other countries. The challenge for small Caribbean countries would be avoiding trade and investment dependence, something even the largest and most powerful countries seek to manage now.

China and CARICOM also share export markets. Caribbean countries must avoid or mitigate the displacement of exports that can occur through

China's competitive capacity. In Chapter 8, it is noted that China presents a competitive threat to CARICOM in terms of merchandise exports.

Chapter 7 discusses the spillover influences of China's growth. It is also clear that CARICOM countries must overcome some structural barriers to competitive capacity and development. It is not just a question of small size. Uruguay is small, yet China has become its main export market.

The structural problems that CARICOM must overcome include an infrastructure deficit, limited participation in the global value chain, and consumer dependence on imports, which is partially, though not entirely, due to structural deficiencies in economic production systems. The lethargy over CSME in CARICOM is a major liability in a world where every country trades and invests wherever possible. So, there is an urgent need for greater integration and synergy within CARICOM and CSME and for meticulously putting in place infrastructural arrangements to ensure ease of implementation and solidification of integration arrangements.

The Caribbean must organize its business in individual countries and as a regional block to do business effectively and beneficially, not only with China but with the rest of the world. As pointed out earlier, the Caribbean is not capitalizing effectively on CBI and CARIBCAN nor arrangements with the European Union or Britain. The region is hard-pressed to benefit from facilitative regional/hemispheric partnerships, which are with traditional European partners with whom beneficial arrangements have been negotiated. In this very Western Hemisphere, the Caribbean exports to and trades little with Central and South America. Therefore, the Caribbean must put its house in order to build out infrastructure, make structural adjustments, build capacity, and grow its economies to improve the quality of life of its people.

This volume proposes a partial scope agreement between China and CARICOM. The problem is that some CARICOM countries have diplomatic relations with Taiwan. Indeed, St Vincent and the Grenadines, whose prime minister, Dr Ralph Gonzalves, will be Chairman of CELAC in 2024, has diplomatic relations with Taiwan.

The CELAC-China summits and the Belt and Road Initiatives, together with the growing presence and influence of China in the Americas, the ongoing geopolitics of China's "One China, Two Systems" policy, and how the China Sea and Taiwan Straits and China-Taiwan-USA issues are managed to resolution, comfort, or conflict, can neutralize Taiwan in this hemisphere and open the door for China's establishment of diplomatic relations with all countries of CARICOM and CELAC. That will improve opportunities for countries out of China's diplomatic loop and open the door to institutional support, including financing, for CARICOM and CELAC.

The USA has responded to China's initiatives and impact in the region since the last Summit of the Americas. The question of ideology came up; some countries were excluded, and the Mexican president, notably, did not attend. However, constructive initiatives were taken to deepen relations with CARICOM, with US Vice President Kamala Harris in charge on the White House end. In addition, hemispheric committees were established in key areas such as Energy, Security, and Investment to address cooperation and coordination against the glaring neglect by the USA of the Western Hemisphere. So, it is not unfair to say that China's push towards the Caribbean and Latin America has elicited a response from the USA that might benefit CARICOM and Latin American countries in the hemisphere.

Apart from China, other countries from outside are active in the Americas. This includes Russia, Iran, Japan, Turkey, and Saudi Arabia, among others, and global terrorist groups may be positioning themselves.

In addition, the ideological divide and the Trump effect, as with Bolsonaro in Brazil and Javier Milei in Argentina, are factors. Cuba presents a problem for the USA because of local political considerations, but no country in the hemisphere shares the US position on Cuba. The Venezuela issue is being managed. Only time will tell if US management of the Venezuelan challenge is indeed effective.

In the challenging economic circumstances that China faces at home, and China's One China, Two Systems policy also being under fire, China may become more aggressive militarily around its borders and in the waters surrounding it but may not necessarily want to provoke confrontation elsewhere. It will continue its strategy towards the Caribbean and Latin America but will likely exercise necessary restraint. Economic challenges at home, though, may make China more adventurous for trade, investment, and development opportunities in the Caribbean and Latin American region, but it may well be more cautious when it comes to financing strategies. China, however, may be highly flexible in its Belt and Road arrangements to harness more countries and projects and offset the slowdown inside China. In addition, China's global strategy for developing countries to effect a restructuring and recalibration of the world order remains a persistent Chinese objective. In like manner, the geopolitical value of strengthening relations with CELAC also remains important in terms of containment of the USA, creating a countervailing capacity within the Western Hemisphere, and in terms of China's global strategy to build a developing world alliance to challenge the status quo and to reshape the global order.

The challenge for the Caribbean is whether these countries can navigate and how well. The Caribbean needs to enhance its relationship with China and win benefits in its own best interest without jeopardizing its good relations with the USA, with Canada (hemispheric neighbours and allies with significant diasporas) with Europe, and the UK (longstanding relationship since colonial times) and with other Central and South American neighbours (good relations generally). This requires some looking inward, fixing and reaching outward, and embracing opportunities from a more competitive platform. If CARICOM, for instance, could make better opportunistic use of CBI, CARIBCAN, EU Partnership, and UK partnership and build a new, formidable collaboration with China as it enhances its relationship with traditional partners and strengthens bonds with Latin America, it could be in an enviable place.

An open area of focus for CARICOM countries could be a collaborative Tourism strategy with China. China is well invested in Tourism in Cuba and is enhancing its involvement with Tourism in the Bahamas. However, it is largely invisible in the tourism sector in the region, while tourism is the number one industry and foreign exchange earner in most Caribbean countries.

Perhaps a collaborative approach could link investment, the Chinese market, in China, as well as, throughout China's diaspora, investment in agriculture, food processing, fish farming, restaurants, entertainment, culture, outdoor activities, including sun sand and sea, swamplands, forests, nature trails, hiking, turtle watching, diversity exposure, and a range of experiences that citizens take for granted in the region and all of which can be effectively packaged and properly managed in an attractive customer-friendly way.

So, there is a course of travel to design and navigate; the Caribbean has to reorganize itself for effective business arrangements; the region needs to identify export products for a successful thrust; we have to balance the interests of those countries on whom the region depends, yet win new opportunities; we need to craft an innovative relationship with China, and we need to make a special effort with tourism and tourism investment and industries and an eco-system built around it.

10.15 The Grand Vision

The Chinese Communist Party and its leaders, in sequence, tend to present grand visions for China to attain and for the world to aspire towards. The current Leadership of the Party and Xi Jinping as president of China, General Secretary of the Party, and Commander of Military Forces is no different. To his name, we have phrases like "economic rejuvenation," "The Belt and Road Initiative," and "The Chinese Dream" associated with it. These phrases are identified with Xi Jinping and this period of Chinese history. In 2019, the Institute of Party History and Literature of the Central Committee of the Communist Party of China published some of the speeches of Xi Jinping under the title "On Building A Human Community With A Shared Future."

In one of his speeches in which Xi Jinping affirms that the Belt and Road Initiative is not empty talk but will lead to tangible successes for countries, this is what he says: "Today the connectivity we need to build is not just about creating roads and bridges or making linear surface connections. Instead, it should be more about three integrated pillars—infrastructure, rules, and institutions and flows of people. It should involve equal priority to progress in five areas—policy communication, infrastructure connectivity, trade links, capital flows, and bonds between peoples. This kind of big connectivity involving every front is multi-dimensional and forms a network that creates an open system enabling dynamism and flows of talent and resources." It is a grand vision of interconnectivity for cross-border inclusion.[80] And again: "… we should build the belt and road into a road of innovation. Innovation is an important force powering development. The BRI is a pioneering undertaking, and we must encourage innovation to keep it moving forward. We should promote innovation-driven development and intensify cooperation in frontier areas such as the digital economy, artificial intelligence, nanotechnology, and quantum computing. We should also advance the development of big data, cloud computing, and smart cities to form a digital silk road of the twenty-first century. We should promote the full integration of science and technology into industry and finance and improve the environment for innovation. And in this age of the internet, we should create spaces and build workshops for young people from different countries to pursue entrepreneurship and realize their dreams."

This is a vision of BRI as a collaborative hand-up to achievement, progress, and success in the twenty-first century. Moreover, there is a vision for 2049, the hundredth anniversary of the founding of the Republic of China. By this time, the Chinese government hopes to "build a modern socialist country that is prosperous, democratic and harmonious." At the same time, the vision is for a "world-class" military because world peace and stability depend on it.

This is the Chinese Dream for a prosperous socialist success story after 100 years of national effort, and the aspiration for BRI is to pull up, pull forward, and enable development, progress, and success for as many countries that can achieve this through the Belt and Road Initiative. What if there would be a convergence? That would be China's celebratory story and victory as a world power—success by their own efforts on the one hand and collective success in the world system for many countries and peoples through collaboration, driven and led by China, on the other.

10.16 Conclusion

While China's immense size and growing influence present significant opportunities for smaller Caribbean nations, it is essential to navigate this relationship strategically. The Caribbean has a history of engaging with larger powers, and the potential benefits of partnerships with China through initiatives like the Belt and Road can be significant. However, balancing these ties with existing relationships with the USA, Canada, and Europe is crucial to avoid over-dependence on any single nation. Yet, the Caribbean must also address its structural challenges, such as limited market size and reliance on imports, to effectively capitalize on these opportunities.

The region's navigation of trade and development partnerships must also occur against global tensions, including the war in Ukraine, Israel's war with Hamas, with the potential for explosion in the Middle East, largely sponsored terrorism everywhere, and the constant threat of nuclear annihilation; the world seems a dangerous and unpredictable place. Venezuela, a Latin American country close to the Caribbean whose shores are washed by the Caribbean Sea, can become a challenge in managing the geopolitics of the Western Hemisphere.[81]

The Donald Trump presidency has brought a robustness and unpredictability to geopolitical engagement by the White House, that is unprecedented. The tarrif impositions on China, met with retaliation by China, has by no means been off set by harsh tarrifs on bordering neighbours of the US, Canada and Mexico nor by those on Europe. In fact it has reversed globalization and stopped free trade in its tracks. "If war is what the US wants--be it a tarrif war, a trade war or any other type of war- we are willing to fight till the end" said a March 5 2025, tweet on X, by the Chinese Embassy in Washington, DC, and as reported by Laura Bicker, BBC News, Beijing. This was on the eve of China's week long National People's Congress and was a direct response to President Trump's speech to a joint sitting of Congress and Senate on March 4, 2025, described as an "unyielding" speech by the Associated Press.

Before the Trump Presidency, avoidance of the Thucydides Trap, was a consistently articulated position of Xi Jinping. We have noted earler, that the Chinese President went out of his way to give comfort to former US Secretary of State, Anthony Blinken, that China expects to be respected, but, that it had no appetite for war with the US, during a period under the Biden administration, when tensions heightened between those two countries over Taiwan, spy balloons over US territory, and related matters. The China statement of March 5, represents an aggressive shift of tone and disposition by China in response to US stridency. The battle for technological superiority has also been an issue between the US and China for some time, but the articulated positions by China and the USA have become sharper if not shriller. The New York Times on March 11, 2025, reported that Xi Jinping at the National People s Congress, set a goal for China to become a technological Superpower. The Chinese unveiling of Deepseek just weeks before, adds some realism to this aspiration.

US President Trump has not been shy about articulating his position that the USA is pursuing dominance in AI. Indeed in his address to Congress, he outlined a broad "America first" vision for dominance in all things including space technology. In that speech he talked about military and technological superiority as well as a protective shield over the USA and the desire to plant an American flag on Mars (Speech of US President Trump to Congress March 4, 2025).

Competition between China and the USA will undoubtedly proceed on trade, technology, and probably all other strategic fronts. Whether it will be a healthy rivalry or lead eventually, to increasing conflict and military confrontation is another matter altogether. What does that mean for the Caribbean and this Hemisphere? President Trump has sent strong signals on the Panama Canal, Venezuela and Cuba in addition to a clearly hegemonic interest in the Western Hemisphere from Greenland to Argentina. This may well be a frame being established for serious dialogue and negotiations with Xi Jinping and China, as negotiations over peace making between Russia and Ukraine set the stage for wider US/ Russia engagement on respective geographical domains of influence, as well as new terms and conditions to avoid escalation of geopolitical tensions and to maintain a peaceful world in which USA, Russia and China cooperate as well as compete. What that will mean for China's continued involvement in the Hemisphere is likely to involve a tension ridden navigation. The question now arises as to how will these tensions affect US engagement within a Western Hemisphere of boundary challenges, ideological clashes, junctures and disjunctures? Moreover how will the US positioning towards the Hemisphere of the Americas, condition it's approach to other regional domains of the global arena where China and Russia are geographically present and exert influence, regionally? In this imminent renavigation of geopolitical terrain, the developing world may well end up as casualties, leading to the marginalisation of the vast majority of developing countries. Life may well turn out to be more difficult for them in a differently conceived multi-polar world. In such an emerging scenario, developing countries may well have, resourcefully and strategically, to engage not only powerful geopolitical rivals but, may also have to resolve to promote strong, more meaningful regional partnerships as well as mutually beneficial partnerships in trade, investment, technical and technological cooperation, across the so called developing world of technologically and industrially, less advanced countries. The countries of the Caribbean, individually and as CARICOM, may well have to pursue a survival and sustainability strategy directed to the developing world, that complements strategic engagement of the larger, more powerful, geopolitical giants. To this end, the geopolitical landscape, influenced by China's ambitions and the ongoing tensions with the USA, necessitates careful diplomacy and constant vigilance. A thoughtful approach emphasizing cooperation, economic integration, and sustainable development will be critical for Caribbean nations to navigate their role in this evolving global order.

Notes

1. World Atlas.
2. Ibid.
3. Ibid.
4. Ibid.
5. World Trade Organization.
6. European Commission.
7. Journal on Eastern Caribbean Studies, "UWI-GLOBAL Belt & Road Research Bulletin: Caribbean Perspectives on the Belt & Road Initiative Issue 1".
8. Annita Montoute, "The State Council, The People's Republic of China.
9. Worldometer, 2024.
10. Ibid.
11. Ibid.
12. Michael Porter, "The Competitive Advantage of Nations" 1990.
13. Socialism with Chinese Characteristics in the New Era 2022. pp. 16–17.
14. Yanling Xu et al. "Impact of COVID-19 on transportation and logistics: a case of China", 2021.
15. United Nations Conference on Trade and Development, 2024.
16. The Maritime Executive, "Chinese Firm Wins Tender to Build Peru's Third Largest Seaport" 2024.
17. The Guardian "What was it for?': the mental toll of China's three years in Covid lockdowns".
18. BBC "Covid origin: Why the Wuhan lab-leak theory is so disputed" 2023.
19. OECD "Economic Impact Assessment of the Global Minimum Tax" 2024.
20. Forbes, "Why Nearshoring Is Closer Than Ever: How Mexico Is Becoming the Next Big Thing In Global Markets" 2023.
21. Emmy Wassenius et al. "A global analysis of potential self-sufficiency and diversity displays diverse supply risks" 2023.
22. https://una.com/resources/article/shifting-manufacturing-out-of-china/#:~:text=Many%20U.S.%20companies%20realized%20the,risks%20associated%20with%20unexpected%20disruptions.
23. https://www.forbes.com/sites/betsyatkins/2023/08/07/manufacturing-moving-out-of-china-for-friendlier-shores/

24. IMF, "China Stumbles but is unlikely to fall" 2023.
25. https://cepr.org/voxeu/columns/trapped-china-and-middle-income-trap.
26. The Economist, "Protests are soaring, as China's workers demand their wages".
27. CNN, 2024.
28. Ibid.
29. https://edition.cnn.com/2024/01/08/americas/china-us-migrants-illegal-crossings-intl-hnk-dst/index.html.
30. Ibid.
31. https://www.washingtonpost.com/immigration/interactive/2024/china-migrants-us-border-san-diego-new-york/.
32. China Leadership Monitor "The Covid–19 Pandemic and China's Economic Slowdown".
33. Brookings "The impact of Taiwan's election in 2024 and beyond".
34. American Affairs "New Era for the Chinese Semiconductor Industry: Beijing Responds to Export Controls".
35. Council on Foreign Affairs "U.S.-Taiwan Relations in a New Era".
36. Ibid.
37. Aljazeera "Biden and Xi hold first discussions since November, talk Taiwan and tech".
38. https://www.lawfaremedia.org/article/the-dangers-of-peak-china.
39. https://www.businessinsider.com/china-problems-has-us-worried-itll-be-more-aggressive-2024-3.
40. Qiushi Journal "Vigorously Advancing High-Quality Development".
41. Reuters "China's choreographed political meet carries a message of control.
42. Nick Carraway, The Diplomat "China's Two Sessions Announces a 5 Percent Growth Target and 1 trillion yuan National Bond".
43. Deccan Herald "Beijing is aware of the Bumpy ride ahead".
44. Bloomberg "China's Xi Urges Focus on Security Amid Simmering US Tensions".
45. Ibid.
46. Aljazeera "Five key takeaways from China's annual meeting of parliament".
47. Ibid.
48. Laura He and Wayne Chang, CNN.

49. Ibid.
50. Ibid.
51. Laura He and Wayne Chang, CNN.
52. Peter Yeung, Aljazeera.
53. Xi Jinping: The Governance of China Volume Four.
54. Xi Jinping: The Governance of China Volume Four P124.
55. Xi Jinping: The Governance of China Volume Four.
56. Ibid.
57. Ibid.
58. Ibid.
59. Ibid.
60. The Dialogue "China, CELAC & China-LAC Relations".
61. Beatrice Rangel "With China it is about Reciprocity not Getting Even".
62. Ibid.
63. The Dialogue "Myers: China's Increasing Involvement in Latin America and the Caribbean".
64. The Dialogue "Anton Edwards: The State of China-Latin America Relations".
65. Ibid.
66. Merco Press "China becomes the first to congratulate Latin-American countries on CELAC".
67. The Diplomat "BRICS: A China-Led Group Looking for Relevance".
68. Congressional Research Service "China's Engagement with Latin America and the Caribbean".
69. Ibid.
70. Ibid.
71. Congressional Research Service "China's Engagement with Latin America and the Caribbean".
72. Ibid.
73. Ibid.
74. Ibid.
75. Alicia Bárcena, United Nations ECLAC.
76. Ibid.
77. https://www.tandfonline.com/doi/full/10.1080/10971475.2024.2350124.

78. https://www.bu.edu/gdp/2024/06/14/feeling-the-stones-chinese-development-finance-to-latin-america-and-the-caribbean-2023/.
79. Council on Foreign Relations "China's Massive Belt and Road Initiative".
80. Xi Jinping: The Governance of China Volume Four pp. 176–177.
81. The impasse over the July 2024 elections in Venezuela has put China and the USA on different sides regarding Venezuela's future. China and several other countries have recognized Nicholas Maduro as the continuing president of Venezuela. Still, the USA and Europe recognize Edmundo Gonzales, who went into exile in Spain. In the circumstances, the USA has begun to roll back sanctions set into motion in the hope that Venezuela would have had free and fair elections. China will give Maduro support as needed. While the Venezuelan president's inauguration ceremony is in January 2025, in October 2024, a Venezuelan application to be a full member of BRICS is likely to be approved at the BRICS meeting in Kazan, and Maduro will be hosting a China-CELAC business meeting in Venezuela in 2026.

References

Al Jazeera and News Agencies. (2021). *Al Jazeera and News Agencies*. Retrieved 2023, from https://www.aljazeera.com/news/2021/5/31/china-eases-birth-limit-allows-couple-to-have-3-children

Amadeo, K. (2022). How the Yuan Could Become a Global Currency. *The Balance*.

Ang, S. a. (2021). Analysis: High LNG prices trigger gas demand destruction in China's downstream sectors. *S&P Global Commodity insights*.

Arostegui, M. (2020). Chinese firm offers to replace faulty test kits sold to Spain. *VOA*.

Atkinson, D. M. (2020). *Competing with China: A strategic framework*. Retrieved 2024, from Information Technology & Innovation Foundation: https://itif.org/publications/2020/08/31/competing-china-strategic-framework/

Bahavna Dave, Y. K. (2018). *China's silk road economic belt initiative in Central Asia: economic and security implications*. Springer Link.

Batista, J. C. (2008). Competition between Brazil and other exporting countries in the US import market: A new extension of constant-market-shares analysis. *Applied Economics, 40*, 2477–2487.

BBC. (2010). China dairy products found tainted with melamine. *BBC*.

BBC. (2011). Mass arrests in China illegal 'gutter oil' police sting. *BBC*.

Beijing Newsroom. (2022). China to extend FX market trading hours to further internationalise yuan. *Reuters*.

Berman, A. S. (2023). The Dollar: The World's Reserve Currency. *Council on Foreign Relations*.

Bernhard, W. M. (2021). Why Might Taiwan's Allies in Latin America and the Caribbean Soon Look to China? *Global Americans*.

R. Hosein et al., *China in the Caribbean*,
https://doi.org/10.1007/978-3-031-71985-1

Bersola, C. (2023). Outbound travel from China set to reach 228 million a year by 2030, says new report. *The Moodie Davitt Report*.
Best, R. (2023). *How the U.S. Dollar Became the World's Reserve Currency.* Retrieved 2023, from Investopedia: https://www.investopedia.com/articles/forex-currencies/092316/how-us-dollar-became-worlds-reserve-currency.asp
Best, R. (2023). *How the U.S. Dollar Became the World's Reserve Currency.* Retrieved 2024, from Investopedia: https://www.investopedia.com/articles/forex-currencies/092316/how-us-dollar-became-worlds-reserve-currency.asp
Blanchard, B. (2012). Xi Jinping's journey from China party elite to party leader. *Reuters*.
Britannica, T. E. (2023). Tiananmen Square incident. *Encyclopedia Britannica*.
British Petroleum. (2021). *Statistical Review of World Energy – 2021.* Retrieved 2023, from BP: https://www.bp.com/content/dam/bp/business-sites/en/global/corporate/pdfs/energy-economics/statistical-review/bp-stats-review-2021-china-insights.pdf
Caribbean Development Bank. (2024). *Non-Borrowing Members*.
Carol Bertaut, B. V. (2021). *The International Role of the U.S. Dollar.* Retrieved 2024, from Board of Governors of the Federal Reserve System: https://www.federalreserve.gov/econres/notes/feds-notes/the-international-role-of-the-u-s-dollar-20211006.html
Carr, E. (2023). China's Engagement In the The Caribbean and The United States' Response. *Forbes*.
Chen, D. M. (2019). 'Foreign Interference'in Hong Kong: China's Own Historical Antecedents. *RSIS Commentaries*.
Chilton, L. H. (1919). *A Brief History of Europe from 1789 to 1815*. The Macmillan Company.
China Labour Bulletin. (2023). Migrant workers and their children. *China Labour Bulletin*.
Chow, E. (2023). In 2023, China's appetite for LNG set to rise amid tepid demand across Asia. *Reuters*.
Congressional Research Service. (2022). *The U.S. Dollar as the World's Dominant Reserve Currency.* Retrieved 2023, from Congressional Research Service: https://crsreports.congress.gov/product/pdf/IF/IF11707
Conversation, M. P. (2023a). How long will the dollar last as the world's default currency? The BRICS nations are gathering in South Africa this August with it on the agenda. *Fortune*.
Conversation, T. C. (2023b). The Chinese Yuan could finally become a fierce competitor for the US dollar. *Fortune*.
Conversation, T. C. (2023c). The Chinese Yuan could finally become a fierce competitor for the US dollar. *Fortune*.
Dai, Y. (2019). *The White Lotus War: Rebellion and Suppression in Late Imperial China*. University of Washington Press.

Daniel Hurst, K. M. (2020). Morrison asks for dialogue with China as other countries pledge support for Australia. *The Guardian.*

Dawnay, K. (2001). A history of sterling. *The Telegraph.*

Eckart, J. (2016). *8 Things you need to know about China's economy.* Retrieved 2023, from https://www.weforum.org/agenda/2016/06/8-facts-about-chinas-economy/

Economics, T. (2024). *Suriname Exports.* Retrieved 2023, from https://tradingeconomics.com/suriname/exports

European Environmental Bureau. (2019). *'Flood' of toxic Chinese toys threatens children's health.* Retrieved from https://eeb.org/flood-of-toxic-chinese-toys-threatens-childrens-health/#:~:text=National%20officials%20blocked%20248%20models,with%20phthalates%2C%20a%20plastic%20additive

Feliz, R. A. (2021). *The Fed Explained What the Central Bank Does.* Retrieved 2023, from Board of Governors of the Federal Reserve System: https://www.federalreserve.gov/aboutthefed/files/the-fed-explained.pdf

Fleming, D. C. (2015). Introduction to the Problem: . *The Gavel.*

Foreign Affairs Committee. (2023). *China Regional Snapshot:The Caribbean.* Retrieved 2023, from https://foreignaffairs.house.gov/china-snapshot-project-the-caribbean/

Freeman, R. B. (2015). *A Labor Market with Chinese Characteristics.* Routledge.

Gisela Grieger. (2020). *China's economic recovery and dual circulation model.* Retrieved from European Parliament: https://www.europarl.europa.eu/RegData/etudes/BRIE/2020/659407/EPRS_BRI(2020)659407_EN.pdf

Golubkova, Y. O. (2023). China 2023 gas demand likely to grow, but LNG outlook cloudy - PetroChina Intl exec. *Reuters.*

Gong Yue, W. Y. (2022). Urbanisation of the Chinese Rural Population:. *China: An International Journal.*

Gonzalez-Agote, M. O.-I. (2023). *China's RMB isn't set to outpace the dollar in Latin America…yet.* Retrieved 2023, from The Dialogue: https://www.thedialogue.org/blogs/2023/06/chinas-rmb-isnt-set-to-outpace-the-dollar-in-latin-americayet/

Green, M. (2018). China's Maritime Silk Road: Strategic and Economic Implications for the Indo-Pacific Region. *Center for Strategic & International Studies.*

Greenberg, A. S. (n.d.). *What Does China Want between 1820 and 1839 the annual shipments of Opium into China increased from 4000 to 40000 chests.* (p. 221).

Gresham House. (2020). *Global Timber Outlook 2020.* Retrieved 2023, from Gresham House: https://greshamhouse.com/wp-content/uploads/2020/07/GHGTO2020FINAL.pdf

Hang, H. C. (2016). *China, imperial: 8. Qing or Manchu dynasty period, 1636–1911*. Retrieved 2023, from Wiley Online Library: https://doi.org/10.1002/9781118455074.wbeoe287

Hao, L. K. (2023). Yuan meets all criteria to be a cross-border trade currency. *China Daily*.

Haque, A. (2023). *Will the Yuan Become the World's Reserve Currency?* Retrieved 2023, from Linkedin: https://www.linkedin.com/pulse/yuan-become-worlds-reserve-currency-ariful-haque/

Hayley, A. (2023). China 2023 oil demand growth seen slower on strong EV sales. *Reuters*.

Hein, M. v. (2018). Xi Jinping and the 'Chinese Dream'. *DW*.

Hesketh, P. Y. (2016). The effects of China's universal two-child policy. *The Lancet*.

History.com Editors. (2009). *History* . Retrieved 2023, from https://www.history.com/topics/asian-history/cultural-revolution

Holcombe, C. (2001). *The Genesis of East Asia, 221 B.C.-A.D. 907*. University of Hawai'i Press.

Homer, W. (2023). China's Demand for Oil Hits Record as IEA Raises Global Forecasts. *The Wall Street Journal*.

Hui He, F. H. (2018). Breaking the "iron rice bowl:" Evidence of precautionary savings from the chinese state-owned enterprises reform. *Journal of Monetary Economics, 94*, 94.

Huld, A. (2023). China's Changing Labor Market – Trends and Future Outlook. *China Briefing*.

Idrees Ali, P. S. (2018). "Significant" consequences if China takes key port in Djibouti: U.S. general. *Reuters*.

Interesse, G. (2023). China's Tourism Sector Prospects in 2023–24. *China Briefing*.

Interesse, G. (2023). China-Australia Trade Relations Growing Stronger (Updated). *China Briefing*.

International Energy Agency. (2023). *Global EV Outlook 2023 Catching up with climate ambitions*. International Energy Agency.

Jain-Chandra, D. A. (2023). *China's Economy is Rebounding, But Reforms Are Still Needed*. Retrieved 2023, from International Monetary Fund: https://www.imf.org/en/News/Articles/2023/02/02/cf-chinas-economy-is-rebounding-but-reforms-are-still-needed

Jenkins, R. (2008). Measuring the competitive Threat from China for other Southern Exporters. *The World Economy, 31*, 1351–1366.

Jenkins, R., & Edwards, L. (2015). Is China 'crowding out' South African exports of manufactures? *European Journal of Development Research, 27*, 903–920.

Joseph Phiri, K. M.-K. (2021). Durability of Zambia's Agricultural Exports. *Agriculture.*

Kang, O. (2004). Higher Education Reform in China Today. *Policy Futures in Education.*

Karl, R. E. (2010). *Mao Zedong and China in the Twentieth-Century World: A Concise History.* Duke University Press.

Karlstroem, B. S. (1967). *How Did They Become Reserve Currencies?* Retrieved 2023, from IMF eLibrary: https://www.elibrary.imf.org/view/journals/022/0004/003/article-A007-en.xml

Khan, S. R. (2015). *Caribbean Economic.* Retrieved 2023, from IDB: https://publications.iadb.org/publications/english/document/Caribbean-Economic-Alchemy-Has-Magic-Returned-to-Bauxite.pdf

Kinjo, D. C. (2006). *The role of embassies and consulates in promoting trade: Does economic freedom in the host economy matter?*

Kissinger, C. C. (2004). *How maoist revolution wiped out drug addiction in China.* RCP Publications.

Knowema. (2022). *Aluminum Price Forecast: 2021, 2022 and Long Term to 2035.* Retrieved 2023, from Knowema: https://knoema.com/infographics/ffzioof/aluminum-price-forecast-2021-2022-and-long-term-to-2035

Kung, T. C.-S. (2019). Why the song dynasty? The rise of a merchant class and the emergence of meritocracy in China.

Lane, R. D. (2008). *Encyclopedia small silver coins.*

Lau, L. (2023). The prospects for the Chinese Economy in 2023 and Beyond. *CHINA US Focus.*

Lavelle, P. (2017). The Historial Roots of China's industrial Revolution. *China Dialogue.*

Lieberthal, K. G. (2023). Cultural revolution. *Encyclopedia Britannica.* Retrieved from https://www.britannica.com/event/Cultural-Revolution

Liu, Z. Z. (2022). China Is Quietly Trying to Dethrone the Dollar. *Foreign Policy.*

Lowe, S. (2021). RUSAL's plan to upgrade bauxite operations here raises other key issues. *Kaieteur News.*

Lynch, Y. H. (2013). *Does Internationalizing the RMB Make Sense for China?* Retrieved 2023, from CARNEGIE: https://carnegieendowment.org/2013/09/01/does-internationalizing-rmb-make-sense-for-china-pub-53119

MacDonald, S. B. (2022). The Caribbean and U.S.-China Strategic Competition: Next Phase of the New Cold War? *China Brief.*

Mao Zedong. (2001). *Microsoft Encrata Encyclopedia.*

Matthew P. Funaiole, J. E. (2018). China's Maritime Silk Road Initiative: Economic Drivers and Challenges. *Center for Strategic & International Studies.*

Megan(2021). Top 8 Fastest-Growing Industries in China 2021. *China Success Stories*.
Miller, I. M. (2013). Rebellion, crime and violence in Qing China, 1722–1911: A topic modeling approach. *poetics*, 626–649.
Ministry of Foreign Affairs, the People's Republic of China. (2023). *US Hegemony and Its Perils*. Retrieved 2023, from Ministry of Foreign Affairs, the People's Republic of China: https://www.fmprc.gov.cn/mfa_eng/wjbxw/202302/t20230220_11027664.html
Munroe, D. S. (2021). Three-child policy: China lifts cap on births in major policy shift. *Reuters*. Retrieved 2023, from https://www.reuters.com/world/china/china-says-each-couple-can-have-three-children-change-policy-2021-05-31/
Nations, U. (2022). *China's structural transformation what can developing countries learn?* Retrieved 2023, from United Nations: chrome-extension://efaidnbmnnnibpcajpcglclefindmkaj/https://unctad.org/system/files/official-document/gds2022d1_en.pdf
NBC News. (2015). *NBC News*. Retrieved 2023, from https://www.nbcnews.com/storyline/2014-year-in-review/analysis-chinas-xi-jinping-amasses-power-huge-corruption-crackdown-n270001
Nicola Coniglio, R. L. (2017). The pattern of structural change: testing the Product Space framework. *Papers in Evolutionary Economic Geography*.
Nikkei Asia. (2018). *Brahma Chellaney: China is ensnaring vulnerable states in debt traps*. Retrieved from Nikkei Asia: https://asia.nikkei.com/Politics/Brahma-Chellaney-China-is-ensnaring-vulnerable-states-in-debt-traps
Nulimaimaiti, M. (2023). China population: 100 million more senior citizens expected in next decade as ageing crisis enters 'crucial juncture'. *South China Morning Post*.
Oakley, S. (2013). Here's What China is secretly planning for the Yuan. *CNBC*.
OECD. (2023). *Population with tertiary education*. Retrieved 2023, from OECD: https://data.oecd.org/eduatt/population-with-tertiary-education.htm
O'Neill, M. (2010). 45 million died in Mao's Great Leap Forward, Hong Kong historian says in new book. *South China Morning Post*.
Ozden, C. F. (2008). Trade Policy and Loss Aversion. *American Economic Review*.
Perlez, J. (2012). Close Army Ties of China's New Leader Could Test the U.S. *The New York Times*.
Pettis, M. (2023). *Can China's Long-Term Growth Rate Exceed 2–3 Percent?* Retrieved 2023, from CARNEGIE: https://carnegieendowment.org/chinafinancialmarkets/89466

Pistilli, M. (2024). *How Would a New BRICS Currency Affect the US Dollar? (Updated 2024)*. Retrieved 2024, from Investing News Network: https://investingnews.com/brics-currency/

Ramachandran, S. (2018). The China-Maldives Connection. *The Diplomat*.

Rodrigue, D.J.-P. (2020). Share of the world commodity consumption, China and United States, c2020. In D.J.-P. Rodrigue (Ed.), *The geography of transport systems*. Routledge.

Rodrik, D. (1997). Globalization, Social Conflict and Economic Growth. *The World Economy*. Retrieved 2023, from United Nations.

Ross, S. (2023). *4 Countries that Produce the Most Food*. Retrieved 2024, from Investopedia: https://www.investopedia.com/articles/investing/100615/4-countries-produce-most-food.asp

Sajid, K. M. (2018). Chinese economy under Mao Zedong and Deng Xiaoping. *Journal of Political Studies*, 169–178.

Schuman, M. (2020). China has dominated the west before. *The Atlantic*.

Shavkat Otamurodov, S. Z. (2016). The role of extensive margin and intensive margin in Kazakhstan's export growth. *Ecoforum*.

Shi, Z. (2017). *Agricultural development in Qing China*. BRILL.

Stanway, D. (2021). China energy crunch triggers shutdowns, pleas for more coal. *Reuters*.

Steinsson, J. (2023). How Did Growth Begin? TheIndustrial Revolution and its Antecedents. *Econometrics Laboratory*.

Strange, S. (1971). The politics of international currencies. *World Politics*.

Su, A. (2020). Faulty masks. Flawed tests. China's quality control problem in leading global COVID-19 fight. *Los Angeles Times*.

Subrahmanyam, V. (2023). China's Digital Currency: The hopes and fears of the e-CNY. *China Currents*.

Sullivan, J. (2023). A BRICS Currency Could Shake the Dollar's Dominance. *Foreign Policy*.

Swanson, A. (2016). Why the industrial revolution didn't happen in China. *The Washington Post*.

Tao, L. Z. (2014). *The Benefits and Costs of Renminbi Internationalization*. Retrieved 2023, from Asian Development Bank Institute: https://www.adb.org/sites/default/files/publication/156336/adbi-wp481.pdf

The Business Research Company. (2024). *Aluminium Global Market Report*. The Business Research Company.

The Diplomat. (2023). Where are Australia–China relations headed? *The Diplomat*.

The Wall Street Journal. (2018). *The Wall Street Journal*. Retrieved 2023.

The World Bank. (2020). *China: Fighting Air Pollution and Climate Change through Clean Energy Financing*. Retrieved 2023, from The World

Bank: https://www.worldbank.org/en/results/2020/06/21/china-fighting-air-pollution-and-climate-change-through-clean-energy-financing
Thomas Costigan, D. C. (2017). The US Dollar as the Global Reserve Currency: Implications for US Hegemony. *World Review of Political Economy*, 104–122.
Thompson, G. (2021). *China becomes the world's largest LNG market*. Retrieved 2023, from Wood MAckenzie: https://www.woodmac.com/news/opinion/china-becomes-the-worlds-largest-lng-market/
Tonga PM Calls on China to Write-off Pacific Debt. (2018). *Voice of America*.
Trading Economics. (2024). *China Minimum Monthly Wages*. Retrieved 2024, from https://tradingeconomics.com/china/minimum-wages
Tran, H. (2022). *Internationalization of the Renminbi via bilateral swap lines*. Retrieved 2023, from Atlantic Council: https://www.atlanticcouncil.org/blogs/econographics/internationalization-of-the-renmibi-via-bilateral-swap-lines/
Tseng, H. Z. (2002). *Foreign Direct Investment in China*. Retrieved 2023, from IMF eLibrary: https://www.elibrary.imf.org/view/journals/003/2002/003/article-A001-en.xml
Tung, W. L. (1964). *The political Institutions of Modern China*. Springer Link.
Veugelers, R. (2017). The challenge of China's rise as a science and technology powerhouse. *Policy Contribution*.
Wang, M. Y. (2022). *Brief: China's Role in Public External Debt in DSSI Countries and the Belt and Road Initiative (BRI) in 2020*. Retrieved 2023, from Green Finance & Development Center: https://greenfdc.org/brief-chinas-role-in-public-external-debt-in-dssi-countries-and-the-belt-and-road-initiative-bri-in-2020/
Wang, N. (1982). Deng Xiaoping. The years in France. *The China Quarterly*, *92*, 698–705.
Wang, Y. (2017). For whom the bell tolls: The political legacy of China's cultural revolution.
Westbrook, S. S. (2023). Chinese banks seize on Russia, oil trade to internationalise yuan. *Reuters*.
WITS. (n.d.). *WITS*. Retrieved 2023, from http://wits.worldbank.org/WITS/WITS/TradeIndicatorsHelp/TradeOutcomes_Help.htm
Wong, C. (2011). The Fiscal stimulus programme and public governance issues in China. *OECD Journal on Budgeting*.
Wood, R. (2021). Australia 'open to dialogue' with China despite new economic hit. *9 News*.
World 101. (2023). *How Did the United States Become a Global Power?* Retrieved 2024, from World 101: https://world101.cfr.org/contemporary-history/world-war/how-did-united-states-become-global-power
World Bank. (2015). *How Important are China and India in global commodity consumption?* Retrieved from The World Bank: chrome-extension://

efaidnbmnnnibpcajpcglclefindmkaj/https://pubdocs.worldbank.org/en/716291444853736301/CMO-July-2015-Feature-China-India.pdf

World Bank Group. (2019). *Innovative China : New Drivers of Growth (English)*. Retrieved 2023, from World Bank: https://documents.worldbank.org/en/publication/documents-reports/documentdetail/833871568732137448/innovative-china-new-drivers-of-growth

Wright, L. (2021). China's Property Sector Has Bigger Problems Than Evergrande. *Foreign Policy* . Retrieved 2023, from https://foreignpolicy.com/2021/09/29/chinas-property-sector-evergrande/

Wroe, D. (2018). China eyes Vanuatu military base in plan with global ramifications. *The Sydney Morning Herald*.

Wu, S. X. (2015). *Empires of coal*. Columbia University.

Xi Lu, S. Z. (2020). Progress of Air Pollution Control in China and Its Challenges and Opportunities in the Ecological Civilization Era. *Engineering*, 1423–1431.

Xin, Z. (2023). China still has lessons to learn in making the yuan an international alternative to the US dollar. *South China Morning Post*.

Xinhuanet. (2024). Retrieved 2023, from http://www.xinhuanet.com//

Yongding, Y. (2023). *Reflections on the RMB Internationalization as the International Monetary System Enters a New Historical Stage*. Retrieved 2023, from CF40: http://www.cf40.com/en/news_detail/13474.html

Yude Geng, S.S.-C. (2020). Impact of forest logging ban on the welfare of local communities in Northeast China. *Forests, 12*, 3.

Zakaria, F. (2023). The dollar is the superpower and Russia and China are threatening it. *The Washington Post*.

Zhang, H. P.-S. (2023). *Renminbi Usage in CrossBorder Payments:*. Retrieved 2023, from International Monetary Fund: https://www.imf.org/-/media/Files/Publications/WP/2023/English/wpiea2023077-print-pdf.ashx

Index

R. Hosein et al., *China in the Caribbean*,
https://doi.org/10.1007/978-3-031-71985-1

The manufacturer's authorised representative in the EU is Springer Nature Customer Service Centre GmbH, Europaplatz 3, 69115 Heidelberg, Germany. If you have any concerns regarding our products, please contact ProductSafety@springernature.com

Printed and bound by CPI Group (UK) Ltd, Croydon, CR0 4YY
01/10/2026
02225924-0006